1

THE SOVEREIGN COUNCIL OF NEW FRANCE

STUDIES IN HISTORY, ECONOMICS AND PUBLIC LAW

EDITED BY THE FACULTY OF POLITICAL SCIENCE
OF COLUMBIA UNIVERSITY

Volume LXV] [Number 1
Whole Number 156

THE SOVEREIGN COUNCIL OF NEW FRANCE

A Study in Canadian Constitutional History

BY

RAYMOND DU BOIS CAHALL, Ph.D.

One-time Fellow in Modern European History
Columbia University
Acting Assistant Professor of European History and Government
Miami University

New York
COLUMBIA UNIVERSITY
LONGMANS, GREEN & CO., AGENTS
London: P. S. King & Son, Ltd
1915

PREFACE

In the summer of 1911, Professor Carlton Hayes, while at the University of Chicago, called my attention to the dearth of information about the government of Canada under French rule. In the present study, I have confined myself to the Sovereign Council and the officials connected with it, in the hope that similar studies will be written by others dealing with the Governor, the Intendant, and the inferior courts of New France. This monograph is designed by its copious footnotes in the original and by frequent references to sources to save the future historians of Canada the trouble of sifting a large mass of material.

The core of the work consists of the last four chapters, which treat of the organization, procedure, functions, and actual achievements of the Sovereign Council. The earlier chapters are designed to describe the events which increased or diminished the power of the Council and to acquaint the reader with the personality of the actors. A disproportionate amount of space is given to the two administrations of Frontenac, because during those years the disputes of greatest significance occurred. Owing to the number of these, several cases have been relegated to appendices.

It is with great pleasure that I take this opportunity to thank those who have shown interest in this modest enterprise. I am grateful to Professor James Harvey Robinson for his careful revision of the proof, to Professor James T. Shotwell for reading portions of the manuscript, and to Professor Edwin R. A. Seligman for co-operating in the publication. I am deeply indebted to Professor Herbert L. Osgood of Columbia University and Professor W. B. Munro of Harvard University for the most helpful criticisms. Among several kind librarians and archivists, my thanks are especially due to Dr. A. G. Doughty, Dominion Archivist, and Mr. Parker, Keeper of Manuscripts in the Archives at Ottawa. Finally I wish to express my deep gratitude to Mrs. William F. Pierce of Gambier, Ohio, for the important part which she has had in the revision of the manuscript.

R. D. B. C.

MIAMI UNIVERSITY, *January 2, 1915.*

TABLE OF CONTENTS

CHAPTER I

The Creation and Early History of the Council

CHAPTER II

The Sovereign Council at its Height

CHAPTER III

The Council in the Eighteenth Century

CHAPTER IV

The Membership and Organization of the Council

CHAPTER V

Methods of Procedure of the Council

CHAPTER VI

The Functions of the Council

PAGE

CHAPTER VII

The Administrative and Judicial Achievements of the Council

CHAPTER VIII

CHAPTER I

The Creation and Early History of the Council

The picturesque history of Canada, dealing with the deeds of hardy adventurers in the depths of the forest-clad interior or on the outskirts of Dutch and English settlement, has not been neglected. With the Governor of New France we are accustomed to associate the war expedition, the pipe of peace, and the courtly ceremonies of the Château St. Louis, that miniature Versailles. In the same way our idea of the Intendant is colored by the turbulent quarrels into which a few Intendants were drawn, and by the spectacular corruption and magnificence which constituted the crime of the unspeakable Bigot alone. Owing to the love of the thrilling and the picturesque, the administrative side of Canadian history has hitherto been inadequately presented. It remains to be shown that the Governor and Intendant spent their time in other occupations than Indian fighting or quarreling with each other; that they shared in the prosaic routine of the domestic government of Canada: and that, in this capacity, they were associated together in an institution which has heretofore almost escaped the attention of the historian. Since this institution of which they were members labored quite as much as they for the preservation of property and the maintenance of good order, no constitutional history of New France should any longer be silent as to the history and functions of the Sovereign Council of Quebec.

This Council functioned from 1663 until the English Conquest but was especially active in administrative and judicial achievement during the seventeenth century. Before taking up the more interesting work of analyzing its procedure and functions, and estimating its value to Canada, I shall trace the history of its formation, growing importance, and decline.

The reader who is tempted to conclude from these narrative chapters that struggles for personal power and broader conciliar jurisdiction made up the life of the Council, has only to turn to the later chapters to realize his mistake; the achievements there chronicled could only result from scores of meetings undisturbed by any dispute. It is with the warning not to take the constitutional struggles to be described as typical of the everyday work of the Council, that the opening chapters are introduced.

The Sovereign Council of New France was the third form of Council given to the Colony. Its predecessors were designed both to aid and check the Governor. Long before an Intendant arrived in Canada, the French government had placed a check upon the autocratic tendencies of the colonial Governor, by associating with him the Superior of the Jesuits and the local governor of Montreal. This action was the result of a careful investigation of representations made by the chief inhabitants of Canada and by the directors of the Company of One Hundred Associates. The Royal Regulation of March 27, 1647, provided that a Council of three, or their deputies, should supervise the detailed administration of the colony and see that the duties of all special officers were properly performed, without using their offices for their own private benefit. The Council was given wide appointive powers and was also to serve as an auditing board. Syndics, that is, persons who looked after the business interests of a city, were to be elected each year in Quebec, Montreal, and Three Rivers, and were to appear in the Council whenever their affairs demanded consideration.[1]

But the inhabitants of Canada desired some representation in the Council and they objected to the financial burden imposed upon them. Accordingly on March 5, 1648, a Royal Warrant was issued altering the constitution of the Council.[2] Thenceforth it was ordinarily to consist of the Governor, the Superior of the Jesuits, —— until the arrival of a bishop in Canada —— and the retiring Governor. In addition there were to be two inhabitants elected every three years by these officers and by the syndics of Quebec, Montreal, and Three Rivers. Where the Governor was retained for a second term of three years, three inhabitants might be elected in this manner to complete the number of five. Although the document named the inhabitants who were to serve for the first three years, it is probable that at the first election in 1651 the three syndics, who were themselves elected by the people, elected their nominees, since they cast three out of the five votes. Thus was a popular element introduced into the early government of Canada.

The Warrant of 1648 granted wide powers to the Council, which was to have the disbursement of the public funds, the regulation of the police, the right to grant or refuse permission to syndics, attorneys, etc., to borrow money, and the right to appoint the captains of the volunteers.[3]

[1] *Collection Moreau de St. Méry*, series F iii, vol. iii, p. 169, *et seq.*

[2] La Chesnaye says in 1676 that this action was taken in consequence of mutual complaints of Governor Avaugour and various families. *Collection de Manuscrits de Nouvelle France*, vol. i, p. 250.

[3] *Coll. Moreau St. Méry*, series F iii, vol. i, p. 184, *et seq.* For paraphrases of the decrees establishing the Councils of 1647 and 1648 in English, see A. Shortt and A. G. Doughty, Canada and its Provinces, vol. i, p. 328, *et seq.*

The records of this Council have been lost but we have various accounts of its activity.[1] La Chesnaye, for example, tells us how the Council was installed and began its work. As an administrative body, it sent out ambassadors, decided peace and war and issued ordinances.[2] As a judicial body, it entertained appeals from the local court of Three Rivers and the ecclesiastical jurisdiction of the Sulpitians at Montreal. From its judgments appeal might be carried to the Parlement of Rouen.[3]

The historian Charlevoix, not knowing how this Council was constituted, describes it as an informal body, called upon exceptional occasions to advise the Governor. "But," he observes, "this Council was not permanent: the Governor General established it by virtue of the power conferred on him by the king, and changed it as he saw fit".[4] This description is not accurate. The Council functioned more widely, and was more stable in its organization than Charlevoix indicates. It met in the absence of the Governor.[5] It participated in the most

[1] A few scanty records are found in *Coll. de Man. de Nouv. Fr.*, vol. i, p. 128. The record for a meeting on June 20, 1651, reads as follows: "Le Conseil assemblé à neuf heures du matin où ont assisté Mon. le Gouverneur, le Rév. Père Supérieur, Messieurs de Godefroy et Mencil."

[2] For the Council's share in the negotiations of 1651 with New England, see *Coll. de Man. de Nouv. Fr.*, vol. i, pp. 127–129.

[3] La Tour's description of this Council tallies with references to it in *Jugements et Délibérations du Conseil Souverain*. See La Tour, *Mémoire de la Vie de M. de Laval*, book vii. On the other hand, Kingsford, History of Canada, vol. i, p. 191, says "with appeal to the King alone."

[4] Charlevoix, *History of France* (Shea's edition), vol. i, p. 67.

[5] The Sieur de la Tesserie is spoken of as "cedevant . . . chef du Conseil en l'absence de Monsieur d'Avaugour." *Jugements et Délib.*, vol. i, p. 281.

important business of government.[1] In fact its participation was deemed to be so necessary to the legality of an act, that a grant of trading privileges made without it was declared by its successor, the Sovereign Council, to be null and void.[2] The same organization of the Council was maintained until its abolition in 1663. Argenson, the third Governor during its existence, "preserved the Council as it was established".[3] Nor is there any evidence until 1662, when Avaugour changed the personnel of his Council, that tenure of office was precarious. According to the Royal Warrant of 1648 others than the Governor shared the power of appointing Councillors. Arbitrary removal by the Governor was thus in some measure provided against. There is little doubt that the Governor upon occasion dominated the Council, neglected to consult it and arrogated to himself its judicial powers,[4] but nevertheless the "ancien conseil" could function and did function independently of him and in his absence.[5] It was not merely a Governor's Council.

[1] The treaty with the merchants of Rouen in 1660 to supply the colony at a fixed profit was made "à la prière du Gouverneur [et] du Conseil du pais." Memoir of La Chesnaye, *Coll. de Man. de Nouv. Fr.*, vol. i, p. 251.

[2] "Le dict Sieur Davaugour de son authorité n'a pû faire le dict traicté de ferme dont est question sans l'advis du Conseil estably par le Roy a Quebecq." *Jugements et Délib.*, vol. i, pp. 10–12.

[3] *Coll. de Man. de Nouv. Fr.*, vol. i, p. 251.

[4] Charlevoix, vol. i, p. 371, says that Avaugour had acquired a reputation for wise judgments based upon natural equity rather than upon law.

[5] A record of January, 1664, in *Jugements et Délib.*, vol. i, p. 94, is interesting: "Il est bien vray que l'esté dernier apres le depart du sieur Davaugour ceux qui tenoient le Conseil sous l'authorité du sieur de la Tesserie avoient faict un tarif [allowing French merchants 50 per cent profit] sans appeler aucun des dicts merchands." This is perhaps an exceptional case. Avaugour was on his way to France, and the new government had not yet been formed.

Its members were bound directly to each other, not through him. It was not ambitious and yet it played a considerable part between 1648 and 1663.

Shortly after Louis XIV began his personal reign, agitation was started for a second change in the composition of the Council. There were several reasons on the King's part for taking such action. In the first place, he was dissatisfied with the administration of justice in the colony. In his secret instructions to Gaudais, who was sent out to Quebec to help install the new Council and watch its workings and the attitude of the people towards it, the minister said: "Up to the present there has been in that colony no regular system of justice the authority of which was universally recognized, and through the weakness of character of those who were charged with rendering justice, the judgments which were pronounced were generally unexecuted. Therefore, His Majesty resolved some time ago to create a Sovereign Council in the said country".[1]

The Governor in his individual capacity had drawn to himself many judicial powers to the detriment of the Council. During Avaugour's administration the Governor rather than his Council became the legal court of appeals; for in 1651, the Company of New France had decided that ordinary justice should be administered under the headship of a Grand Sénéchal, in first instance by a lieutenant-general, and, upon appeal, by the Governor General, who was empowered by His Majesty to judge finally.[2] In 1659 the King ordered resort in first instance for all civil, criminal, and police actions demanding prompt and exemplary punishment, to be had to the

[1] *Edits et Ordonnances*, vol. iii, p. 26.

[2] Doutre et Lareau, *Le Droit Civil Canadien*, vol. i, p. 38.

local judges established by the Company, and upon appeal to the Governor[1]. There were many enemies of the Governor to point out the abuses of this system and to influence the King to create as supreme court of appeals a body of which the Governor should be but one, with the vote of an ordinary member.

In the second place, the King was influenced by the ecclesiastics. Among those who called loudest for a change and for the recall of Governor Avaugour were Bishop Laval and the Jesuits[2], and the chief cause for these demands was the question of the traffic in liquor with the Indians. Hitherto the ecclesiastical power had dominated the colony, but in 1661 the Governor, partly by chance, partly by intention, found himself in opposition to the ecclesiastics upon the matter of bartering brandy for skins. On May 5, 1660, the Bishop had excommunicated those who persisted in the sale of liquor to the Indians[3]. He had obtained a law punishing such sales with death. Shortly after he assumed control Avaugour had been forced to shoot two men and flog another for transgressing this law[4]. But when a woman was caught in such traffic and was protected by the Jesuits, the Governor was exasperated. The ecclesiastics had insisted upon punishment: now they withheld from punishment. The Governor declared that he would be

[1] Deutre et Lareau, *op. cit.*, vol. i, p. 44.

[2] Says La Tour in his *Mémoires de la Vie de M. de Laval*, book vii: "Quoique l'établissement d'une cour souveraine ne soit pas du ressort de l'Eglise, le Conseil souverain de Canada fut l'ouvrage de son premier évêque," and the King confessed in his instructions to Talon that the Jesuits had complained so often of Avaugour that he had resolved not only to recall him but to permit them to choose his successor. *Coll. de Man. de Nouv. Fr.*, vol. i, p. 177.

[3] *Mandements des Evêques de Québec*, vol. i, p. 14.

[4] *Journal des Jésuites*, October 7, 1661.

no respecter of persons: none should henceforth be punished for bartering liquor with the Indians. About him grew up such a party that Laval deemed it expedient in January 1662 to suspend his excommunication,[1] but on February 24 the Bishop renewed the excommunication owing to alleged murders, and injuries to innocent persons, committed during the intervening weeks. This time he extended it to all those who were in any way the cause of drunkenness among the Indians[2]. But the situation had passed beyond his control, and realizing the futility of his efforts to prevent what he termed the "augmentation des désordres", he set sail for France on August 12, 1662, to obtain the removal of the Governor General and to curtail the power of his office. He pressed upon the King's attention the abuses in administering justice in Canada and the defects in the system, and the ultimate form of the Sovereign Council bore witness to the success of his mission. The new Council was to be chosen by Governor and Bishop jointly, and the Governor was to be stripped of his power to entertain appeals. Thus the struggle over the sale of liquor to the Indians may be classed as the second cause for the erection of the Sovereign Council.

In the third place, the King was dissatisfied with the administration of the Company of One Hundred Associates, which had been formed in the time of Richelieu. Being financially unable to support the country with supplies, it had in 1644 returned the trade in peltries, which was the only advantage it drew from Canada, into the hands of the inhabitants, upon the sole condition of an

[1] *Journal des Jésuites*, January, 1662. "Le jour de St. Matthias, on fut obligé de rélever l'excommunication à cause des troubles et desordres extraordinaires."

[2] *Man. des Ev. de Queb.*, vol. i, pp. 42–43.

annual quit-rent of 1000 beaver skins. By 1662 the number of shares had dwindled from 100 to 45.[1] The holders of these shares were unable to stand the expense necessary to develop their colony from which they were drawing no profit.[2] Weakened by the resignation of many of its members, the Company had been unable to send soldiers and colonists to New France. According to one decree the colonists were so few in number that they were on the point of being expelled by the Iroquois. It was necessary therefore to think of maintaining and protecting them and adding to their number. On February 24, 1663, the officers and a dozen of the stockholders met in Paris. They had learned that His Majesty was desirous of obtaining possession of the country and seigniory of New France and as a mark of their profound respect and entire deference to his wishes surrendered their rights.[3] The Company thus had the opportunity both to get rid of a white elephant and to oblige Louis XIV. In March the King accepted the cession of the Company's rights explaining his resolution to take the country into his own hands.[4] This resumption, constituting New France a royal province, aimed at the resuscitation of the colony.

The resumption of the colony was probably a good reason for the establishment of a provincial form of tribunal. There were at this time so-called "Sovereign Councils" at Ensisheim, Perpignan, and Arras in France, but it must be pointed out that the Sovereign Council of New

[1] Many influences were brought to bear upon the King to overthrow this tottering Company. Avaugour advised him to dissolve it. Garneau, *Histoire du Canada*, vol. i, p. 146.

[2] This is the résumé in the instructions to Talon. *Coll. de Man. de Nouv. Fr.*, vol. i, p. 177. See also (Clément) *Lettres, Instructions et Mémoires de Colbert*, vol. iii, pt. ii, p. 389.

[3] *Edits et Ord.*, vol. i, pp. 30, 31.

[4] *Ibid.*, p. 32.

France was not modeled entirely upon them. For example, the edict establishing it made no provision for an intendant. On the contrary, it was like the "ancien conseil" of 1648 in many ways, differing chiefly in the way Councillors were chosen and in having much greater judicial power. Louis XIV and Colbert had had no experience in forming courts and consequently they adapted the Council to Canadian needs. They were so pleased with this experiment that they established some nineteen months later similar Councils in Martinique and Guadeloupe.[1]

The form of the Sovereign Council reflected the absolutist notions of the young King. The Council of 1648 was not in accordance with such theories. The Council of 1663 was to be constituted by the two highest officials in Canada. The syndics were no longer to help elect Councillors. Henceforth, these men looked to those above, rather than those below, them for appointment and continuance in office. The King was drawing the reigns of government into his own hands.

In addition to being a step towards absolutism, this appeared like a victory for the ecclesiastics. The Edict provided that the Bishop, or the first ecclesiastic in the country, should share with the Governor General the power of appointing the other members of the Council. These were five Councillors, an Attorney-General, and a clerk. What formerly constituted in great measure the functions of the Governor, was given to the Council, in which he had but one of the seven votes cast. In certain actions final judgment had rested with the Gover-

[1] Arras (1530–1641–1677), Perpignan (1660) and Ensisheim (1657). Desmaze, *Le Parlement de Paris*, p. 473. Letters patent creating sovereign Councils at Martinique and Guadeloupe, dated October 11, 1664.

nor; now, final appeal in all actions was had to the Sovereign Council. It also had wide powers of administration, of regulating the judicial system in the country and of appointing officers of justice. In fact, the creation of this Council, in conjunction with the dismissal of Avaugour and the appointment of Augustin Saffrey de Mésy[1] was clearly an ecclesiastical triumph.

On September 18, 1663, the new Council entered upon its century-long career. At the first session the Edict of Establishment was registered and in the afternoon session the commissions of Governor de Mésy and M. Gaudais-Dupont were likewise registered.[2] As Mésy was strange to the Canadians this first Council was made up wholly at the suggestion of the Bishop. He chose orthodox Catholics, prominent in the affairs of the colony. The names of the first Councillors are worth remembering as these men played leading rôles in the province for many years. The Councillors were commonly known by the names of Villeray, La Ferté, Auteuil, Tilly, and Damours; the Attorney-General was Jean Bourdon and the clerk Peuvret de Mesnu.[3]

[1] The Jesuits, allowed to choose the successor of Avaugour, "jetèrent donc les yeux sur le dict Sr de Mésy, Major de la ville de Caen, qui faisoit profession d'estre devost, et qu'ils croyoient sans doute qui se conduiroit par leurs sentimens." Instructions to Talon, *Coll. de Man. de Nouv. Fr.*, vol. i, p. 178.

[2] *Jugements et Délib.*, vol. i, pp. 1-3.

[3] As they assumed names from lands they possessed, they appear in their commissions as Louis Rouer, Sieur de Villeray; Jean Juchereau, Sieur de la Ferté; Denis-Joseph Ruette d'Auteuil, Sieur de Monceaux; Charles le Gardeur, Sieur de Tilly; Mathieu Damours, Escuyer, Sieur Descaufour; Jean Bourdon, Sieur de St. Jean and St. François; and Jean Baptiste Peuvret, Sieur de Mesnu. Even in the struggling colony, men prized titles. In 1667, Talon and Tracy asked that four of the above should be given letters of noblesse. Later others received such patents. See Munro, *The Seigniorial System in Canada*, chap. ix.

The earliest events in the life of the Council indicate that a change in its constitution was not sufficient to assure "bonne et briefe justice". In the following case the Sovereign Council seems to have withheld justice in order to protect some of its members. The Company of One Hundred Associates some years before had sent out Péronne Dumesnil to investigate the frauds which it believed were regularly practised upon it. The commissioner thought he had gathered evidence sufficient to convict some of the leading members of the colony, among them Villeray and Bourdon. The day after the arrival of Mèsy, Dumesnil begged the Governor not to appoint these two men to the Council until they should make satisfactory statements of the Company's money that had passed through their hands,—basing this request upon the decrees of March 27, 1647 and May 13, 1659.[1] The suspected men were nevertheless appointed on the following day. At the second meeting of the Council the said Bourdon, now Attorney General, represented that a certain Péronne Dumesnil had caused an agent to force the window of the study of Auteuil, former secretary of the Council, and to carry away several papers, including some from the Council's registers, which he had used for purposes of intimidation, forcing signatures from some persons and withholding concessions from others. The other suspected member, Villeray, now First Councillor, was commissioned to search the house of Dumesnil, seize the alleged stolen papers and enclose them in a strong box.[2] Villeray, if we may believe Dumesnil, executed his commission in an unnecessarily harsh manner. Breaking into Dumesnil's house in the

[1] Kingsford, vol. i, p. 306, *et seq.* The author has had access to the Dumesnil account of the affair.

[2] *Jugements et Délib.*, vol. i, p. 4.

early evening with a file of ten soldiers, he forced the place of deposit and extracted the papers while Dumesnil was held to a chair. The outraged man appealed to Gaudais, who presented his complaint to the Council accusing four of its members,—Villeray, La Fertè, Tilly, and Auteuil. The petition was referred to Gaudais [1] and was evidently suppressed as no report of the case was ever made. The Councillors had succeeded in burying the investigation of Péronne Dumesnil in oblivion.

This one incident excepted, the new Council showed remarkable moderation in its first operations. Even while granting Bishop Laval the desired decree forbidding the sale of liquor to the Indians, it reduced the penalty of death to 300 livres for the first offence, and the whip and banishment for a repetition.[2] During the deliberations all interested parties were consulted, among others the Jesuit fathers.

The same moderation was shown in the attitude of the Council towards the political work of the former Governor, Avaugour, the Bishop's old enemy. On October 2 a lease that he had made of the trade of Tadoussac to a number of Canadians was annulled upon the ground that the Governor had failed to get the consent of his Council.[3] There was no hint of personal spite in this action, and this was the only case in which Avaugour's good judgment was attacked. Four actions arose on October 13, November 24, and December 1, 1663, and on January 16, 1664, which involved the question of sustaining or reversing his judgments, and in no case did the Council do more than modify them. Not one was reversed,[4] although the words "sans avoir esgard au jugement de M. d'Avaugour" which appear several times in the

[1] *Jugements et Délib.*, vol. i, p. 6.
[2] *Ibid.*, p. 8.
[3] *Ibid.*, pp. 9 12.
[4] *Ibid.*, pp. 25, 64, 75, 93.

record might indicate the Council's desire to arrive at a judgment independently.

The first few months were filled with the work of settling many disputes, for the most part of a petty nature; and only occasionally did signs of friction become apparent. On November 28 Governor de Mésy confessed in Council meeting that there had been some difficulty between M. the Bishop, M. the Intendant,[1] and himself concerning his salary and "appointments". He proposed that the Sovereign Council should vote to him what any one of the last three Governors of New France had received. The Council did as requested, electing to give him the salary and "appointments that had been granted to Argenson."[2]

Meanwhile the question of local government for Quebec created some dissatisfaction. On October 7, 1663, a mayor and two aldermen had been elected by the citizens of Quebec and vicinity at the instance of the Council.[3] These officers had neglected their duties and the mayor had declared to Tilly that he intended to present his resignation to the Governor. He should have addressed the Governor directly. On November 14 the Council, in consideration of the failure of these local officers to do their duty and of the informal character of the resignation,[4] ordered that the former election of mayor and aldermen should be disregarded, that these

[1] *Jugements et Délib.*, vol. i, p. 67. Although Gaudais did not receive the title of Intendant in his commission and secret instructions and is not accounted the first Intendant of New France, he is here spoken of as "Monsieur l'Intendant."

[2] *Ibid.*, p. 78.

[3] *Ibid.*, p. 15.

[4] "Et que mesme le pais n'estant encor qu'en tres petite consideration pour le petitesse de son estendue en deserts et nombre de peuples, Il seroit plus a propos de se contanter d'un scyndicq Eu esgard au peu d'affaires qui concernent le devoir de ces charges." *Ibid.*, p. 57.

offices should be abolished, and that the people should proceed to elect a syndic. There is no evidence that Mésy was present at this meeting. In any case the mayor should have been encouraged to obtain his release from the Governor before the Council took this step. In view of the trouble that ensued over the local government of Quebec, one must conclude that already ecclesiastical influence was at work to prevent any other government for Quebec than the sway of Bishop and Seminary.

In December a difficulty arose between the Governor and Villeray. The latter had been ordered by the Council to investigate and report a number of causes and had already introduced several. Notwithstanding this order of the Council, on February 4, 1664, public notice was given by the Governor notifying parties who had petitions to present, to address themselves to him when the business concerned the interests of the King, and to the Council in open meeting when it concerned justice or police, alleging that the practice was an innovation introduced at the instigation of certain members of the Council.[1] Any member who should suppress a petition was to be liable to exclusion from the Council. This notice was posted up "to beat of drum" by Angouville, Major of Fort St. Louis. On the 13th, this same military officer was sent by Mésy to announce to the Bishop the Governor's intention to exclude from the Council Villeray and Auteuil, Councillors, and Bourdon, Attorney-General, and to have their successors elected in a "popular assembly." Laval was asked to acquiesce in this arrangement, but instead he protested against the registration of such a document as a dangerous precedent.

[1] *Coll. Moreau St. Méry*, series F iii, vol. i, p. 292.

Angouville answered that the Governor would have it published without registration.[1] The same day the Governor obtained an ordinance of Council[2] signed by himself, Tilly, La Ferté, and Damours, suspending Villeray and Auteuil from their positions as Councillors. For a few weeks the Governor and these three members conducted the administration of justice, but as the need of an Attorney-General was felt, the Governor proposed the erection of the office of deputy Attorney-General.[3] The Bishop opposed this project. He could not acquiesce in the removal of former Council members unless convinced of their crime, nor proceed to the choice of a deputy Attorney-General. Nevertheless on March 10 the Council permitted the registration of letters from Mésy granting the office of deputy Attorney-General to Louis-Theandre Chartier, Sieur de Lotbinière.[4] The Bishop again protested against the creation of an office to the prejudice of the Attorney-General.

The "rump" Council thus provided with a deputy Attorney-General heard many causes during the next month. After a time the old members were re-admitted, and a general reconciliation took place on April 16. The Governor erased certain phrases from the ordinance of February 13, declared that it should be considered null and void, and re-established all as before its promulgation.[5] The deputy Attorney-General gracefully resigned and the reunited Council gave itself uninterruptedly to the business of administration.

[1] *Jugements et Délib.*, vol. i, p. 121.

[2] This document accuses two Councillors and the Bishop of usurping the authority of the Governor and of fomenting sedition. *Supplement Canadian Archives Report*, 1899, p. 53.

[3] March 5, 1664. *Jugements et Délib.*, vol. i, pp. 127–128.

[4] *Ibid.*, p. 129.

[5] *Ibid.*, p. 170.

In June the Council instituted an innovation, which, in view of the somewhat electric condition of the atmosphere, was not well-considered. It sent letters dated the 13th and written by the hand of Villeray to the King and minister. These were signed by "le Conseil Souverain Etably a Quebecq".[1] The topics treated were such as the Governor generally discussed in his letters to the home government. There is no evidence that Mésy showed resentment at this encroachment upon the time-honored duties of the Governor, but he must have seen in it a revival of the "Cabal" under the influence of Laval for the purpose of undermining his power.

During the next three months events occurred in the Council meeting which shook the foundations of the government. On July 28 the Attorney-General had asked the election of a syndic for Quebec, which, following the Council's ordinance, duly occurred, resulting in the election of one Charron by a majority vote. As there were but twenty-three electors present, and as Charron was a merchant and inclined to consider only the interests of his class, certain citizens were prompted to petition the Council for his removal. This was effected without injury to Charron's feelings and another election was ordered. The second meeting was more poorly attended than the first. In fact so few were present that no election was attempted. The Governor began to realize that "the Cabal of the Council," as he called it, was determined not to allow the election of a syndic and to that effect had used every effort to keep people away from the elections. He determined to outwit his opponents. He issued writs to a numerous electorate without stating the purpose of the proposed meeting, and under the

[1] *Jugements et Délib.*, vol. i, pp. 201-206.

supervision of himself and Councillor Damours the meeting was held and a syndic was successfully elected.[1]

But the "Cabal" was not to be outwitted. The Bishop was at this time masking behind the Sieur de Charny, who usually attended the Council in his stead to lead the opposition. No sooner then was the syndic-elect presented to the Council to be installed in his office than objection arose from various Councillors. Charny, La Ferté and Auteuil (Villeray being absent on a voyage to France) succeeded in excluding Tilly and Damours from the deliberations and were about to reject the candidate when Mésy postponed the consideration of the subject until another day. A second time the Governor summoned the syndic-elect before the Council to take the oath, and again Charny interfered as spokesman of the "Cabal." La Ferté and Auteuil joined in the attack, when the Governor, mindful that their term of office was nearly expired, began negotiations with the Bishop for their removal.[2] On August 25 an exchange of notes took place. Mésy asked the Bishop to agree to the choice of new Councillors to replace Villeray, La Ferté and Auteuil, Bourdon, Attorney-General, and Peuvret de Mesnu, clerk. He offered to make nominations from any twelve persons whom the Bishop might propose; or himself to propose twelve persons from whom the Bishop might make the selections. The Bishop replied that he could not consent to the election of Councilors

[1] See *ibid.*, pp. 278–280, where the greater part of this account appears as a review of the case. This review is substantially in accordance with information gathered from other records in the same collection and from the *Coll. Moreau St. Méry*.

[2] The Edict of Establishment authorized the Governor and the Bishop conjointly to dismiss from, and refill offices of Councilors at the close of each fiscal year.

until the arrival of M. de Tracy,[1] who had been appointed viceroy of New France and the West Indies. Driven to the wall, the Governor on September 19, 1664, declared four seats vacant. All four men accepted their dismissal in good part, except Bourdon, the Attorney-General, who shouted out in haughty and insolent disdain that he did not consider himself dispossessed of his office. A violent scene followed, during which Bourdon was maltreated and put out of the Council chamber, as a salutary warning against further insubordination.[2] Mésy had gained the day. He reappointed Damours and Tilly for a second year, and a week later filled the other vacancies in the Council.

Mgr. Laval[3] had occupied a strong position. While

[1] Had Mésy consented he would have had a hostile Council until the middle of the summer following. These letters are found *in extenso* in *Coll. Moreau St. Méry*, series F iii, vol. i, pp. 316, 317.

[2] A copy of this record of September 19 is found in the above collection; also a factum by the Bishop, in *Canadian Archives Report*, 1905, p. 506, where Bourdon's chastisement is set forth as follows: "M. de Charny having asked M. de Mésy the reason of his refusal to enter on the registers the deliberations of the Council, he got into a frenzy and said to the whole Council: 'I dismiss you, go out; I do not suspend you only, I dismiss you, go away from here,' threatening them with insulting words, a stick in his hand and looking at the registrar and the Sr. Bourdon, Procureur General, he said, 'I dismiss you also.' M. Bourdon retorted: 'As to me, Sir, I must not consider myself as dismissed; the decree of the establishment of the Council does not enact that I may be removed; I ask you, if you please, that it should be read.' Hearing this, M. de Mésy rose up out of his chair, took M. Bourdon by the throat and pulled him out of his place by force, hit him on the head with his stick, drew out his sword and struck him many times, when the Sieurs D'Amours and D'Auteuil covered him, thus enabling the said Bourdon to retire. He went out. M. de Mésy followed him outside, hit him again repeatedly with his stick and with the flat side of his sword and wounded one of his hands, saying, 'I will kill you.' Sr Bourdon retired without saying a word and called on a surgeon to get his wound dressed."

[3] The Roman Catholic Church preserves the memory of ancient epis-

his proxy and his partisans in the Council drove the Governor most ardently to desire their dismissal, the Bishop refused him the one legitimate way out: he declined to coöperate in changing the personnel of the Council, a personnel that the Governor could no longer tolerate. He forced Mésy into the adoption of violent measures that placed him in the wrong before the King[1] and before posterity.

The new Councillors appointed by Mésy served from September 24, 1664, to July 6, 1665. During that time there was energetic and concerted action. The struggle between Governor and Bishop was now waged outside the Council chamber walls, the opposition being offered both by the Bishop and by his adherents. It was the intention of the Governor to establish the authority and prestige of the new Council. Four days after its first meeting, proclamation of its establishment was published at the door of the church, without making mention of the opposition of the Bishop, but next day Laval from

copal sees which have lapsed through the decline of population or through falling into the hands of infidel or heretic nations, by bestowing their bishoprics as honorary titles upon coadjutor and suffragan bishops, apostolic vicars and delegates, etc. Such bishoprics are called bishoprics *in partibus infidelium*. As Quebec was not erected into a see until 1674, its first vicar apostolic, François-Xavier de Laval-Montmorenci, held the title of Bishop of Petraea *in partibus infidelium*, from, it is said, a decayed city in Arabia. The great Italian authority Moroni claims, however, that Petraea has given the title of *archbishop* ever since the days of Baldwin, king of Jerusalem, who restored the ancient see; while Petra, a city in Asia Minor, has always given the title to a *bishop*. A doubt may arise, therefore, as to the correctness of title Bishop "*de Petraea*," which the bull expressly accords Laval. See Moroni, *Dizionario de erudizione storico-ecclesiastica*, under "*Vescovi in partibus infidelium*," and "*Mandements des Evêques*," vol. i.

[1] See the grossly unfair accounts of Colbert in instructions to Talon and also La Chesnaye's Memoir written in 1676. *Coll. de Man. de Nouv. Fr.*, vol. i, pp. 178, 260.

the pulpit destroyed any illusions that might be entertained on that score. On October 5 a proclamation of Mésy against the Bishop and his partisans was promulgated to the sound of the drum. Laval retaliated; or at any rate the Governor claimed that he was refused confession and absolution.[1]

Several evidences of the struggle appear in the Council records. On October 1, at the suggestion of the Governor, Tilly was appointed to investigate the denunciations of the Sieur Pommier uttered from the pulpit of the parochial church in Quebec.[2] On November 19 the Governor declared that he would oppose Messieurs the Ecclesiastics receiving any funds until they acquiesced in the reorganization of the government.[3] But the Bishop nevertheless continued his opposition. In November he refused the repeated requests of the syndic of Quebec to publish a warning against those who sequestered merchandise and kept it out of the market. This monopoly had proved so harmful that on December 17 the Council authorized the monitory letter of the syndic, and on the last day of the year gave it the force of law.[4]

Subsequently the struggle languished. As Mésy sickened and approached his end he made his peace with the ecclesiastics. He died on May 5, 1665. To him justice has never been done. His papers disappeared after his death and Talon made no report concerning his conduct. The Intendant possibly thought it more politic to spare the feelings of the living than to preserve the reputation of the dead.

[1] *Journal des Jésuites*, October, 1664.

[2] *Jugements et Délib.*, vol. i, p. 283. Tilly is to inform himself of "plusieurs choses . . . contre le service du Roy et bien public comme affiches et autres pratiques Caballenzes."

[3] *Ibid.*, p. 300.

[4] *Ibid.*, pp. 305, 309.

The whole struggle turned upon the desirability of a syndic in Quebec. The Bishop opposed the election, installation, and functioning of the syndic, probably for two reasons. In the first place, he was probably jealous of any other than the ecclesiastical government of Quebec. In the second place, he desired the mercantile class to remain without a leader as only thus could he hope to keep the ban upon the liquor traffic with the Indians. The opening of this trade effected under the leadership of Talon proved the wisdom of his fears.

Jacques Leneuf de la Poterie, the Lieutenant Governor, had been authorized by Mésy to conduct the government until the arrival of new officials, but his right was denied by the Council. It refused to admit him as its "Chief and President" and limited his functions to the management of the militia.[1] It was alleged that the Governor had not the right to nominate a substitute; that the power of appointing First Presidents for his parlements rested with the King. Having thus stated their constitutional grounds and incidentally shown that their sense of obligation to Mésy had not outlived him, the Councillors pushed forward repairs on the Château St. Louis and the palais de justice, for the reception of his successors.

On July 6 the Sovereign Council was honored by the presence of the Marquis de Tracy, Lieutenant General of all the Americas. At the meetings on this day the commission of Tracy was registered; so also was the edict of establishment of the Company of the West Indies, the King having tired of his experiment and established a new Company.[2] This was the last session of Mésy's reconstructed Council. Thus terminated that

[1] *Jugements et Délib.*, vol. i, p. 350. *Edits et Ord.*, vol. ii, p. 25.

[2] *Jugements et Délib.*, vol. i, pp. 363-364.

part of the Council's history, which concerned New France as a royal province.

Nearly a year and ten months before, the Sovereign Council had been erected in the midst of a turbulent, scheming, grafting, frontier community. Almost every American colony, English, Dutch or French, possessed the same characteristics: the shrewd pushing element bent on rising by any means and with glaring lack of public integrity; and the wild, irresponsible class that freedom from routine-work and the presence of an inferior race produced. But in Canada the presence of still a third class, the ubiquitous Jesuit and ecclesiastic, by no means lessened the difficulties of government.

Sometimes a reflection of the turbulence of the community appeared within the Council chamber, where there was a fair display of give and take. There was no morbid nursing of enmity however. Governor and Bishop, the principals in this struggle, exchanged amenities even so late as New Year's Day of 1664. Most of the Councillors had "played the game," and knew what a "square deal" meant, and once in power they applied this knowledge to a surprising degree. With some few exceptions they displayed a keen sense of justice and and moderation in judgment. The Sovereign Council did good service during this period, of which we have chronicled only the exceptional incidents.

The narrative of the succeeding years of the Council's history must be supplemented by the imaginative intelligence of the reader. I shall content myself with indicating the unusual events in its life, leaving the weeks, months and years, in which judicial and administrative business was carefully though monotonously performed, to be presupposed. The tale of how many judgments, *arrêts*, and *règlemens* were issued in each term and the nature of this business is not the subject of this chapter, although such a narrative would most truly represent the average life of the Council.

During the decade following the arrival of Tracy the government of New France was in the hands of the Company of the West Indies. In reality the change from royal to proprietary government was merely nominal, and affected the Sovereign Council but little. In return for part payment of the costs of government the Company was authorized to make nominations to the Council, and might be represented in that tribunal by its general agent.[1] The burden of the first provision was not evaded, while the privileges of the second and third provisions were not fully enjoyed. Le Barroys, the general agent of the Company, rarely attended the Council meetings,[2] and it was not until 1674 that the representatives of the Company attempted to influence the personnel of the Council by using their right of nomination. In actual working the government was still that of a royal province. The King poured men and money into the country and kept in closest touch with its chief officials.

The new régime began in the autumn of 1665. On September 12 Daniel de Remy de Courcelles, Mésy's successor, arrived in Quebec. Upon the same vessel came Jean Talon, the first Intendant of New France. A commission for this office, dated March 21, had been given to Louis Robert in 1663, but he failed to cross the Atlantic. If he had come, what position would he have held in the Council—because the Edict of Establishment

[1] Le Barroys conducted most of his business with Tracy, Courcelles and Talon. There is proof of his attendance at the first meeting of the Council in September, 1665.

[2] *Edits et Ord.*, vol. i, pp. 51-60.

made no mention of an Intendant? Gaudais came to New France in that year, exercised some of the functions of Intendant and was occasionally spoken of as such, but he was not given the title either in his commission or secret instructions. On the other hand, Talon's commission and instructions gave him a very strong position in the Sovereign Council. He was the first Intendant *de jure et de facto*.

Thus augmented by the presence of lieutenant-general, Intendant and general agent of the West India Company, the Council held its first meeting on September 23, and at this meeting the commissions of Governor, Intendant and general agent were registered.[1] The proportion of more dignified officials to ordinary Councillors was much larger than during Mésy's day: there were six of the former and only four of the latter, as is shown by the fact that the minutes of this first meeting were signed by Tracy, Courcelles, the Bishop of Petraea, Talon, Le Barroys, and Villeray as First Councillor. The presence of Villeray in his old position indicates that those whom Mésy had dismissed had been reinstated.[2] This does not mean the unqualified triumph of Bishop and Jesuits, because from 1665 until 1674 appointments to the Council were made by Governor and Intendant.[3] On the con-

[1] *Jugements et Délib.*, vol. i, p. 364.

[2] At the annual installation of the Council, December 6, 1666, both Auteuil and La Ferté were dropped. The others are spoken of as continued in office. Therefore they must have been appointed in 1665. *Ibid.*, p. 367. Abbé Ferland, *Cours d'histoire du Canada*, vol. ii, p. 58, says that Villeray, Gorribon, Tilly, Damours and La Tesserie were appointed.

[3] Tracy, Courcelles and Talon were empowered to make what changes they thought desirable in the Council. Instructions to Talon, Doutre and Lereau, i, 147; also (Clément) *Lettres, Instructions et Mémoires de Colbert*, vol. iii, pt. ii, p. 389, *et seq.*

trary, the decline of ecclesiastical influence in the affairs of government became more and more apparent.

This decline between 1665 and 1672 was due to the dominance of Talon in the counsels of the Sovereign Council. The question at issue was again the liquor traffic with the Indians. The prohibition party, led by Bishop Laval, now very faithful in his attendance at Council meetings, gradually lost ground. No ordinances imposing stringent punishments could be obtained. The Council was half-hearted in its measures and was slow to prosecute offenders. For example, on December 6, 1666, the Council abolished the death penalty and substituted discretionary fines and corporal punishment.[1] A decree of January 5 to the same effect was followed in April by the appointment of Gorribon to investigate reported infractions in the neighborhood of Three Rivers and Cape Magdeleine.[2] On June 20 three men were surprised while attempting to trade with the Indians. The Council awarded the money obtained from the sale of the confiscated liquor to the denunciator, but made no effort to prosecute the delinquents further.[3] On February 29, 1668, an ordinance was passed instructing local judges to keep the Council informed of the contraventions of its ordinances and the crimes and disorders that followed upon the drunkenness of the Indians. It ordered these judges to imprison the delinquents until a member of the Council could be sent to conduct the trial of the accused.[4] It forbade persons to carry drink or merchandise into the woods, without however restricting those who wished to hunt game for the "boiling-pot". No

[1] *Jugements et Délib.*, vol. i, p. 368.

[2] *Ibid.*, p. 588.

[3] *Ibid.*, p. 410.

[4] *Ibid.*, pp. 474-476.

record of prosecutions follows. Earlier in the month the Bishop had complained that since he had been compelled to raise his excommunication, the people had forgotten that it was a mortal sin to sell drink to the savages.[1] As regards this matter Laval was losing ground both within and without the Council chamber.

Meanwhile Talon was gaining ground in the Council, where he was gradually entrusted with many commissions. On July 30, 1667, the Council referred the syndic of Quebec to the Intendant to consider measures to reduce the prices asked by French merchants.[2] On August 20 it ordered that all petitions tending to commence a suit should be addressed to Talon to be by him assigned to the Council or to the local court of Quebec, or retained to be judged by himself independently.[3] The Governor protested against this ordinance as encroaching upon his authority. Again, on October 17, the Council requested Talon to write to the Court concerning the organization of a company of inhabitants for monopoly of trade.[4] On January 16, 1668, the Council ordered the execution of its decree of August 20, 1667, providing that judicial business should be distributed by the Intendant. This action of the Council was taken against the protest of of Governor de Courcelles and at the instance of Talon.[5]

Finally, on November 5 the Council wrote a short

[1] *Mand. des Ev. de Queb.*, vol. i, p. 72.

[2] *Jugements et Délib.*, vol. i, p. 433.

[3] *Ibid.*, pp. 447, 448.

[4] *Ibid.*, p. 457.

[5] *Ibid.*, p. 469. The matter was referred to the Crown, and Colbert refused to allow Talon to exercise this prerogative, saying that reference to the Council or the Intendant of all petitions would greatly complicate judicial business; and that the judges of the lower courts should take cognizance of all matters within their competence, and that from their judgments appeal might be carried to the Sovereign Council. (Clément) *Lettres, Instructions et Mémoires de Colbert*, vol. iii, p. 542.

letter to Colbert which shows the degree of confidence it reposed in Talon:

"Monseigneur,

Since M. Talon has resolved to return to France, esteeming his health strong enough to support the fatigues of the voyage, we shall add nothing to the letter which we have had the honor to write to you. Since he is perfectly enlightened concerning everything that relates to the welfare of this country, he will be able to give you true information. We relie entirely on him (*Nous nous en remettons entiérement à luy*). And however, we shall not cease to pray God for the continuance or your prosperity and good health as being,

Monseigneur,

Your very humble, very obedient, and much favored servants,

The Sovereign Council of New France".[1]

Five days later the Council declared trade in liquor with the Indians open to all French inhabitants of New France. Talon witnessed the triumph of his policy before he sailed for France. The evil effects of drink upon the savages were freely admitted in the Council chamber, but the measure was urged in order to give the better class of citizens profits that men of the lowest character were clandestinely enjoying, and to treat the Indians more fairly in trade and to form a closer union with them.[2] Talon felt the evils that strong drink brought on the colony, and had begun the construction of a brewery in order that "nourishing and wholesome" beer might replace brandy and wines, the common

[1] *Jugements et Délib.*, vol. i, p. 531. The high respect in which Talon was held was even better shown in the humiliating punishment and 300-livre fine meted out to one of his detractors, October 1, 1668. *Ibid.*, p. 518.

[2] *Ibid.*, p. 534.

liquors of the country, and had obtained an ordinance from the Council placing heavy restrictions upon the importation of these liquors as soon as the brewery should be completed.[1] From the end of 1668 to January 2, 1671, Talon was absent from the meetings of the Sovereign Council. While at Court he obtained the confirmation of Louis XIV to the measure of the Council granting freedom of trade. Meanwhile Bishop Laval, defeated in the Council on this matter, had made the sale or gift of liquor to the Indians a *cas réservé*, that is, a case for which absolution could not be granted by the parish priest, but must be referred to the bishop for judgment.[2] But the people took their chances with the Bishop and enjoyed unrestricted trade with the Indians, and so the matter rested during the second term of two years that Talon served in New France.[3]

Jean Talon's land policy was alike successful. As an example to other seigniors, he had cleared lands and had built up three towns. During the last few months of his stay in New France, Talon received letters patent erecting these towns into a barony. It was a proud day when these letters patent were registered in the Council, and Talon received the congratulations of the Councillors upon his title. He bade adieu to the Sovereign Council on October 17, 1672.

During the years 1666 to 1672 the personnel of the

[1] *Jugements et Délib.*, vol. i, p. 477.

[2] *Mand. des Ev. de Queb.*, vol. i, p. 77.

[3] La Chesnaye says that Talon asked permission to return to France because of difficulties with Courcelles, and that a recurrence of similar disagreements with Frontenac resulted in his leaving for Franee without the royal permission. Nothing so unceremonious happened. In a letter dated May 15, 1669, the King gave him permission to return to France at the expiration of two years. *Supplement Canadian Archives Report*, 1899, p. 247.

Council had changed somewhat. Auteuil and La Ferté had been dropped in 1666 and had been replaced by Gorribon and La Tesserie, and in 1668 Mouchy had been made deputy Attorney-General in the absence of Bourdon. The death of Gorribon in 1669 and the dismissal of Villeray resulted in the advancement of Mouchy to be Councillor and in the appointment of Dupont as Councillor and of Lotbinière as deputy Attorney-General. This is the Council, consisting of Tilly, Damours, La Tesserie, Dupont, and Mouchy, Councillors, Lotbinière, Attorney-General, and Peuvret, clerk, that met September 17, 1672, to listen to the inaugural address of Louis de Baude comte de Paluan et de Frontenac.

CHAPTER II

The Sovereign Council at its Height

The entrance of Count Frontenac into the Sovereign Council meant additional pomp and ceremony. The little court took on some of the aspects of the Parlement of Paris. As representative of the greatest monarch of Europe, Frontenac opened the meeting of September 17, 1672 with a speech " from the throne ". After thanking the Councillors for the courtesies of his reception, he dwelt upon the glorious victories of His Majesty's arms in the war with Holland. " All these prodigies," he continued, " which are almost unexampled, ought to increase the love and veneration that we should have for this Incomparable Monarch, whom we see to be so visibly favored by God; and they ought to urge us more and more into giving greater proofs of our obedience and fidelity.

" Although in this regard His Majesty has never had cause to doubt, he has nevertheless commanded me that on my arrival in this country, I should have you take a new oath at my hands, and that I should urge you to acquit yourselves of the duties of your office with every sort of vigilance and integrity. It is through justice that the best established states are preserved, and those which have just been born have still more need that it be quickly and carefully rendered. This is why, Messieurs, you ought to use your best endeavors to respond to the intentions of His Majesty, since it is one of the things which may contribute most to the progress of the colony, the growth of which he so strongly desires.

"For myself I shall try to give you an example of it by being no respecter of persons, by always protecting the poor and feeble against those who wish to oppress them, and by carefully seeking means to procure the advantage and satisfaction of those whom I see to be intent upon the good of the country and the service of His Majesty." [1]

The Governor then administered the oath to the Councillors, who sometime later marched in solemn procession to the church of Notre Dame, to attend upon a Te Deum, sung in honor of His Majesty's victories against the Dutch. To increase the Council's train of attendants, all the court ushers were ordered to be present thenceforth at all ceremonies and assemblies on pain of fine and loss of office.[2] To sue for Divine guidance, mass was said in an adjacent church upon the days that the Council met.[3] These ceremonies were designed to impress Councillors with the dignity and responsibility of their office and with the high position of Frontenac. The Governor sought above all to impress the people with the importance of the Sovereign Council, that they might the more readily heed its judgments and respect its members.[4]

As New France had no Intendant for the next three years, and as Bishop Laval was in France, Frontenac became the undisputed leader of the Council. He filled vacancies with his followers and reminded Councillors in his annual speech of 1674 that their continuance in office depended

[1] *Jugements et Délib.*, vol. i, p. 689. [2] *Ibid.*, p. 695.

[3] September 5, 1682, order to pay Messire Pierre Thury, priest, the sum of 240 livres for six years that the mass was said for the Council on the days it assembled. *Ibid.*, vol. ii, p. 821.

[4] His instructions urged the principle upon Frontenac, but left the means to be devised. See *Documents of the Colonial History of New York*, vol. ix, p. 88.

upon the favor of the Governor.[1] Accordingly, for some time his wish was law.

It was under these circumstances that the Council undertook the trial of such a high official as Jean-Marie Perrot, Governor of Montreal, nephew of Jean Talon, and Premier Valet de Chambre to His Majesty and of such a prominent ecclesiastic as the Abbé Fénelon, a brother of the great Fénelon. In both cases the Governor was insulted and the jurisdiction of the Council challenged. Under the leadership of its Chief, the Council was successful in establishing its jurisdiction against the most astute defense of the accused.

Perrot was heavily interested in the fur trade and was hand in glove with those who traded and hunted without the license of Frontenac, thus conniving at the infraction of the ordinances of the Council.[2] In accordance with one of these ordinances, the local judge of Montreal arrested two coureurs de bois, said to have trading relations with one of her prominent citizens, M. Carion. This man effected the escape of the prisoners and insulted the judge. Accordingly Frontenac sent the lieutenant of his guard to arrest Carion. Lieutenant Bizard should have given Frontenac's letters to the Governor of Montreal before making an arrest in his territory, but he failed to do so until after the arrest. He was immediately confronted by Perrot with judge and notary to investigate his conduct. Having simply obeyed his orders, Bizard refused to be questioned and was consequently imprisoned over night. Next day he drew up a legal statement of what had occurred. One of the witnesses to this statement was thrown into prison by

[1] *Jugements et Délib.*, vol. i, p. 693.

[2] This is Frontenac's initial statement, which facts brought out in the trial confirm. See *Collection Moreau St. Méry*, series F iii, vol. ii, pt. i, p. 212, *et seq.*

Perrot and kept there to the detriment of his business; the other fled to Quebec. Frontenac ordered Perrot to come to Quebec. The latter being led by the Abbé Fénelon to think that reconciliation with Frontenac was possible complied, but was immediately placed under arrest.[1]

From January 30, 1674, until the middle of November, the Council persisted in the investigation of the case, gathering such an array of evidence that the King gave Perrot three weeks in the Bastille in addition to the nine months he had suffered in a Quebec prison.

More bitter and dramatic was the trial of the Abbé Fénelon, which grew out of the Perrot affair. The case involved the settlement of the question whether or not the Sovereign Council could try an ecclesiastic, whether or not the clergy were subject to the jurisdiction of the temporal court. It shows so well the intricacies of a legal battle that I include it in detail as follows. The Abbé Fénelon had been largely responsible for Perrot's coming to Quebec. After he saw his friend imprisoned by Frontenac, when he had been led to expect a peaceful settlement, he became very hostile to the Governor. On Easter Day he preached a sermon on the ideal magistrate which was aimed at Frontenac. He insinuated corruption in the matter of the Indian trade and referred to the treatment of Perrot and the forced labor of the people on a recent expedition of the Governor, etc.[2]

[1] For the process of the trial before the Council, see Appendix A.

[2] These subtle yet obvious insinuations were couched in the following general terms: "That he who is vested with authority should not harass the peoples who are subject to him; but he is bound to regard them as his children, and to treat them as a father; that he should not disturb the trade of the country, by ill-treating those who do not give him a share in the profits they may make; that he should be satisfied with honest gains; that he should not trample upon the people nor harass them with forced labor on roads, which benefit none but him; that he should think of something else than providing himself with servile creatures to sing his praises everywhere, etc., etc." *Coll. Moreau St.*

This sermon created a furore. Information and declarations were gathered from ten witnesses as early as May 2. In the beginning the Abbé had no clerical backing, for on May 16 the priests of the Seminary of Montreal expressed their regret at his conduct. Fénelon had not been content with preaching his anti-Frontenac sermon but had gone about collecting favorable declarations from certain inhabitants of Montreal respecting the government of Perrot. The Council appointed Tilly and Dupont to be commissioners in this matter. These commissioners called upon the Abbé to produce these declarations and the original of his sermon. He answered that he did not recognize in the Council, which was the mere creature of Frontenac, the power to compel him to produce his sermon.[1] After ignoring two summonses to appear before the Council, he finally came to the meeting of August 21 where he behaved in the most turbulent manner.[2] He was held a close prisoner in

[1] These early stages in the trial are described in *Coll. Moreau St. Méry*, series F iii, vol. iv, pt. 1, p. 308, *et seq.*; 349-352; 352 *et seq.*; 280 *et seq.*

[2] The record of this meeting in *Jugements et Délib.*, vol. i, pp. 817-819, is well summarized by Kingsford, vol. i, p. 428. On entering the Abbé Fénelon proceeded to take a seat. The Governor told him that he must remain standing. Fénelon replied that he could not act in disregard of his privileges as an ecclesiastic, and sat down at the end of the table. He claimed also the right to sit covered. The Governor replied that there was a distinction between ecclesiastics summoned to give evidence and those arraigned for crime. Fénelon replied by placing his hat upon his head. He then walked up and down the room and said his pretended crime was in the head of the Governor, and was without foundation. The Governor, for the third time, explained that the Council in no way desired to attack the privileges of the clergy, as they existed in France, and that which was now asked was only what was customary there, and that Fénelon ought not to be deficient in respect to the head of the Council. Upon this remark, Fénelon replaced his hat which he had temporarily removed, and answered that the Governor should not be deficient in respect to his character as an ecclesiastic. Fénelon was requested to leave the room.

his lodgings under charge of an usher of the court. On the 23rd, he was again arraigned before the court. He protested that the Bishop alone had the right to try him. In the absence of Bishop Laval, the Council asked the Vicar General to serve as clerical representative, in order that Fénelon might enjoy full justice. A dispute arose, however, as to how this official should be received and where he should sit. On the 29th, the Council refused him the Bishop's place at the Council board.[1] On September 4 it was hard to see how the matter would terminate, Fénelon insisting that he recognized no other judges than his ecclesiastical superiors, so long as these did not hand him over to the secular arm, and the Council insisting that he make his defence before it and produce the offending sermon. On the same day he challenged Peiras and Vitré in particular because, as he said, " they were appointed to the Council by M. de Frontenac alone, without the Council; that both were the creatures of the Governor; without legal knowledge, of little intelligence, etc."[2] The Council responded to this attack by appointing two others to fill the places of those challenged.

Four entries concerning the case appear under date of September 5, the written work so exhausting the Abbé Fénelon that he asked for delay, which was granted. He challenged those who replaced Peiras and Vitré and the Governor appointed Villeray and Auteuil as commissioners to pass upon these challenges. On September 7, Fénelon challenged these commissioners also, but the Council disregarded his objections. On the 10th the Council thus constituted considered the prisoner's exceptions to Peiras and Vitré and to the Governor. Frontenac briefly explained

[1] *Jugements et Délib.*, vol. i, pp. 821, 824, 829.

[2] *Coll. Moreau St. Méry*, series F iii, vol. iv, pt. i, pp. 487, 490, 492, 494, 496, 503.

the misconstruction put upon his actions by the Abbé Fénelon. He added that he could not be recognized as a party to a criminal suit because Fénelon might evade punishment by challenging Councillors on the ground that his enemy had appointed them.[1] The Council doubted this statement. Article XVI, section 24, of the Great Ordinance of 1667, it was argued, provided that no president of a court should serve as such in any case in which he was challenged; that in case of an order for further examination of the case, the process of the suit should be reported by one of the other presidents or judges.[2] It would seem, then, that the Governor as president of the Sovereign Council could be successfully challenged. The Council voted to ask the King whether he intended this article to apply to his Governor and lieutenant general in New France and if a suit by Fénelon against Frontenac could be entertained.[3] This action marks the beginning of an independent attitude towards the Governor.

In the afternoon session the Governor urged the Council to take some step in regard to Fénelon's accusation that he had prevented a free vote in the Council. Upon his with-

[1] "Personne ne peut ny ne doibt estre receu à le prendre à partie lorsqu'il agit du Service du Roy ou de l'Interest public, Et que si l'on y estoit receu, ce seroit un moyen a ceux qui commettent des crimes d'en Esluder la punition en proposant des moyens de recusation contre les officiers du Conseil qui jusques icy ont esté par luy *nommez* ou *continuez*." *Jugements et Délib.*, vol. i, p. 842.

[2] "ce que nous voulons avoir aussi lieu à l'égard de celui qui présidera en l'audience, nonobstant l'usage ou abus introduit en aucunes de nos cours où le président réccusé reçoit les avis, et pronounce le jugement, ce que nous abrogeons en toutes cours, jurisdictions et justices: et en cas d'appointment, l'instance sera contribuée par celui des autres presidens ou juges à qui la distribution appartiendra." *Edits et Ord.*, vol. i, p. 180.

[3] "Et si en consequence il peut estre pris à partie par le dict sieur de fénélon aux cas susdicts suivant la dicte requeste et moyens portez par icelle." *Jugements et Délib.*, vol. i, p. 843.

drawal, that body argued over the matter until nightfall and adjourned to meet at seven o'clock the next morning. On September 11 the Council finally promised that it would pass upon Fénelon's accusation before the departure of the vessels for France. Two weeks later Villeray began to be disaffected. He begged to be excused from judging the Abbé, because of his obligation to Talon, the uncle of Perrot, whose champion was the accused in this case.[1] He was permitted to retire on October 22. However, increased folly on Fénelon's part caused a reaction against him. A petition for a writ of error (*d'apel comme d'abuz*) was declared to be impertinent and unreasonable. His refusal to pay the usher for his maintenance was met by a peremptory order from the Council.[2]

The Council, having now been reduced to three unchallenged members, was unable to consider the most recent petition of the Abbé.[3] On October 29, the Governor reminded the Council of its promise of September 11, and Frontenac having retired, the court declared unanimously that the Governor had not sought to bend it to his will or to interfere with freedom of voting.[4] The whole mass of records of this trial was sent to France with Fénelon and Perrot about the middle of November. While the Council never succeeded in making Fénelon produce his sermon and petition, about the criminality of which the real trial would have centred, yet its jurisdiction over eccle-

[1] *Jugements et Délib.*, vol. i, p. 850.

[2] "que le dict sieur de fenelon sera contrainct par toutes voyes deues et raisonnables au payement de la dicte somme de trente sept livres." *Ibid.*, p. 869.

[3] *Ibid.*, p. 871.

[4] Le Conseil "declare unanimement qu'il n'a point esté cognu que le dict Seigneur Gouverneur aye voulu persuader quoyque ce soit, ny empesché la liberté des suffrages de personnes de la compagnie." *Ibid.*, p. 878.

siastics was successfully asserted. While unable to try him on the charge of inciting to sedition, it had patiently collected enough evidence to influence Louis XIV to prohibit the Abbé Fénelon's return to New France.

Yet Councillors felt that this measure of success was bought at a considerable price. They were growing restless at the leadership of the Governor. He had put pressure upon them during the Fénelon trial, and they resented it. He had insisted upon taking a very active part in a case in which he was the injured party. He had forced Councillors to vote whether or not he had intimidated them or influenced their votes. They felt that they could never act with the proper impartiality and independence as long as the Governor could remove them from office in case they did not do his will. They therefore sought royal commissions, which they obtained in the following way.

Villeray and Auteuil had re-entered the Council as substitute judges during the trials of 1674, and anxious to enjoy their old positions, had gone over the head of the Governor by persuading the Company of the West Indies to nominate them *to the King,* making representation that the Council was too small in number. Accordingly, on October 2 and 3, 1674, royal commissions were registered making Lotbinière a Councillor, and Auteuil Attorney-General.[1] At the same time, various letters from the King and West India Company showed that Villeray had been given a commission as First Councillor, although the document itself did not appear.[2] The Council agreed to seat him as

[1] *Jugements et Délib.*, vol. i, pp. 856-862.

[2] Villeray received this appointment by impressing the minister with his commercial activity; for on May 17, 1674, Colbert wrote Frontenac that Villeray of all Canadians applied himself most to commerce, sending his vessels to trade with the Islands of America. Frontenac replied that the minister was deceived, for Villeray had not even a bark on the St. Lawrence, far less, vessels trading with the Antilles. (Clément) *Lettres, Instructions et Mémoires de Colbert,* vol. iii, pt. ii, p. 580.

an ordinary Councillor until the arrival of the belated commission; but Villeray angrily refused to attend until he could do so in the capacity of First Councillor.[1] The other Councillors besought the Governor to write to the Court for similar commissions for them. Frontenac did so to his own detriment,[2] for September 23, 1675, the day on which these commissions were registered and Councillors became independent of the Governor, marked the real beginning of the decline of his influence in the Sovereign Council.

A second cause of the decline of the Governor's power at this time was the arrival of Bishop Laval and Intendant Duchesneau, whom the King had sent to New France to check Frontenac's domineering attitude towards the Council. The new Intendant began at once to win over Councillors. From January until May, he worked with them each Monday afternoon upon police regulations, which finally appeared as forty-two ordinances.[3] Meanwhile, in the morning sessions, the Intendant acted as president, introducing much business and signing the minutes. An occasional flash of arrogance showed that Frontenac regretted the loss of functions which he had previously exercised in the Council. Still he was just as interested as before in up-

[1] There is evidence that Frontenac disliked Villeray. In 1673, under pretext of being an adherent of the Jesuits, he had deprived him of the post of collecting the ten per cent duty, entrusted him by the Company. Now it was upon his advice that the Council acted. He said "qu'il n'estime pas se pouvoir dispenser pour un manquement de formalité et un oubly qui peut estre arrivé par accident et par negligence de les executer, Et de leur declarer qu'ils ayent a restablir conformement aux dicts ordres le dict sieur de Villeray dans la charge de premier Conseiller". *Jugements et Délib.*, vol. i, p. 860.

[2] See Frontenac's speech of January 1675: "Messieurs, La Commission que j'ay bien voulu prendre à vos prieres en me chargeant d'écrire à la Cour pour faire obtenir de Sa Majesté des provisions de vous charges," etc. *Ibid.*, p. 889.

[3] *Ibid.*, pp. 63-73.

holding the jurisdiction and dignity of that court, when he considered it to be threatened by the ecclesiastical power. It was upon his advice that Father Morel, having repeatedly refused to appear before the Council, was seized and lodged in the Chateau St. Louis.[1] The ecclesiastics claimed the right to try the prisoner, and showed such convincing titles to their ecclesiastical court (officialty), that the Council surrendered him and recognized the court—recognized that there was one class of persons, who might escape justice at its hands.

Meanwhile the Council exerted itself to better effect in maintaining its preëminent position in church. On the Feast of the Purification of the Virgin, it had been humiliated by the church wardens who had been given precedence, and accordingly, on March 4, 1675, ordained that officers of justice should be given places next after the Governor or seigniors, and that whenever present officially, they should receive the *pain benit* (or eulogiae), the pax, the incense, the tapers, and so forth, immediately after them.[2] A month later, the Council suggested that it receive these next after the clergy from the hands of the officiating priest rather than from the beadle. The Grand Vicar agreed and the Council was thenceforth given honorable treatment in the churches of Quebec.

But there was trouble in other communities about the decree of March 4. On April 22, the Governor produced a report of the captain of the seigniory of Lauson, confirmed by a legal statement made by an usher of the Sovereign Council, to the effect that the parish priest and church wardens in that place had rebelled. Peiras was commissioned to gather additional information. Other unpleasantness had caused the matter to be referred to the King

[1] *Jugements et Délib.*, vol. i, pp. 948-949. [2] *Ibid.*, pp. 904, 922.

for settlement. Pending that decision, the ecclesiastics of Montreal gave the church wardens precedence of the judicial functionary of that place at the Feast of the Purification of the Virgin in 1677. In retaliation the Council ordered that the wardens be deprived of all honors until the arrival of the vessels from France by which the King's will should be known. A fine of 300 livres was to be laid upon any warden who received any church honors until that time.[1]

In 1676 the King had written to Frontenac that members of the Sovereign Council (and officers of justice in Montreal, etc.) should take precedence of the church wardens, when they were in a body and on solemn occasions, but not under ordinary circumstances.[2] In 1677 the vessels brought a letter from the minister to Duchesneau to the effect that the Bishop had the right of offering incense to all the members of his clergy before offering it to the Councillors even though present in a body.[3] This did not, however, affect the position of the Council as regards church wardens. The Council had practically won its contention, and its dignity in church ceremonies was thenceforth assured.

Yet it was difficult for the Council to follow a course independent of ecclesiastical or of commercial influence. The Intendant was warned by the minister against the Bishop. The Bishop, he wrote, was assuming an authority a little too independent; it would perhaps be well that he should not have a seat in the Council. The Intendant was to seek every opportunity, and on all occasions to take every means practicable, to wean the Bishop from the craving for attending the Council. Far from doing as directed, Duchesneau

[1] *Jugements et Délib.*, vol. ii, p. 116.

[2] King to Frontenac, April 15, 1676. *Coll. Moreau St. Méry*, series F iii, vol. iv, pt. ii, p. 773.

[3] *Ibid.*, vol. v, p. 20.

became a friend and supporter of the Bishop. In the spring of 1677 the King instructed Frontenac to point out to Duchesneau that he was too eager to follow the advice of the clergy.[1] But no correction on the part of the Governor had apparently been accepted; for Duchesneau, upon his own responsibility, regulated the tithes in a way very favorable to the clergy. He ordered that no Huguenots should remain in Canada during the winter.[2] Moreover, he used his influence in favor of the Bishop, when the latter's policy of chastising those who traded with the Indians forced him into an unpopular position.

The Bishop, for example, had ordered his parish priests to refuse absolution to such traders.[3] In several cases scenes of violence attended such refusals. The Council investigated these cases, but refused to prosecute a priest or to involve the Bishop. The most interesting case is that of the trader François Noir Rolland, of Isle Mont Royal, who was refused absolution by his priest, Father Guyotte, after making his Easter confession in 1676. Hearing that Father Guyotte was about to denounce him for not making his Easter Communion, Rolland sought out the Jesuit Father Fremin, who expressed satisfaction with the state of his soul and gave him a letter to his priest. A complicated

[1] A letter from the King to Frontenac, written in 1678, is typical of the correspondence during these years. "Quoyque je ne doubte pas que tous les Ecclesiastiques ne se contiennent dans l'estendué de leur pouvoir, je ne laisse pas de vous dire, que mon Conseil Souverain, auquel vous presidez, doubt toujours donner un soin particulier à ce qu'il ne soit rien entrepris contre mon autorité ny celle de mon justice.

"Le mesme Conseil doit aussy tenir la main que les dixmes soient regulierement payées aux Ecclesiastiques sur le pied de reglement qui en a esté cy devant fait comme Chef et President de mon Conseil Souverain exciter les officiers qui le composent a la rendre bonne et briefve [justice]." *Archives des Colonies*, series B, vol. vii, pp. 188-189.

[2] Ordinance of May 11, 1676. *Jugements et Délib.*, vol. ii, p. 72.

[3] *Mandements des Evêques de Québec*, vol. i, pp. 77, 82, 88.

situation developed, the result of which was that the priest interrupted the celebration of mass, and, after a dialogue with Rolland, commanded the kneeling worshipers to eject the offender. As one excommunicated, he was beaten, insulted, and dragged by the hair from the church. Rolland appealed to the Council, which, on December 19, commissioned Lotbinière to go to the scene of the affair and to make investigations. The trader did not wish to sue his assailants for damages, but seems to have thought that the Council could restore his religious privileges. Consequently, having been assured by the Bishop that his assailants would pay for his trip to Quebec, that he might make his confession there and later to the Jesuit Father Fremin, Rolland returned to Montreal, where he reported his interview to the ecclesiastics. They affected to discredit his story, since the Bishop had not informed them of his promises, and refused him permission to go to Father Fremin for confession. Father Guyotte induced his parishioners to sign a statement against him, and from the pulpit, exhorted those who had ejected him not to repent of their deed.[1]

A second time Rolland came down the ice to Quebec, but his petition to the Council was condemned by the Bishop as insulting and untrue. Rolland was overwhelmed at having made an enemy of the Bishop and besought the Court to erase the objectionable terms. He said that possibly the Bishop himself had not promised to have him reimbursed, but he was not ignorant that others had given him such assurances. He referred to Father Custode, a Récollet, for the truth of his other statements, since that ecclesiastic had been present during the interview. But Father Custode asked to be excused from testifying because as a friar he

[1] *Jugements et Délib.*, vol. ii, pp. 97, 103-105.

was dead civilly and could not give evidence in a law court, nor according to canon law could he depose against his Bishop. Furthermore, he could not divulge what he had learned in the secrecy of the Bishop's closet. The witness evidently had damaging evidence to give. Undoubtedly Laval had tried to buy off Rolland with promises which he did not care to acknowledge, since such promises meant disavowal of a priest who was acting in accordance with the episcopal policy. Led by Duchesneau, the Council avoided any such revelation by excusing Father Custode from testifying and by erasing the Bishop's promises from Rolland's petition.[1]

With the same show of tenderness, the priest, who had ordered the attack upon Rolland, was not even summoned; although his agents were prosecuted throughout the spring and summer of 1677.[2] While a certain Quesneuille was fined 100 livres for inducing the people to sign another petition against Rolland, the author was simply ordered to confine all future petitions to purely religious matters. Nevertheless from France came encouragement to deal impartially with such cases in the future. King and minister berated Duchesneau for partiality to the Bishop and directed the Sovereign Council to keep the clergy within bounds.[3]

As this trial illustrates, Frontenac's influence in the Council was weakening.[4] There seems to have been a concerted effort during the next few years to cut him off from

[1] *Jugements et Délib.*, vol. ii, p. 108. [2] *Ibid.*, p. 133.

[3] King to Frontenac, May 12, 1678 and Minister to Duchesneau, May 15. *Supplement to Report on Canadian Archives for 1899*, p. 262.

[4] His advice that Rolland's assaillant should appear and justify his conduct was ignored. "Monsieur le Gouverneur a esté d'advis . . que le dit S Guyotte y sera mande pour luy ouy estre ordonné ce que de raison." *Jugements et Délib.*, vol. ii, p. 133.

active participation in its deliberations. The Governor had lost the power to appoint Councillors, harangue them and administer the oath of office. During 1679 the Council forced him to dispense with the title of "Chief and President", and some time later established the right of its eldest Councillor to act as vice-president. Thenceforth the Governor never served as president either when the Intendant was present or absent. It only remained for the Council to assert its right to act against his advice and to bring him within its jurisdiction by considering petitions against him, unembarrassed by his presence, to reduce the Governor to the position of an ordinary Councillor. This was the tendency of the long disputes, which occupied the Council for weeks at a time, to the exclusion of ordinary affairs. The more important ones will be given in detail.

In 1679 a dispute arose as to the respective titles to be given to the Governor and the Intendant in the minutes and registers of the Council. The Governor had had occasion to look over some old minutes and had been reminded that he was no longer styled "Chief and President of the Council". He therefore ordered Peuvret du Mesnu, the clerk of the Council, to return to the old formula. In the minutes of February 20, 1679, the Governor is described in these terms, while the Intendant is spoken of as functioning also in the capacity of president, in accordance with the declaration of the King of June 5, 1675.[1] This declaration, which was issued by the King as a confirmation of the powers of the Council when he withdrew Canada from the jurisdiction of the Company of the West Indies in 1675,

[1] "La Cour Assemblée où astoient Monsieur le Gouverneur chef et president d'icelle, Monsieur de Bernières grand vicar de Monsieur l'Evesque de cette ville de Québec, Monsieur l'Intendant faisant aussi fonction de president suivant la declaration du Roy du cinc juin 1675." *Ibid.*, p. 277.

provided that the Intendant, although below Governor and Bishop in point of dignity, should perform the functions of acting president in the Council.[1] Unfortunately for the peace of the Council, the commission of the Intendant failed to provide that he should serve as president during the presence of the Governor.[2] On the other hand, royal despatches of April 15, 1676, and May 12, 1678, and a memoir of May 24, 1678, make mention of the Governor as "Chief and President of the Council".[3]

At the third meeting of the Council which he attended upon his installation in 1675, Duchesneau had ordered Peuvret du Mesnu to use the words "Chef du Conseil" after Frontenac's name in the minutes and had sent him with a note to this effect to Frontenac, who refused the proposal. Duchesneau had persisted and the poor clerk had been running to and fro between the two until his departure for France.[4] Becquet then became clerk. For three months he had kept the minute books at the house of the Intendant, where he roomed, and the Governor asserted that he had not seen the headings of the minutes during the two years that Peuvret du Mesnu was away. Duchesneau contradicted

[1] "que l'intendant . . . aura la troisieme place comme president du dit Conseil, demande les avis, recueille les voix et pronounce les arrêts et ait au surplus les mêmes functions et jeuisse les mêmes avantages que les premiers presidents de nos cours." *Édits et Ord.*, vol. i, p. 84.

[2] It simply stated as his duty: "présider au Conseil Souverain en l'absence du dit sieur de Frontenac"; "que le Conseil Souverain auquel vous présiderez ainsi que dit est", etc., etc. *Ibid.*, vol. iii, p. 42.

[3] "Comme Monsieur le Gouverneur est chef et president du Conseil Souverain, il doit tenir la main à ce que la justice soit bien rendue bien examinée et bien establie"; "que Monsieur le Gouverneur doit aussi . . . comme chef et president du dit Conseil exciter les officiers qui le composent à rendre la [justice] bonne et briefve". *Jugements et Délib.*, vol. ii, p. 313.

[4] See the account of Peuvret du Mesnu, *Jugements et Délib.*, vol. ii, p. 281.

Frontenac flatly by saying that he must have seen the minutes, since he presided in the Intendant's absence and signed the records of the meetings. The Governor had been content for over three and a half years with the title of "Chef du Conseil", which had early been agreed upon. Frontenac claimed that it had not been definitely settled, and the clerk confirmed his view of the matter.[1] These conflicting statements were confusing to the members of the Council, but a detailed list of the minute headings, made by the Intendant from the record, enlightened them. There had been no fixed practice. Peuvret, Becquet, the first usher Roger, and again Peuvret, had in turn served as clerk. These scribes had written: Monsieur the Governor, President of the Council, Monsieur the Intendant also functioning as President of the Council; or simply Governor and Intendant. When the Governor was absent, the Intendant was several times spoken of as presiding over the Council, and once, as President of the Council; or when the Intendant was absent, the Governor was mentioned as presiding. On February 6, 1679, the clerk gave the Governor the title of "Chief of the Council", and on the 20th enlarged it to "Chief and President of the Council".[2] Thus Frontenac temporarily gained his point.

The Intendant claimed that this formula was an innovation. On March 7 the Governor presented his despatches while the Intendant cited the royal declaration as mentioning only one president of the Council, that is, himself. On March 20 the Council passed a decree requesting Governor and Intendant to waive the question of title until the King should rule concerning it. Meanwhile, in the minutes, they

[1] Minutes of March 3 and 4, 1679. *Ibid.*, pp. 279-288.

[2] *Ibid.*, pp. 284-285.

were to appear simply as Governor and Intendant.[1] The Intendant acquiesced, on the ground that the administration of justice had suffered during the disputes; but the Governor, although he knew that the decree had been unanimously passed, refused to accede to it. He exhorted the Councillors to deliberate again upon the subject and not oblige him to have recourse to the authority which the King had put into his hands to have his wishes executed, since he would not be sorry to make use of that last road after having hitherto employed the road of persuasion, of gentleness, of remonstrance.[2]

Thus the issue was joined. The Council held to its *arrêt* referring the matter to the King for settlement, while the Governor attempted to wrench the title he desired from the Council by force. On March 24, the Council decreed that the Governor be requested again to uphold it. On March 27, Frontenac declared in the King's name that henceforth the Council must give him the same treatment and the same titles that it pleased the King to accord him. He ordered the clerk to entitle him "Chief and President of the Council" in all minutes and registers for the last three and a half years.[3] The Intendant supported the position that the Council had taken, claiming that the Governor was master of the Council only on questions of war and public safety, and that in this case Frontenac was opposing the execution of two *arrêts* that had no concern with these matters. Duchesneau warned them that the Governor intended to employ force to destroy justice utterly, and that if the Council yielded now, its subserviency was assured for the future, and that it would see itself forced to petition

[1] *Jugements et Délib.*, vol. ii, p. 299.

[2] *Ibid.*, p. 300.

[3] *Ibid.*, p. 305.

the Governor to pronounce as a sovereign upon all business that came before it.[1]

By a unanimous vote the speeches of Governor and Intendant were referred to the Attorney-General for his conclusions. On April 11, Auteuil was ready with his report; but he refused to give it so long as the Governor insisted upon being present while his claims were under consideration. The Governor insisted upon obedience to his order of March 27 and refused to allow the subject of titles to be discussed. A ridiculous scene followed.[2] The Governor refused to withdraw; the Councillors then determined to leave him, but they were ordered to remain. They obeyed; but sat in silence in the Council chamber until the hour of adjournment.

[1] For a paraphrase of the significant parts of Duchesneau's rambling speech of March 27, see *Jugements et Dé ib.*, vol. ii, pp. 306-307.

[2] The details of this session are very amusing. While the clerk was copying the opinions of the Governor and Attorney-General, the Intendant left the table for the chimney seat and sent for his favorite book. Frontenac insisted upon proceeding to the affairs of justice, and asked the Intendant to return and inquire if any one had causes to introduce. In answer to the Intendant, each Councillor replied that he had such business to present but would wait until after the controversy was settled. Tilly offered his resignation, and so also did Vitré, saying that he would rather not be a Councillor than be forced into disobedience. As it was apparent that nothing could be done that day, the Governor demanded that a day be named before the spring recess on which to judge private causes; but the Attorney-General replied that the sowing had already commenced and that it was necessary to declare a recess at once.

When it became apparent that Frontenac would not retire and permit an unbiased decision upon his claims to the title of chief and president, and that the clerk was giving him that title, the Councillors rose to leave the chamber, since they said "all liberty was taken away." "Upon being ordered to remain," continues the account of the Intendant and Councillors, "we took the resolution to speak no longer, which was carried out until noon, which is the hour of the end of the Council session. I attest all the above to be true," (signed) Bernière, Villeray, Tilly, Damours, Bermen, Vitré, Auteuil. *Coll. Moreau St. Méry*, series F iii, vol. v, pp. 288, 305, *et seq.*

No agreement was arrived at in the succeeding sessions of April 17 and April 24. Councillors Tilly and Vitré had threatened to resign; and in the meeting of April 17 the Governor said that Tilly had only to hand in his commission. Tilly replied that he begged to be allowed to keep it as a mark of the honor shown him by the King.[1] At both sessions the argument was maintained with great spirit and acrimony until the noon hour, the whole Council apparently being arrayed against Frontenac.

At this juncture, the Governor ceased to attend the Council meetings but ordered the clerk to bring him the minutes after each session, that he might ascertain whether or not he had been given the title he had ordered. Even this the Councillors and Attorney-General opposed as an attempted restraint upon free expression of opinion in the Council. During this deadlock the spring vacation occurred. Upon reassembling the Council persisted in its decrees, referring the matter to the King; and the Governor, in consequence, meditated the banishment of its leaders. On July 4 he issued orders for Villeray to retire to the house of Berthelot on the Isle St. Laurent pending further orders to proceed to France to give an account of his conduct to the King.[2] Tilly was likewise ordered to the house of his

[1] "Apres quoy le dit sieur de Tilly auroit dit qu'il estoit facheux de demeurer dans cette contrainte et qu'il auroit mieux sortir et se retirer du Conseil, et en effect seroit sorty et Monsieur le Gouverneur luy auroit dit qu'il n'avoit qu'a raporter ses provisions et qu'il les recevroit. A quoy led. Sieur de Tilly auroit répliqué qu'il le privit de trouver bon qu'il les gardast comme un tictre à sa famille de l'honneur que le Roy luy avoit fait. J'ateste ce que desus veritable, Le Gardeur de Tilly.' *Ibid.*, vol. v, p. 314, *et seq.*

[2] "Il est ordonné du sieur de Villeray, premier conseiller au Conseil Souverain de ce pays de se retirer dans l'Isle de Saint-Laurent, en la maison du Sieur Berthelot, deux fois vingt-quatre houres après le présent ordre receu et d'y attendre celluy de passer en France, pour rendre conte au Roy de sa conduite, faisant deffences aud. Sieur de Villeray de venir en cette ville sans nostre permission." *Coll. Moreau St. Méry*, series F iii, vol. v, p. 288, *et seq.*

brother-in-law, the Sieur of St. Denis. The Attorney-General Auteuil was ordered to his house of Monceaux at Sillery.

On July 5, in a meeting at the house of Duchesneau, the Council resolved not to be intimidated by the Governor, but to persist in its policy of referring the question of titles to the King. Every effort was made to keep Villeray, Tilly, and Auteuil in Quebec until the departure of the ships. The Governor's order permitted them forty-eight hours' grace before they should retire to the places assigned. During this time the Council met and addressed a petition to the Governor to permit the suspended members to attend the Council until their departure for France, inasmuch as the ordinary affairs of justice, which required a full Council, were very pressing. On the 10th Duchesneau too sought to obtain this favor for them, but Frontenac refused. Further petitions were sent to the Governor and he authorized La Ferté to interview Villeray, Tilly and Auteuil, who agreed to participate in the ordinary business of justice and to give the Governor the title he desired, provided that the protests of Intendant and Attorney-General should be entered on the minutes at the same time. On July 22, La Ferté made his report to the Governor, who was dissatisfied with the reservation and refused to allow the absent members to return.[1]

At a meeting on October 16 the Council gained a considerable triumph. It had been agreed before this meeting, which was the first one attended by the Governor for six months, that there should be no mention of any subject that might give rise to disputes. After the clerk had written

[1] In the collection of records called *Jugements et Délibérations*, there is a gap between March 27, 1679 and August 14, which we have filled by collating chance references from the later minutes and from the documents of the *Moreau St. Méry Collection*.

the heading to his minutes, Duchesneau asked him to read it. The clerk had written as Frontenac had formerly ordered: "Monsieur the Governor, Chief and President of the Council". The Intendant protested that the difficulty would recommence if the Governor insisted upon retaining the title that the clerk had written. Frontenac said he would rather retire than make any difficulty, in order that the Council might proceed to business.[1] The Intendant also retired and the Council decreed that the Governor and Intendant be requested to agree that no one should be named in the headings which might be made, and that the words "the Council assembled" should alone appear. Both Governor and Intendant agreed to this temporary solution of the difficulty. Thus after seven months of debate, banishment, and strife, the Council succeeded in forcing the Governor to forego the cherished title of President in its minutes. This rule was enforced until October 29, 1680, when a ruling made by the Council of State was adopted. Thenceforth Frontenac was to appear as Governor and Lieutenant-General of the country, and Duchesneau as Intendant of justice, police and finance.[2] This ruling, backing up the Council's contention, was the definitive settlement of the dispute about titles. Frontenac no longer held even the title of President of the Council.

During the next few weeks several changes occurred in the personnel of the Council. Villeray sailed for France. Tilly was too ill to attend the meetings, and Auteuil died. The death of the Attorney-General stirred up more trouble in the Council. Auteuil had been ailing for some years. Duchesneau, fearing his death might cause a halt in the

[1] "Monsieur le Gouverneur a dit que pour ne point faire d'incident il aymoit mieux se retirer, afin la Compagnie pust passer a travailler et expedier les affaires." *Jugements et Délib.*, vol. ii, p. 318.

[2] *Edits et Ord.*, vol. i, p. 238; *Jugements et Délib.*, vol. ii, pp. 423, 427.

business of the court, obtained a blank commission from Colbert dated 1677,[1] but Auteuil had rallied and had performed his duties to the end. The Intendant now proposed to fill out the blank commission of deputy Attorney-General with the name of Auteuil's son, a youth of twenty-two, who had been admitted to the bar of the Parlement of Paris and who had since been associated with his father in the work of his office.[2] The Governor objected to this appointment because the commission now three and a half years old had expired, and because the youth of Auteuil rendered him ineligible. The Governor proposed that one of the members of the Council should serve in the capacity of Attorney General. The Council however decreed that the Intendant should fill out the commission with whatever name he pleased. Even without the old leaders, the Council thus assumed an attitude independent of the Governor. They had summoned Frontenac and Duchesneau to hear their deliberations, without fear of intimidation; had ignored the Governor's recommendation; and had declared for the Intendant.

The events of 1679 undoubtedly made for the independence of the Council. Frontenac's action in banishing the Councillors had not obtained for him the coveted title, nor was he supported at the French court. In April 20, 1680, Colbert wrote that His Majesty, after having examined all

[1] Duchesneau possibly wished to provide that one of his friends should obtain the office. He gave however as his motive for seeking the commission, that "voyant le dit Sieur procureur general fort incommodé de la poitrine et d'une fluxion sur les yeux, Et aprehendant qu'il moutust, ou qu'il tombast dans un estat dans lequel il ne pourroit plus exercer sa charge, Il se crût obligé d'en donner avis a Monseigneur Colbert, etc." *Ibid.*, p. 341.

[2] Duchesneau states as Auteuil the younger's qualifications: "qui depuis deux ans a travaillé sous son père, et qui est *seul* dans le pais *apourvoir* de charge qui ayt fait son cours de droit et qui soit recou advocat en la Cour de parlement de Paris." *Ibid.*, p. 342.

the papers, was of opinion that Frontenac's conduct was deserving of great blame, and that he had abused his authority. He would be maintained in his office for another year however, in the hope that he would alter his conduct. He had no right to the title of Chief and President of the Council, and he deserved that an indemnity, taken out of his emoluments, should be paid to the Councillors whom he had banished.[1] Just one year before, the same minister had written in a very different tone to Duchesneau: "When the Governor votes anything in the Council, you have but to submit. The Council can only make representations to the Governor, and if he does not take heed of them, refer them to the King. But, even in that case, you must first submit to the Governor all your complaints against him, that he may be in a position to answer them."[2] Without taking either letter at full face value, it is evident that there was a reaction at Court in favor of the Sovereign Council and in favor of rendering it independent of the Governor. The appointment made by Duchesneau of M. François Magdeleine Reuette, Sieur d'Auteuil, to the place of his father, was confirmed by letters patent of the King, dated June 2, 1680.[3] On May 29, the King gave Duchesneau the right to appoint the ushers to the Council and the clerk of the Maréchaussée of Canada.[4] The Governor's influence was

[1] "Sa Majesté m'ordonne encore de vous dire qu'elle ne peut approver en aucune manière l'ordre que vous avez donné aux deux con^ers^ et au procureur gn'al de se retirer, et que si ce n'etoit pas qu'Elle espere encore que vous chargerez de conduite elle leur auroit adjugé un dedommagement assez considerable a prendre sur vos appointemens parcequ'elle ne peut jamais autoriser une violence de cette nature sans aucun fondement." *Archives des Col.*, series B, vol. viii, pp. 39-40.

[2] *Coll. Moreau St. Méry*, series F iii, vol. v, p. 353, *et seq.*

[3] *Jugements et Délib.*, vol. ii, p. 422.

[4] *Coll. Moreau St. Méry*, series F iii, vol. v, p. 503.

to be counterbalanced by that of the Intendant, while the Sovereign Council was to be dominated by neither.

In 1681, a dispute resulted in the Governor's surrendering the functions of vice-president to the eldest Councillor. On March 9, 1676, he had requested the approval of the Council to his withdrawal, since it was not in accordance with the dignity of his office to preside in the absence of the Intendant, whereupon Tilly as the eldest Councillor presided. At another time, Duchesneau and Villeray being challenged withdrew from the Council chamber; and then Frontenac desired to collect the votes, but, on the remonstrance of Tilly, desisted. On March 7, 1678, in the absence of the Intendant, the Governor desired again to collect the votes and pronounce the judgments, whereupon Villeray reminded him of his statement that it was not in accordance with the dignity of his office to preside in the absence of the Intendant. The Governor indicated that he had changed his mind. It appears that the principle was propounded that the functions which the Intendant had a right to exercise to the exclusion of the Governor, should not, in his absence, devolve upon the Governor, but upon the eldest Councillor present.[1]

On February 3, 1681, the Governor and five Councillors constituted the Council. Because they were interested in a certain action, the Governor and Peiras retired. As the trial of a cause at that time required five judges, the Council requested the Governor to return to complete the quorum. The Governor, upon his entrance, told Villeray the First Councillor, that he might take the opinions. Villeray asked for the opinion of the Governor fourth in order, but he preferred to give it last. Villeray stated that the functions which the Intendant exercised included the determining vote and that, in the Intendant's absence, the eldest Councillor

[1] *Jugements et Délib.*, vol. ii, p. 286.

had a right to this prerogative. The Governor replied that Villeray might demand the opinions, collect the votes and pronounce the decisions, but that his claim to deliver his opinion last was contrary to the King's wishes. At the conclusion of the meeting Frontenac pointed out how Villeray had executed all the functions of the Intendant, including the nomination of a reporter, while he, the Governor, had delivered his opinion last.[1] On March 10, 1681, this procedure was definitely adopted.[2]

A rapid sketch of a number of cases will show that the Council sought, during the next twenty months, to reduce the Governor to its jurisdiction. For three months a contest was waged in the Council chamber between Frontenac and his old enemy Villeray over the latter's right to the title of Esquire in a certain writ. The Governor exhorted the Council to order Villeray not to use a title which he could not prove belonged to him; and cited a decree of the Council of State of May 29, 1680, by which the King prohibited Councillors from assuming titles other than those he specified in their commissions.[3] Villeray replied that the usher alone was responsible for the term in the one writ where it occurred, and Autueil, the Attorney-General, concluded that the decree of the Council of State referred only to titles used in the Council chamber and its minutes and registers and not to those used in private business.[4]

[1] *Jugements et Délib.*, vol. ii, pp. 466-468.

[2] "Et qu'il s'y arrestast tant pour le present que pour l'avenir Et sans y déroger Encor que dans les occasions qui pourroient se presenter cy parez elles ne fussent renouvellées, a quoy Monsieur le Gouverneur ayant consenty le dit Sr de Villeray a dit son advis, Monsieur le Gouverneur sien ensuite et le dit sieur de Villeray a prononcé l'arrest, etc." *Ibid.*, p. 477.

[3] *Ibid.*, p. 478.

[4] *Ibid.*, p. 506. The decree of May 29, 1680, was the one which settled the difficulty as to what titles should appear in the minutes. It abolished "Chief and President", etc.

Having forced the Governor to retire[1] to permit of unbiased consideration of the case, Auteuil now asked the Council to request the Governor to cease complaints prejudicial to the expedition of justice, and to refrain from invalidating legally-worded writs until His Majesty should express his will upon the subject.[2] Upon this impudent recommendation the Council passed a decree validating Villeray's papers. Frontenac was furious, more especially as he had that morning served an order upon Villeray, enjoining him from using the title of Esquire in writs of any character. Villeray had not told and Councillors unanimously declared that they had known nothing of Frontenac's order. The Governor held up Villeray's petition, list of titles, responses, etc., and refused to give them up. At the same time Tilly rose as an ally; said the Governor was not within the jurisdiction of the Council; said that he would not grant an act to Villeray against the Governor since the Council had refused such acts on several occasions. The majority thought differently and sustained the act.[3] The Governor had been treated as an ordinary Councillor: his exhortation had been treated not as a mandate but as a debatable proposition. It was not met by obedience, but by an inquiry into the alleged abuse, which was decided to be no abuse.

Again in the trial of Thomas Vaultier, pressed during

[1] "Sur quoy Monsieur le Gouverneur a dit que pour ne point apporter de trouble, sans préjudicier au rang qu'il a plû au Roy luy donner dans le Conseil ny a ce qu'il est obligé de faire pour s'en acquicter Il se retire, protestant de donner avis a Sa Majesté de la maniere dont les affaires se traittent au Conseil." *Jugements et Délib.*, vol. ii, p. 483.

[2] "de finir ses plaintes qui pourvient estre prejudiciables au bien de la justice; de n'empescher que les exploits dont est question n'ayent leur effect dans de pareilles affaires, atendu qu'ils ne sont point contraindre de faire les recherches susdites, qu'apres il sera plu Sa Majesté faire savoir sa volonté sur ce sujet." *Ibid.*, p. 490.

[3] For this trial, see *ibid.*, pp. 507, 522, 597.

April, 1681, the Council attempted to sit in judgment upon the Governor. Vaultier, a servant of Duchesneau, had come into collision with partisans of Frontenac and violent recriminations ensued. Frontenac had him imprisoned. Duchesneau committed him to trial before the Council, which asked the Governor to show cause why Vaultier was imprisoned. Frontenac replied that the King should know of the conduct of the Council; that the intention was apparently to embroil him with the Council and make him amenable to its court of justice. Such action implied that the Council could without request from him constitute itself judge of outrages committed against him and of safeguards taken by him, even after he as Governor had taken cognizance of complaints addressed to him. On April 29, the Council decided not to press the suit but to send all the papers of the trial to the King for his judgment.[1]

Councillors Tilly and Peiras supported the Governor's position that the Vaultier affair was not within the jurisdiction of the Council. They refused to take part in that trial or any other until their written opinions should be read. Between April and August the Attorney-General failed to give his conclusions upon these protests, and the majority was left to do as it liked. But Frontenac wanted his friends in the Council and effected their return on August 11, when the Council voted to send the dangerous protests unperused to the King.[2]

On the following morning Frontenac imprisoned Mathieu Damours, one of the leaders of the opposition, on the charge of clearing a boat on a permit that had been granted for another purpose. Did the Governor aim at destroying the majority against him in the Council? Dupont might be counted upon for occasional support, and Tilly and

[1] *Jugements et Délib.*, vol. ii, pp. 552, 553, 554.

[2] *Ibid.*, pp. 490, 522, 531, 535, 537, 582-584, 623.

Peiras, annoyed at their recent treatment, would be steady supporters. With the Governor's, the votes of these three would counterbalance those of the Intendant, Villeray, Vitré and Martinière. At any rate, Frontenac kept Damours *hors de combat* for two months during which time his party prevented the passage of a number of hostile measures. This was his only gain, for his friends were in the minority when the Damours trial came up because the Governor was excluded as the accuser.[1]

The imprisonment of a Councillor by the Governor called for a consideration of the rights of the case. The opportunity to make Frontenac party to a suit was too good to miss. Duchesneau and Auteuil hurried to ask if they might summon the Council to try Damours. The Governor replied that it was no affair of the Council's, but upon their suggestion, the prisoner petitioned that body to conduct his trial in the ordinary way. Frontenac was furious at being thus outwitted, and protested to the end of the trial that he could not be made a party to a suit. No judgment was reached, but the first steps of the trial were successfully taken and the documents obtained sent to the King.

In the meantime Councillors asserted their right to decide how the coureurs de bois should be treated. Frontenac and Duchesneau supported very different policies. The former wished not to crush out this class of hardy and enterprising adventurers, but to utilize them in pushing the French outposts into the wilderness. It was the business of the Intendant, on the other hand, to draw these men back into farming pursuits, since he was responsible to the King for the annual increase of *arpents* cleared and cultivated. Frontenac therefore wished merely to overawe the coureurs de bois, Duchesneau to root out the whole class.

[1] For the process in detail of this very interesting case, see Appendix B.

The majority of the Councillors favored the latter policy. When, in December, 1680, Duchesneau's commissioner, Martinière, made so many descents upon the coureurs de bois and raised much excitement with confiscations and arrests, the Council assumed the responsibility and voted high pay to the commissioner. On April 25 it decreed that the accused should appear before its tribunal and summoned twenty-seven witnesses to appear before its commissioner, to whom it delegated the widest powers.[1]

On May 2, the receiver of the King's domain complained of the expense of this commission system and argued that the Intendant should do that work. The Attorney-General replied that there were good grounds why Governor and Intendant should not leave Quebec for Montreal and distant places; that the Intendant could not serve as commissioner and then as president in the court of appeals; that the Council had full power over the coureurs de bois and could delegate the trial in first instance to whom it pleased. Frontenac offered to save the receiver all the expenses of travel by furnishing canoes, canoeists, etc., and proposed reducing commissioners' rates. He claimed that Martinière's investigations had caused such widespread excitement that the presence of himself and the Intendant would be necessary to authorize those measures, to arrest insolence, and to assure obedience. To make an example of the ringlead-

[1] For full particulars, see *Jugements et Délib.*, vol. ii, pp. 441-445, 545, 547.

"le sieur de la Martinière a esté commis pour se transporter a Montreal Et autres lieux, Et ouys plusieurs personnes adjournées personnellment pour l'affaire des dits coureurs de bois, Et pour informer de nouveau, Interoger, recoler Et confronter, de metter d'adjournement personnel ou de prise de corps, Et faire tous actes que besoin sera jusques a arrest diffinitif exclusivement atendu l'esloignement des lieux Et pour accelerer l'Instruction du proces dont le retardement pouroit estre prejudiciable Et pour Esviter a plus grans frais." *Ibid.*, p. 576.

ers, to spare the others, and to bring all back to a sense of duty were, he claimed, his objects.

The Intendant, on the other hand, asserted that only the total destruction of the coureurs de bois could increase the profits of the King's "farm," prevent the ruin of the colony, and banish licentiousness from it. He said that the Council and he would be surety for both the expenses of the undertaking and the good order of the people.[1]

The Council rejected Frontenac's proposals and despatched Martinière and its own Attorney-General upon a second circuit. But the Governor also traveled beyond Montreal, cross-questioned eleven witnesses at Chambly before the lieutenant general of Three Rivers and upon their evidence ordered the capture of two canoes. The raids were successful and the prisoners were lodged in the prisons of Quebec. On July 14 the Council took cognizance of their cases. The question of competence was raised. Since the offenses concerned the King's revenue and the commissioners of the Council had not conducted preliminary investigations, they were held to be within the jurisdiction of the Intendant. Duchesneau, however, yielded in favor of the Council.[2] On July 28, the lieutenent general of Three Rivers was ordered to submit the minutes of his investigations, that the Council might be enabled to proceed expeditiously with the trials. During the intervals between other disputes the crusade against the coureurs de bois was vigorously pushed, until the arrival of the King's amnesty in August.

[1] *Jugements et Délib.*, vol. ii, pp. 569-572, 575-577, 587.

[2] "Il se retranchoit apres la Compagnie de s'en retenir la connoissance Et de se trouver bon qu'il la juge avec elle, n'estimant pas que dans une autre occasion elle veuille tirer a consequence, . . . Et a Esté arresté que le Conseil prendra connoissance de l'affaire en question." *Jugements et Délib.*, vol. ii, pp. 608-609.

The publication of this document gave rise to another dispute concerning the scope of the Council's jurisdiction. On August 18, the Attorney-General demanded that the amnesty be promulgated in the villages of Nipissing, Sainte-Marie du Sault, St. Ignace, Lake Huron, St. François-Xavier, and in the Baye des Puants, in order that all Frenchmen who traded with the Indians might learn its provisions and subsequently return to civilized communities.

The Governor affirmed that the Council proposed to promulgate the amnesty beyond its own jurisdiction in regions where there were no established judges with appeal to the royal *prévôtés* and the Council; that the territory beyond was within his jurisdiction, whither he alone could send his own or the King's commands. He promised that he would himself execute at once the amnesty in that country, abolish trading licenses and open trade to all the inhabitants.[1] The Attorney-General answered that he only asked for the same process of promulgation that had been adopted on October 15, 1676.[2] Frontenac replied that, whereas he had had his reasons for consenting to it then, he had other reasons now for objecting. The Council nevertheless decreed the promulgation of the amnesty in the manner and places recommended by the Attorney-General.[3] One of its own ushers was despatched to post copies in the farthest settlements and posts. Apparently the Sovereign Council thought that its jurisdiction extended to the boundaries of New France.

That there should be no rival jurisdiction to its own, the Council took a significant step in November of 1681. Owing to the great distance from France and the inevitable ruin to Canadians who should be compelled to plead in French

[1] *Jugements et Délib.*, vol. ii, pp. 653-654.

[2] *Ibid.*, p. 73.

[3] *Ibid.*, p. 655.

courts, the Council asked the King to forbid the carrying elsewhere of any cases that concerned persons dwelling in the country.[1] As all the seigniories had been included within the jurisdiction of local courts, from which appeal was had to the Council, that tribunal would thus be assured of the ultimate consideration of all private business involving inhabitants of the country.

But the Council aspired also to a larger control of public business. The registration and promulgation of the King's edicts was public business. The consideration of currency problems was of the same nature. During 1681 and 1682 the Council reasserted its right to fix the currency of the country. This was done largely upon the initiative of the Intendant and Attorney-General. After several ordinances relating to the currency had been enacted by the Intendant in agreement with the Governor, the subject was introduced by the Intendant in Council meeting without previous conference with the Governor. At this meeting on December 2, 1680, the Council passed an act which was entirely in accordance with former ordinances.[2] Later, Duchesneau admitted that he introduced the business simply to restore to the Council an old power.[3] "He thought that having the honor to perform the functions of president, he ought not only to preserve to the company the advantages which they enjoyed, but even to increase them as much as should be in

[1] *Jugements et Délib.*, vol. ii, p. 725.

[2] "Dit a esté que doresnavant les pieces de quatre sols et sols marquez ainsy que toutes autres sortes de monnoye n'auront cours en ce pais que sur le mesme pied des Louis d'or Et Louis d'argent a raison du tiers en montant, ainsi qu'il est en usage depuis plusieurs années." *Ibid.*, p. 440.

[3] "et luy Intendant ayant apris que le Conseil estoit en porcession de faire les Reiglemens des monoyes comme il luy dut justifié par celui qui avoit esté fait en mil six cent soixante sept le dixiesme janvier." *Ibid.*, p. 752.

his power". He had therefore not consulted with the Governor, because he did not care to have Councillors think that they were doing no more than vote upon a prearranged proposition. He wanted to have them feel that they were the authors of the currency regulation.

The Governor doubtless understood the situation in December of 1680; but he said nothing until May 2, 1681, when he expressed surprise that the Council had not informed him of the nature of the business to be considered. The clerk who came to invite him to "come and take his place" should have prepared him. In the matter of the coureurs de bois the Intendant had done wrong in introducing the subject before he and the Governor had agreed as to what should be done. It was evident to the Council that Frontenac was sensitive upon the subject. When, therefore, in September the Attorney-General complained that the country was flooded with underweight coins, a temporary regulation only was passed owing to the absence of the Governor. On January 12, 1682, the Governor was given a week's notice that the regulation of the currency would be considered.[1] Frontenac returned an indignant note. In it he expressed astonishment that the clerk had come to him just one-half hour before the meeting of the 6th with the announcement that the Council would consider the regulation of the currency, thus treating him like an ordinary Councillor. According to the King's orders the Intendant should have conferred with him concerning general affairs, in order that they might have decided and presented to the Council their unanimous opinion.[2] Thereafter

[1] "Et que mon sieur le Gouverneur sera prié par le greffier de la part de la Compagnie de venir prendre sa place au premier jour affin de reigler l'affaire des monnoyes, ou de faire connoistre sil desire y estre present ou non." *Jugements et Délib.*, vol. ii, p. 741.

[2] *Ibid.*, p. 751.

the Council no longer failed to give notice of prospective business, but Frontenac declined to participate. The Councillors delayed taking action on the currency until February 16, when they definitely confirmed the regulation of September, 1681, to take all foreign money at one-third above its face value.[1] Councillors passed this measure by unanimous vote. Even Tilly and Peiras believed the Council could " fix the currency ".

The years 1679 to 1682 are more full of significance for the student of the Sovereign Council than any other period in the history of New France. During that time the Council broke away from the leading strings of the Governor. On the other hand it usually accepted the guidance of the Intendant and Attorney-General. To keep such leadership these officials planned to exalt the Council. The jurisdiction of the court was extended to comprise all persons, even the Governor, in all parts of the country. The share of the Council in public administration was also recognized. Within its organization the Governor was made practically an honorary member; his functions as vice-president were exercised by the eldest Councillor present. It was more than the Governor's Council, more than the supreme court of appeals. It almost justified its title of *Sovereign* Council.

In consequence of their quarrels both Governor and Intendant were recalled to France, Frontenac returning in 1689 for his second administration. During this interval of seven years the Council was associated with two Governors and two Intendants. These high officials came and went; the Councillors' terms of office ended only with their deaths, which stability of tenure increased their influence. Men newly arrived from France and ignorant of Canadian conditions naturally sought advice from officers who had

[1] *Jugements et Délib.*, vol. ii, p. 760.

been for years conversant with the public affairs of the colony.

The new régime opened auspiciously with promise of peace and union. On October 9, 1682, the Council met to install the new officials. Duchesneau, although he had been informed of his recall, presided over the Council until the last minute. The letters patent of Le Febvre de la Barre, the new Governor, were registered. Then the Council proceeded in a body to beg him to "come and take his place". The whole Council attended him. This mark of consideration led to further demonstrations of amity. The Governor told how the King had especially directed him to establish peace and quiet, to unite persons estranged through dissensions, in order that each might apply himself to the duties of his office with single-mindedness and good-will.[1] He begged the Councillors to restore Tilly to office since his exclusion had been the result of difficulties between Governor and Intendant.[2] He drew out of his pocket letters patent and commission according the office of Intendant to Jacques de Meulles. At this moment Duchesneau left the room. The Council consented to receive Tilly and registered the papers of Meulles. A committee of two was delegated to escort the new Intendant to the Council chamber.[3]

In 1684, the Council made the first of two notable at-

[2] "Ce que l'oblige, ayant apris que le sieur de tilly l'un des Con^ers^ introduire afin que chacun pûst s'employer aux functions de sa charge avec une application entière Et une reunion des coeurs et des Esprits." *Jugements et Délib.*, vol. ii, p. 828.

[2] "Ce que l'oblige, ayant apris que le sieur de tilly l'un des Con^ers^ de ce Conseil se trouvoit privé de l'honneur de sa Seance pour des causes que le Conseil auroit trouvées raisonnables, Etc." Tilly had last attended at the morning session of February 23. On March 2, the Council assigned special duties formerly performed by him to other Councillors. *Ibid.*, p. 771. The clerk said Tilly returned the public papers to him after the close of the last session. [3] *Ibid.*, p. 829.

tempts to establish the right to enact important legislation without the participation of the Intendant as well as the Governor. During their absence meetings were called at the instance of the Attorney-General on August 14 and 16. At these meetings the prices of wines and brandy were considered and the Council passed a decree upon the matter. The Bishop of Quebec attended both meetings. On August 21, the Intendant called a meeting, at which he protested against the enactment of a decree upon such an important subject during the absence of Governor and Intendant. Although the debate occupied both morning and afternoon sessions, the Council refused to reverse its decision.[1] It offered, however, to compromise, but the Intendant refused and issued an ordinance giving the merchants complete liberty to charge what they pleased. On March 10, 1685, the Council of State annulled the decree of the Council and forbade it to make any regulations in the absence of Governor and Intendant. During the time of Frontenac the Council had dispensed with the consent of the Governor to various public measures, but now it overreached itself when attempting to act independently of both Governor and Intendant. It met with rebuff, because the Court considered its action as a usurpation of the ordinance-making power.

In 1685 Canada received a new bishop. His arrival presaged stirring events in the Council. Laval had grown wise with increasing years. He had steadily championed the cause of the Indians. His arguments against the traffic in liquor with those primitive peoples are most convincing.[2]

[1] "Sur ce qui a esté remontré a la Cour par Monsieur L'Intendant afin de voir s'il n'est pas apropos de ne pas faire executer L'arrest rendu en icelle le seize de ce mois touchant la taxe du vin Et de l'Eau de Vye, Il *n' rien esté arreste.*" *Jugements et Délib.*, vol. ii, p. 960.

[2] For the clearest exposition of his position, see *Mand. des Ev. de Québ.*, vol. i, p. 149, *et seq.*

Yet he had seen the need of concession and compromise. The result of labors extending over a score of years was the limitation of the liquor traffic to towns and trading posts. Men were restrained from going into the forests to live with the Indians, baiting them with drugged brandy and getting their peltries for almost nothing. The traffic was to go on only in towns and under the ordinary conditions of commerce. This edict, if executed effectively, would have been some compensation for Bishop Laval, although the sale of liquor was not proscribed. Nevertheless the Bishop saw that he must be content for the time being. He made concessions as to the discipline of his clergy and in his later years he avoided any open collisions with the temporal power. In 1684 he returned to France, a man prematurely worn and aged by his strenuous work in Canada. In his stead came Bishop St. Vallier, unmellowed by age and experience, and filled with his own ideas as to the position of the ecclesiastical power and the discipline of the clergy. Bishop Laval had adjusted the clergy to the circumstances of the communities in which their work lay. Bishop Saint Vallier thought these adjustments unwise and upset them. Consequently, in 1688, Bishop Laval wrote to the Pope that his successor was "the greatest scourge and chastisement that could befall the Church in Canada".[1]

The introduction of Bishop St. Vallier into political circles in New France was promising. He had made the passage with the Marquis de Denonville, the Governor nominate, and entered the Council under the new Governor's auspices. On August 3, 1685, the letters patent of Denonville were registered, to the great chagrin of La Barre who affirmed that His Majesty had not informed him of his

[1] Gosselin, *Vie de Mgr. de Laval.*

recall.[1] As his successor was escorted into the Council chamber by three Councillors, La Barre rose and gave him his seat, withdrawing in discomfiture from an assembly which had welcomed him with acclaim less than three years before. Denonville announced that the Abbé St. Vallier, appointed Bishop of Quebec by the King, had come upon his invitation to take his place in the Council. He had remained in the office of Sieur de la Barre, judging that his entrance would be inopportune as he had brought from France no brevêt of nomination. Denonville asked the Council to install Bishop St. Vallier without the brevêt, saying that there could be no doubt about the truth of the nomination and that His Majesty would be happy to see the Councillors give this proof of their regard for a person who so richly merited it.[2] The Council consented to give His Majesty so much pleasure, voted to receive the Bishop, and delegated Tilly and Dupont to accompany him to the hall. At the next meeting of the Council the Intendant proposed to send two Councillors to the Governor's lady to express the joy of the assembly that she had been willing to expose herself to the dangers of the sea, and their satisfaction that the country should possess a person of her rank and courage. Villeray and Vitré carried this message. With these delicate compliments was the administration of Denonville inaugurated.

Few events interrupted the harmony of the administration. Nevertheless beneath the surface there were feelings that were not made apparent to the public. For instance, Denonville's friendship for Bishop St. Vallier was several

[1] "Sa Majesté ne luy ait point fait savoir par aucunes de ses depesches qu'elle desire le rapeller en france." *Jugements et Délib.*, vol. ii, p. 1011.

[2] *Ibid.*, p. 1012.

times subjected to some strain. The Bishop, not content with admonishing the people about their follies and vanities, sent the Governor a five-page treatise regulating the conduct of that functionary, his family and his retinue.[1] Denonville, pious and orthodox, probably felt this advice to be tactless and unnecessary. At any rate in a letter to the King he expressed a desire for the return of Bishop Laval.[2] Still there is evidence that Governor, Bishop, Intendant and Council were closely united at this time.[3] For example, when Meulles was about to leave for Acadia to see about establishing fisheries, he expressed the desire to stand in the good graces of the Council, praying it to continue its friendship for him and to permit him to take Councillor Peiras with him. He would like to take another Councillor as a second adviser, but the smallness of their number

[1] *Mandements des Evêques de Québec,* vol. i, pp. 169-174.

[2] King to Denonville and Champigny, *Supplement Canadian Archives Report,* 1899, p. 277.

[3] La Hontan was a Frontenac sympathiser. Naturally he exaggerated somewhat the ecclesiastical influence and scored the Council with which Frontenac had come into conflict. Nevertheless his testimony is of some value. Writing in 1684 he dwelt at length upon the influence of Bishop and Jesuits over Governor Denonville. It was good policy, he said, for parents to gain their good will, for they would influence the Governor to procure suitable husbands for their daughters, and favorites too might receive one of the twenty-five trading licenses at the disposal of the Governor. Of the Councillors this sharp-tongued writer said: "When they have nice points under consideration they usually consult the priests or Jesuits; and if any cause comes before them in which these good fathers are interested, they are sure not to be cast, unless it be so very black, that the cunningest lawyer can't give it a plausible turn." La Hontan, *Voyages,* Thwaites' translation, vol. i, p. 263. The records of the Council indicate that there is some truth in this account. Formal consultation with the Jesuits is recorded, and the miscarriage of justice where ecclesiastics were concerned was illustrated by the Rolland case and will be shown by others.

and the coming trip of Villeray to France, obliged him to deprive himself of that pleasure.[1]

In September, 1686, this amiable Intendant was superseded by the Sieur de Champigny, who assisted the Council in preparing several series of police ordinances. The effective operation of the Council was interrupted, however, in 1689 by the blundering Indian policy of Denonville. This had resulted in the surprise and burning of Lachine by the Iroquois. Even the Council in distant Quebec adjourned in alarm to give Councillors and litigants a chance to harvest crops and take precautions against the fifteen hundred savages then hovering about.[2]

It was into this Canada of war and confusion that Frontenac returned. His letters patent were registered by the Council on November 28, 1689, but he failed to attend any meetings until late in the following spring. During the intervening months, a brisk interchange of messages occurred concerning the reception of the Governor. Frontenac desired the same honors as those accorded to the King by his Parlement. If his position was to be only that of an honorary Councillor, the Governor intended to make it as respected and dignified as possible. At last he was satisfied with the ceremonies proposed for his initial and later entrances, and on May 3, 1690, Dupont, Peiras, Villeray, his *bête noir*, and Damours, his erstwhile prisoner, marched in state to the Château St. Louis and returned to the Council chamber with Count Frontenac in their midst. The personnel of this delegation seems to indicate a commendable desire to let bygones be bygones.[3] From 1690 to June 28, 1694, the Governor attended an ever larger pro-

[1] *Jugements et Délib.*, vol. ii, pp. 1035-1037.

[2] *Ibid.*, p. 353.

[3] *Ibid.*, pp. 389-392, 397, 405.

portion of meetings,[1] where he was always conducted to his chair by two Councillors.[2] This courtesy was shown rather to the great man, who had brought Canada through a grave crisis,[3] than to the Chief of the Council.

The disputes which had disturbed Frontenac's first administration were not repeated for some years. In 1694, however, one of the most interesting cases in Canadian history arose. The Bishop struck at the practice of presenting skeptical plays by having the leading man imprisoned. The Governor, who was responsible for the plays thus condemned, watched with some impatience the trial of the prisoner. When, after some months, he became convinced that the trial was not fair, he condemned the Council and released the prisoner by force. The details of the process before the court are as follows.

The Sieur de Mareuil, a lieutenant on half-pay, had been admonished by the Bishop and others appointed by him, to discontinue his alleged blasphemous words against God, the

[1] The incomplete records at my disposal show that he attended three meetings in 1690, four in 1691, eleven in 1692, ten in 1693, and fourteen in 1694. After 1694, he attended only the hearings of the Lamotte-Cadillac trial in 1698.

[2] This is the shortest of the announcements: "La Compagnie Esté advertie que Monsieur le Gouverneur venoit prendre sa place, Mrs de Tilly Et Damours Conèrs ont Este deputez pour l'aller recevoir, Lesquels estant partis Le dit sieur Gouverneur Est ensuite Entré a la chambre Et apris sa place."

[3] In 1690, the Council was again forced to adjourn: "Sur ce qui a esté remontré par le Procureur General du Roy, qu'atendu le pressant besoin de continuer les travaux des fortifications de cette Ville, pour la mettre en estat de resister aux desseins que les Anglois nos Ennemis ont formé de la Venir attaquer cette année et faire tous leurs efforts pour s'en rendre les Maistres; Et ayant receu plusieurs avis qu'ils estoient en Mer avec une flotte considerable, qui pourroit arriver dans peu." *Jugements et Délib.*, vol. iii, p. 754.

Holy Virgin, and the saints.[1] Upon his continued disobedience his case was referred to the Council. On February 1, the Attorney-General made an eloquent speech, dwelling upon the danger of impiety to the country and to the Church.[2] The Council decided to take cognizance of the case, and ordered Auteuil to ascertain the facts and Villeray to conduct the preliminary hearings. Mareuil in a very boldly worded petition accepted the jurisdiction of the Council. He asked that the Bishop's mandate of interdict against him be annulled since it was contrary to canon law, which provided that a man be warned several times in the presence of two or three witnesses before the infliction of such a penalty. He challenged the Bishop to prove that he had ever admonished the accused or had authorized any person to admonish him. He asked for a speedy and public trial, with a chance to justify himself, maintaining that otherwise the procedure would be worse than the Inquisi-

[1] Lamotte Cadillac thus describes the only crime he admits that Mareuil had been guilty of: "Il est vrai quil y a environ deux ans que le Sr de Mareuil a son arrivée icy s'etant trouvé en debauche dit quelque chause indecente, M^r^ le Comte en fût âverti, qui luy en fit une severe reprimande, voila le procès qu'on luy fait aujourdhuy, voila le zele pastoral reveille apres un silence de deux annees, et la veille d'une comedie qu'on voulut aboli a quelque prix que ce fût et dont l'authorité ecclesiastique ne voulloit pas avoir le dementi.

"Il est incontestable et on ne peut nier sans rougir que Mareuil depuis ce tems la n'ait eu recours a la penitence, il s'etoit confessé et a communié diverses fois, il tomba meme dans une maladie dangereuse ou il receut les sacremens, et il a continué à faire le devoir d'un chretien et d'un honete homme." *Correspondance Générale*, series C xi, vol. xiii, p. 230, *et seq.*

[2] "Il dit que sil y a lieu au monde où doive veiller a ceque limpietté soit bannie, ce doit estre en ce pays, puisque ne Comment ç'aut qu'a se former outre le scandalle qu'ell Cause, ceux qui en seroienattaints peuvent facilement alterer les dogmes de la foy et Corrompre les Moeurs. etc." *Jugements et Délib.*, vol. iii, p. 830.

tion, which had never been introduced into France.[1] The petition was referred to the Attorney General for his conclusions.

The real reason for the mandate of the Bishop became apparent only after later hearings. In January it was proposed to play Molière's *Tartuffe* during the Carnival.[2] On the 17th Bishop St. Vallier denounced all comedies and tragedies and prohibited all persons in the parish from attending the presentation of *Tartuffe* on pain of excommunication. At the same time he issued his mandate interdicting Mareuil, who was to play the title rôle, from entering a church or receiving any of the sacraments. Mareuil was not the person to submit to this treatment. Having sought justice from the Bishop in vain, he planned to appeal to the Governor and Council. But the Bishop forestalled him by himself calling upon the Council to punish the offender. He intended that ecclesiastical should be supplemented by secular punishment. The evident joy with which Auteuil had accepted the supposition that the accused was guilty, and his failure to recognize the possibility that the Bishop might have been wrong in pastoral and mandate, indicate that Bishop and Attorney-

[1] *Jugements et Délib.*, vol. iii, p. 832.

[2] The presentation of plays was not unusual in Canada. The *Cid* by Corneille had been given in 1646, again in 1652, and the *Heraclius* of the same author in 1651. Other plays followed and Bishop Laval does not appear to have objected. St. Vallier however asked Governor de Denonville not to have a dramatic evening at the time of the Carnival. Although Denonville acquiesced Frontenac was not so complaisant, for in the early days of January 1694 the *Nicomède* of Corneille and the *Mithridate* of Racine were given with great success. It was then proposed to be a little more daring and give a presentation of *Tartuffe*, which had already been driven from the French stage. See Abbé Gosselin, "Un Épisode de l'Histoire du Théâtre au Canada," *Transactions and Proceedings of the Royal Society of Canada*, series ii, vol. iv.

General were in collusion.[1] Mareuil was to be punished; the Bishop's actions were to be left unquestioned. Mareuil had beaten the servant of Villeray and yet the Council deputed Villeray to make an impartial inquiry into the facts of the case.

On March 15, the Governor urged the speedy completion of the legal investigation as the accused was in a very distressing situation. Mareuil was probably not so much distressed by being kept away from church, as he was anxious to justify himself at the expense of the Bishop. On June 11, the Governor asked the Council to decide whether or not the Bishop had passed the bounds of his authority and jurisdiction to the prejudice of the King's. He demanded that each one should commit himself on this subject by having his opinion recorded in the register. On June 28, this demand was answered by the Attorney-General. He admitted that opinions had been recorded but asserted that this method had hampered the freedom of the Councillors. Recorded opinions could only serve to embarrass the Council and to intimidate it in the execution of justice.[2] The Council resolved to vote *viva voce*. No record of this vote appears on the books of the Council.[3]

At this same meeting a petition of Mareuil was presented asking once again for the consideration of the Bishop's

[1] Frontenac, according to Cadillac, said "que les conclusions precipitees du procureur general avoient été prises dans le Cabinet de Mgr L'Evesque avec qui il avoit été en conference toute la veille du Conseil Souverain." *Corres. Gen.*, series C xi, vol. xiii, pt. i, p. 238.

[2] "avoir lieu de craindre dans la suitte quelque chose de facheux, si leurs dits avis n'estoient trouvés tels qu'on l'auroit desiré." *Jugements et Dé ib.*, vol. iii, p. 892.

[3] Mr. Edouard Richard, who abstracted folios 186-270, vol. v, series F, of the *Collection Moreau St. Méry*, says that the Council thought the Bishop went beyond his powers except in issuing his pastoral warning people against attending the presentation of *Tartuffe*.

mandate against him. The petition was referred to the Attorney-General who straightway pigeon-holed it. On October 4, the Attorney-General and First Councillor made their reports and upon the strength of them the Council imprisoned Mareuil on the 14th and seized and invoiced his possessions. In prison he was interrogated by Villeray but refused to answer, taking formal exception to that Councillor as reporter of his case on the ground that Villeray was his enemy. The Council found his objections frivolous and inadmissible and maintained Villeray as reporter. A deadlock ensued. A month later the prisoner was denied communication with any of his friends.[1] The Council was determined upon trying him and upon not hearing his countercharges against the Bishop. On November 22, it was ordered that if Mareuil persisted in his refusal to recognize Villeray as reporter of his case, he should be tried unheard.[2] At this point Frontenac intervened. He entered the Council chamber on the following Monday and ordered the registration of a review he had written of the case and of a petition which Mareuil had addressed to him. The Intendant deprecated such an abuse of authority to frustrate justice. The Attorney-General predicted that Mareuil's petition would be found to be filled with misrepresentations and proposed to inform the King that the Council did not support its registration. The Council accordingly ordered that this registration should be considered as prejudicial to the authority of the King and of the Sovereign Council.

Mareuil's petition to the Governor was a remarkable ar-

[1] "deffences sont faittes a l'archer a la Garde duquel il est, de la laisser Communiquer avec qui que ce soit." *Jugements et Délib.*, vol. iii, p. 939.

[2] "son process sera instruit comme a un muet volontaire." *Ibid.*, p. 94[illegible].

raignment of Attorney-General and First Councillor. Auteuil had delayed presenting the prisoner's petitions, had kept one in his possession from March 15 until October 14; had suppressed one date March 18, so that the Council acted without hearing his side of the story. The Attorney General was therefore guilty of obtaining the decree of March 18 by artifice. The petitioner claimed that the maintenance of Villeray as his commissioner was in contravention of two articles of the ordinance of 1670. The Council had refused to consider his objections to Villeray and he accordingly appealed to the Council of State to annul this decision. The decree of November 22 was likewise obtained surreptitiously from the Council, Attorney-General and Villeray acting in collusion to prevent knowledge of his last petition from reaching that body. Bishop St. Vallier should not have been received as his accuser, having just decreed against him as his ecclesiastical judge. The Attorney-General should have demanded the mandate with the alleged denunciations, instead of posing at once as his accuser. The whole procedure indicated the existence of a scheme to cover over the false steps of the Bishop to the ruin of the petitioner.[1] They had stooped to the lowest devices to obtain evidence against him for they had solicited persons to depose against him. The Attorney-General had actually imprisoned one witness in order by prison fare and threats to obtain the evidence he desired. Others he had threatened to chastise and expel from the city, unless they deposed what they were supposed to know. Mareuil besought the Governor to deliver him from prison as it would be some time before the decision of the Council of State upon his appeal could reach Quebec.

[1] "Ce procedé donc assez évidemment La parcialité et Caballe formée par le dit sieur procureur General pour Tacher a Sauver les fauces demarches de Monseigneur l'Evesque par la ruine du Supliant." *Jugements et Délib.*, vol. iii, p. 951.

The Governor in his writings referred to the irregularity of the proceedings of the Council and to his attempts to prevent these false steps. It was not a desire to palliate crimes but the evident miscarriage of justice that prompted his intervention. He spoke of the attempts to gloss over the affair and bring the trial to a premature end by inducing Mareuil to escape to France on the last ship disguised as a sailor. He said that he would not be doing his duty if he did not suspend the trial until the Council should be willing to conduct it according to the forms of law; heretofore personal animosity had colored all its proceedings.[1] He indicated his intention of delivering Mareuil from prison, pending the decision of the Council of State upon his appeal.

At the next meeting of the Council, the jailer was summoned to report whether or not the Governor had made good his words. Unable to find the jailer, the usher brought the jail-record, where the words "discharged by Sieur de la Vallière, Captain of the guards of Monsieur the Governor" were found on the margin opposite the name of Mareuil.[2] It was, however, a principle of the Council not to reverse any of its decrees, so it voted that Villeray should remain reporter of the Mareuil case ac-

[1] "Il est visible qu'elle n'est remplie que de partialitez, de Caballes, et de passions particulieres, et qu'elle ne tend qu'a opprimer par quelque biais que ce puisse estre, un homme dont on hait peut estre encore plus la personne, que le Crime qu'on pretend qu'il a Commis." *Jugements et Délib.*, vol. iii, p. 953.

[2] The full marginal note was: "aujourdhuy 29e Novembre, de l'ordre de Monsieur le Comte de frontenac, Gouverneur et Lieutenant General pour le Roy en ce pays, Nous Capitaine de ses Gardes, avons déchargé le present Registre et L'ecroue cy a Costé de la personne dud. sieur de Mareuil aussy que la Recommandation faitte au baz dud. Escroue, Et en Consequence Enjoignons au Consierge de ses prisons d'ouvrir les portes aud. Sieur de Mareuil, a quoy il a satisfait a lheure meme, et me la remis entre les mains, signé de lavalliere." *Ibid.*, p. 954.

cording to the decree of October 18 and November 18 and 22.

The length of the trial, caused by the persistence with which the Council sought to force Mareuil to accept Villeray as his reporter, and its sudden end brought about by military force, meant humiliation and loss of prestige for the tribunal. The affair does not smack of premeditated injustice, for the partisan statements of Frontenac, Mareuil and Cadillac are all highly colored. The Councillors were, however, prejudiced against Mareuil: first, because he belonged to the military class and to the small and brilliant circle about Frontenac, with which the Councillors were out of sympathy; second, because Frontenac's championship of his cause aroused the traditional hostility of the Council towards the Governor; and, third, the attempts to condemn the Bishop as having gone beyond the bounds of his authority brought out the high respect for that religious arbiter and great feudal prince to the detriment of his accuser. Still the trial was carried on honestly and correctly, as far as the common Councillors were concerned, and would possibly have had a different ending, if Auteuil had not, probably, suppressed the prisoner's petitions. The important point about the trial is that Frontenac wrested a prisoner from the Council's jurisdiction by force, during the process of the trial, and the Council had no recourse.

At the same time the Council voluntarily turned over to the King several cases involving the Bishop,[1] and showed great timidity in a case involving another one of Frontenac's officers. This last affair was the only one that drew the old Governor to the Council chamber after the Mareuil episode, possibly to see that justice was done to Captain Antoine Lamotte Cadillac. In the dispute of the latter with

[1] For these cases, see Appendix C.

Joseph Moreau, Champigny, who was still Intendant, was made reporter. Cadillac claimed that Champigny was not an impartial person to investigate the case, because he had threatened the petitioner with heavy fine and had given advice to Moreau. Upon the refusal of the Council to appoint another reporter, he appealed to the King and Frontenac asked that the trial be suspended until the King's decision should be heard. The failure of the Council to act upon this suggestion brought out such threats from the Governor that on March 21, 1698, the court asked the Intendant to excuse it from taking cognizance of the case. Frontenac was well pleased, while Champigny in his chagrin declared that he would judge the case alone as Intendant of justice, etc.[1] Thus while the jurisdiction of the Sovereign Council during the first administration of Frontenac was an expanding jurisdiction, the reverse was the case during his second term as Governor General of New France.

The death of the dignified old "Chef du Conseil" on November 28, 1698, was undoubtedly regretted by the majority of the Councillors. On December 19, a solemn service was held in the church of the Recollets for the soul of the deceased. The Councillors marched in a body to the church to pay a last tribute.[2] No Governor ever obtained such marks of deference from the Council as Frontenac. After his death, the ceremony of sending two Councillors to meet the Governor on ordinary days of meeting was abolished, nor did any Governor venture in later times to style himself "Chef du Conseil".

[1] *Jugements et Délib.*, vol. iv, pp. 165-168, 175, 182.

[2] It was Frontenac's most consistent enemy Auteuil who proposed this mark of respect to the dead "pour faire connoistre par cette ceremonie la consideration qu'il a toujours Eue pour la personne de mond. Sieur Legouverneur." *Ibid.*, p. 246.

In actual administration of affairs the Council had received little help and encouragement from Frontenac. During the last four and a half years of his life he had attended but three or four Council meetings. That tribunal however enjoyed during his second administration the independence which it had gradually won during his first term as Governor. The twenty years of his administration saw the Governor reduced from president and chief of the Council to the position of an honorary Councillor. Although he might still obstruct Council work, he had no part in its constructive policy either as a judicial or as an administrative body. Although the Council risked in a measure its high repute for justice in its regard for the Bishop, the most effective period of its operation coincided with the two administrations of Frontenac.

CHAPTER III

THE COUNCIL IN THE EIGHTEENTH CENTURY

THE successor of Frontenac was not named until after an interval of five months. Letters patent had been granted to Louis Hector de Callières, who had shown himself to be the most enterprising officer in Canada. Upon May 27, 1699, the King wrote to inform him of his appointment. On September 13, the Council sent a delegation to congratulate him upon his arrival at the Château St. Louis. Six weeks later, he made his first appearance in the Council chamber, Villeray and Dupont preceding and Peyras and Vitre following him. This ceremony of the new governor's initial entrance, first practiced in 1690, thus became the customary mode of procedure. Likewise the initial entrance of the new Intendant with an honorable escort of two Councillors and the ushering out of the old Intendant by a similar escort became the practice in 1702, when M. de Beauharnais replaced Jean Bochart de Champigny.

In the year 1700, a conflict between temporal and spiritual authority enlivened judicial routine. The Council for a time acted with spirit but the attachment of the Attorney-General for the Bishop ultimately led to an accommodation, no definite victory for the Council resulting. Ignace Gosselin, guardian of the children of Thomas Rosseau, had lent the funds in trust for his wards to a merchant at a rate of interest authorized by ordidinance. He did this in order to clothe and educate his wards. His parish priest, having learned of his investment, repeatedly refused him absolution, on the ground of usury. The priest reported the case to the Bishop, who issued a mandate and several special orders, refusing absolution to those who were engaged in such business. Gosselin carried his case to the Bishop, who replied that absolution had been refused by his order. Torn by his desire to do his duty to his wards and by fear for his soul, Gosselin appealed to the Sovereign Council to maintain him in his obedience to its laws, or discharge him from his office of guardian. M. Reverin, who was acting as Attorney-General in the temporary absence of Auteuil, confirmed the petitioner's story concerning the Bishop's action. Some days before, he said, he had been in the parish church in Quebec, when a mandate of the Bishop was promulgated, in which among other things the Bishop condemned the loans, which merchants made to Indian traders, exacting over thirty-three per cent although the current rate of the kingdom was only eight per cent. Reverin asked that two Councillors be sent to ascertain from the Bishop his grounds for such a mandate and whether he thought that putting money of wards out at interest was usury. On April 5, 1700, the Council appointed such a commission. On April 19, Villeray reported that the Bishop would explain his reasons after he had reviewed the case. To Auteuil, present at this meeting, was referred the petition of Gosselin. At this next meeting, Villeray presented the written opinion of the Bishop.[1] The case is not again mentioned in the records. The issue was clearly joined; the encroachments of the Bishop were undeniable. Perhaps Auteuil lost the papers submitted to him for his

[1] For this case, see *Jugements et Délibérations*, vol. iv, pp. 418, 429, 432. The Bishop's writing was not incorporated in the minutes.

decision; probably the case was accommodated. The lack of records is exasperating.

In the same year the influence of the Intendant upon the judgments of the Council was shown in the De Louvigny case. The accused was a captain of the Marine stationed at Fort Frontenac. There, it was alleged, he had traded with the Iroquois in contravention with his Majesty's ordinance. The Intendant referred the case to the Council, which decided on September 27 to take cognizance of it. The Iroquois had petitioned the Governor to set Louvigny free, because he had clothed their nakedness. De Callières answered that he had imprisoned him because of disobedience and that he would put another commandant at Fort Frontenac. Martinière, who was reporter of the case, had some difficulty in getting any one to testify. Finally, sufficient evidence was obtained, the tell-tale peltries were seized and confiscated and sold at auction. The Governor was most active in the prosecution. The case was worthy of such solicitude, for it involved several other persons, Laperottière, Godefroy, Desruisseau, etc.—upon similar indictments. On October 23, Callières produced the last pieces of evidence and four days later the judgment of the court was reached. Governor de Callières gave this dissenting opinion: that Sieurs de Louvigny and Laperottière ought to be judged finally in accordance with the orders of the King for the sake of the example; concerning Godefroy he advised less stringent measures:[1] that the person Desruisseau should be condemned to a fine of 500 livres for having purchased the peltries at the fort. Whether any of the Councillors held the Governor's opinion is unknown. The judgment representing the majority of opinions was

[1] " . . . il aura provision de sa personne." *Ibid.*, p. 503.

that Louvigny and Laperottière should be sent to His Majesty to be judged; that Godefroy, Cullerier, and Garras should be released because they were not old offenders, and that Ruisseaux be condemned to a fine of 300 livres.[1] Thus the Council itself punished no one but the purchaser of peltries. The Council had failed to convict the worst offenders and even though supported by Governor de Callières, who favored vigorous measures, had shifted the responsibility of judgment to the King. The situation was entirely reversed from that of 1681, when it was the Council which was grasping at the chance to extend its jurisdiction and favoring stringent measures against the coureurs de bois; and it was the Governor who then sought to limit its power and favored a policy of moderation. The refusal of the Intendant to judge the case and the tone of His Majesty's letters indicate that that official was largely responsible for this lenient judgment.[2] The King complained of the evident partiality of the judges.[3] The Mareuil case had brought

[1] " . . . attendu leur peu d'Experience." *Ibid.*, p. 503.

[2] In a royal memorial to Callières and Champigny this partiality is condemned. Louvigny was to remain captain of his company in consideration of his services, but his office of mayor of Three Rivers was taken away. Perottière was reduced for the same offence. *Supplement Canadian Archives Report*, 1899, p. 355.

[3] The minister wrote to Champigny that he showed partiality towards Louvigny. It was asserted that Madame de Champigny, through mistaken principles of charity, prevented the punishment of guilty persons by her entreaties. He must forbid her to meddle with such matters. At the same time the King wrote: "Je ne puis me dispenser de vous dire que vous avez marqué beaucoup de partialité dans l'affaire du Sr de Louvigny, et il paroist, par la maniere dont elle a esté instruite, que vous ne vous en estes chargé que pour prouver le moyen d'esluder l'éxécution des ordonnances de Sa Majesté cette conduitte ne convient point a aucun officier et encore moins a un intendant, dont la principelle fonction est de tenir la main à l'execution des ordonnances de Sa Maj^té et je vous prie de prendre garde de ne pas tomber dans ces sortes de fautes." *Archives des Colonies*, series B, vol. xxii, pt. ii, p. 325.

forth a like complaint.[1] The prestige of the Council was somewhat damaged. The strongest, most vigorous period of its existence was passed, There was no marked decline, but such trials as the one chronicled above show that the Council was no longer aggressive. It was in a defensive position.

In 1702 Champigny was replaced by M. de Beauharnais. In the following year Governor de Callières died and Philippe Rigaud, Marquis de Vaudreuil, was commissioned as Governor General of New France. Vaudreuil had been in the King's service as soldier, and Governor of Montreal for thirty-two years. He now held the first place in the province until his death in 1725. During this period Beauharnais, the two Raudots and Bégon acted successively as Intendant. A detailed description of the Council under these presidents is unnecessary for our purpose which is to describe only those events in its history, which indicate a rise or fall of its power or a change of standing in public opinion. It will be possible, therefore, to describe the chief events of the administration of Vaudreuil (1703–25) in the briefest manner.

The old members of the Sovereign Council had nearly all died in office. In 1679 Autueil died and was succeeded in the office of Attorney-General by his son. In 1696 Charles Aubert, Sieur de la Chesnaye, had been appointed to the office of Councillor left vacant by the death of Tilly. In the same year Damours died and was succeeded by his son Bernard Damours, Sieur de Plaine et de Freneuse. In 1700 Villeray died in harness, having

[1] The minister had written to Champigny, "Thus you were on bad terms with the Bishop until he fell out with M. de Frontenac, and then you left the latter to act alone in procuring justice for those who appealed to the courts, on the ground of abuse of power against the Bishop's proceedings." *Supplement Can. Archives Report*, 1899, p. 310.

presided as First Councillor and signed the minutes almost to the day of his death,[1] and in the summer of 1691 Peiras attended his last meetings. Council sessions became so slenderly attended that it was no longer possible to marshal a working quorum. On June 27, 1701, the Council passed a decree permitting two judges to summon a third from the attorneys (*practiciens*) when but two Councillors were present or left unchallenged.[2]

The King offered a better remedy however in 1703 by increasing the number of Councillors by five.[3] Lotbinière, who had been a Councillor from 1660 to 1677 and had then occupied the important position of lieutenant general of Quebec, was made First Councillor, Claude de Bermen, Sieur de la Martinière being given his position. Monseignat and Hazeur were appointed to the two vacant seats in the Council. The five new Councillors were MM. de la Durantaye, de Répentigny, de Villeray, son

[1] "Estant arrivé que Me Louis Rouer de Villeray premier Conseiller aud. Conseil seroit decedé L'undy dernier Sixisme du present mois sans avoir pu signer les arrests de la Sceance du 29r 9bre dernier a laquelle il avoit presidé, ainsi que quelques autres arrests qu'il n'a non plus Eû le temps de signer sur le Registre layant cependant fait sur le plumitif apres les assembléés ausquelles il Sestoit trouvé president." *Jugements et Délib.*, vol. iv, p. 513.

[2] Il "a esté arresté aud. Conseil que dans les assembléés d'Iceluy qu'il sera pris Et appellé un troisieme Juge lorsqu'il ne s'y trouvera que deux des Coners En Iceluy affin d'administrer la Justice a l'ordinaire, ou que sy Estant trouvé plus grand nombre Ils auront Esté obligez de se retirer, ce qui pourra Estre vollablement fait par les deux presens non recusez." *Ibid*, p. 585.

[3] "Mais l'expérience a fait connoitre que le nombre de juges étoit trop petit, d'autant par l'absence ou par maladie d'aucuns d'iceux, ils se sont trouvés au nombre inferieur à celui réglé par nos ordonnances, en sorte que nous avons résolu de joindre encore cinc conseillers au sept etablis en vertu de notre declaration," etc. *Edits et Ordonnances*, vol. i, p. 300.

of the late Councillor, and Aubert, and the Abbé de la Colombière. Of the old members only Lotbinière and Dupont had participated in the events of the Talon and Frontenac regimes. Upon the death of Villeray in 1700, Dupont had been elected First Councillor by the Council subject to the confirmation of the King, who compensated him with various offices when he put Lotbinière into his place.[1] Auteuil, as we have seen, succeeded his father as Attorney-General, and shortly after this period obtained assurance of the reversion of the office to *his* son. Alexandre Peuvret had succeeded his father as secretary or clerk of the Council. In 1702 a man who was to be a very active member, Mathieu Martin Delino, was installed. The commission of Répentigny was never received by the Sovereign Council and he never served as Councillor. The list of active Councillors was thus Lotbinière, First Councillor; Dupont, dean and keeper of the seals; Riverin, Delino, Monseignat, Hazeur, La Durantaye, Aubert de la Chesnaye, Villeray, La Columbière, with Auteuil as Attorney-General and Peuvret as chief clerk.

The five new Councillors served without pay. Gratuitous service in a busy community is likely to be performed in very perfunctory way, but it was not so in this case. For a time the attendance of the reinforced assembly was steadily good. Often the eleven active Councillors were all present, and the average attendance of the next decade was eight. Later, even when all except the

[1] The minister wrote to Dupont on June 14, 1704. It was not from dissatisfaction with him that the King appointed Lotbinière First Councillor, but on account of the long and important services rendered by Lotbinière as lieutenant general of the Prévôté. He has given him the office of Councillor and keeper of the seal. *Supplement Can. Arch. Report*, 1899, p. 378.

clerical Councillor received salaries, the attendance gradually dwindled. The royal declaration which authorized the increase in the Council's membership spoke of the "Conseil Superieur". Henceforth the Council was no longer the Sovereign but the Superior Council.[1]

A change in the character of the Councillors may perhaps be noted at this time. In earlier times, Councillors were allowed to hold no other office. Martinière had had to choose between the position of Councillor and service with the Trading Company of Hudson's Bay, and Villeray had been severely criticised for selling meat in his house. The worst thing that could be said about a public official was that he was in trade, or connived at the trade of others, with the Indians. Frontenac vigorously defended himself against such charges. But beginning with the eighteenth-century public opinion and conciliar conscience permitted the frank combination of public duties and commercial projects.

In the spring of 1700 a petition was addressed to the King by the grantees of the south shore of the St. Lawrence below Quebec, respecting the right to trade with the Indians. It was signed by Villeray, Damours, Peiras and Vitré, Councillors, and Auteuil, Attorney-General, and eighteen others. The King consented to the forma-

[1] Following Chereul, vol. ii, p. 100, in his Old Régime in Canada, Parkman says that this change of title was part of a general movement throughout the kingdom; that the Grand Monarch could not tolerate the word *sovereign* applied to another institution. On the other hand, Desmaze, *op. cit.*, p. 473, shows that Sovereign and Superior Councils in France were entirely different courts, the latter being instituted by Louis XIV in Arras, Blois, Châlons, Clermont, Lyons and Poitiers, to remedy abuses in the lower courts, and to prevent the extension of the jurisdiction of the Parlement of Paris. The old Sovereign Councils were retained. It is evident that the Canadian tribunal did not receive its change of title (for the change went no farther) as part of this movement in France.

tion of a company, which was incorporated under the name of the "Company of the Colony of Canada" (La Compagnie de la Colonie du Canada). On October 15, Auteuil, Lotbinière, Riverin, Hazeur, Gobin, Macart and Peire were elected directors and La Chesnaye and Délino delegates for France. On May 21, 1701, the minister sent Auteuil his congratulations that he had been selected as manager of this new company for the beaver trade. But the affairs of the Company did not prosper. In order to make beaver hats popular the price was reduced, and, as the Indians had to be paid at the previous rate to keep them from selling their skins to the English, the middleman suffered. The Company therefore through its agent Délino asked that the duty of one-quarter the beaver skins be abolished and be replaced by a duty on draper's goods, merceries, groceries and millinery. The petition was granted, but even with this encouragement the Company was not successful. The minister wrote that as Lotbinière was First Councillor and director of the beaver Company, he ought to endeavor to put an end to the cabals existing in the Company. Commerce and justice went thus hand in hand. The most dignified members of the Council traded. Vaudreuil was, according to Auteuil, in the business, while Bégon in 1715 admitted that he had traded.[1]

La Compagnie de la Colonie proved to be a bad venture. People refused to subscribe to its shares and it gradually became insolvent. Meanwhile in a letter dated June 17, 1705, the minister informed Auteuil that its board of directors was abolished. On December 15, Raudot, the Intendant, directed an account to be rendered by the former directors. Auteuil and the other

[1] *Supplement Can. Arch. Report*, 1899, pp. 122, 391.

directors held that the management, having been suppressed, did not exist and therefore could not order the clerks to make the desired report. Raudot held that the erstwhile directors were able and were under obligations to do so.[1] He ordered the clerks of the Company to render their accounts to the said directors and instructed the directors to hold a meeting in order to receive them. Bad management, ignorance and dishonesty were disclosed. The agent of the Company, Délino, was interdicted as Councillor in 1706 as penalty for his commercial failure; but he was reinstated in the following year.[2]

The irritation caused by allowing officers of justice to involve themselves in the vicissitudes and struggles of commercial enterprise, was at the same time increased by various episodes in a suit brought by Berthelot against Madame de la Forest for recovery of the Island of Orleans. Madame de la Forest had paid but 4.000 livres of the purchase price of 31,000 livres. As early as 1702 Berthelot had informed the minister that he had taken proceedings to recover the balance or get the sale canceled.[3] The minister instructed Beauharnais, then Intendant, to see that the Council should grant him a prompt and effectual remedy. Raudot, the successor of Beauharnais, pushed the suit, but it was not until December 7, 1705, that the Council condemned the defendant to *restore* the estate to the plaintiff.[4] Autueil was the brother-

[1] *Sup. Can. Arch. Report*, 1899, pp. 99, 101, 108, 111, 353, 382, 383.

[2] Raudot was loathe to remove Délino from the Council, as he said that he was its most able member. The minister, however, wrote on June 10, 1706: He has deceived the company and the writer himself; on his arrival in France he must stand trial, and the King will deprive him of the office of Councillor. *Ibid.*, p. 202.

[3] The minister to Callières, May 30, 1703. *Ibid.*, p. 367.

[4] *Jugements et Délib.*, vol. v, p. 201.

in-law of Madame de la Forest and was largely responsible for the delays in the trial and for the unruly behavior of the lady. He was irritated that the Intendant's conduct concerning the Compagnie de la Colonie du Canada had been approved by the minister. His conduct in the Berthelot-La Forest affair was due to this chargin and to a desire to champion his sister-in-law's cause.

Judgments had been given against her in the provost court of Quebec, the Superior Council and the Châtelet of Paris. Finally on January 18, 1706, she appealed to the Council of the King, expressed objection to all Councillors, judges and advocates in Canada and laid the documents in the case on the Council table. They were referred to Raudot the younger to report upon. Later in the week Madame de la Forest obtained them from Raudot upon the promise to return them before the Council meeting on January 25. This she failed to do, and the Intendant had to place a guard in her house (*mettre Garnison chez elle*) before she would yield. At the meeting on January 25 she challenged the Intendant, stating that he had issued an order against her and was therefore not competent to be her judge. The Council decided otherwise. At the same time it was found that Auteuil had written some parts of this act of challenge and interlined others. Upon being summoned to acknowledge his handwriting he wrote out his justification for the act. Raudot condemned this course of conduct as lacking in respect toward the Council. Auteuil replied that if he failed in respect to the Council, the Intendant had done likewise inasmuch as he had supplied the places of the challenged Councillors by nominations made without consulting the Council, alleging that Madame de la Forest made no objection to them, whereas he knew perfectly well that she had objection to any official in Canada. The Council declared through the mouth of Raudot that his accusations were without proper evidence, that his conduct in writing parts of a paper designed to make the Intendant party to a suit was not in keeping with the duties of an Attorney-General, that he should not in future draw up such papers for litigants, and that he should display more respect for the Council.

Eventually the Council of State reversed the decisions of the Council, Châtelet and Provost Court. On July 7, 1708, it issued a decree, ordering Berthelot to pay 20,000 livres in damages, which reduced the sum due him to 7,000 livres, for the payment of which a delay of one year was granted to Madame de la Forest.[1]

As for Auteuil, his actions led to his dismissal from office. On June 9, 1706, the Minister wrote him that Raudot was right in preventing his exceeding the limits of his duties.[2] On June 30, 1707, he was dismissed from office. M. Macart served as Attorney General until 1710, when Sieur le Duc was commissioned to fill that office. He died however fourteen days after his arrival in Canada, and M. Macart continued to perform the functions of the office until October 17, 1712, when Mathieu Benoît Collet was regularly installed.[3]

Auteuil had in part been the cause of increasing the Council's jurisdiction during the years 1679 to 1682: he had always been the champion of freedom of deliberation in the Sovereign Council, but his later conduct would

[1] The decision simply indicates the King's wish. His minister had repeatedly urged accommodation of difficulties, and indicated that the King was unwilling that the defendant should be severely dealt with. *Ibid.*, pp. 216–222.

[2] *Sup. Can. Arch. Report*, 1899, p. 391.

[3] *Jugements et Délib.*, vol. vi, p. 523.

seem to indicate that personal ambition, not deliberate endeavor to increase the Council's power, was the mainspring of his actions. Duplicity in business and partiality to relatives ill-became an Attorney-General of the King. Still with all his faults, and Raudot has taken good care to exaggerate them,[1] he represented perhaps most truly the free-thinking Canadian native, fighting in the person of Governor and Intendant an undesirable political machine.

Throughout this period Vaudreuil worked in harmony with the successive Intendants in the Superior Council. Governor and Intendant if united exerted great influence over its proceedings. This was evidently the case in the proceedings just chronicled. It was also evident in the events of 1714, which deserve brief description. Martinière, appointed lieutenant of the provost court of Quebec, when Lotbinière became First Councillor, had had trouble with Raudot. He complained that the Intendant encroached upon the privileges of the Council and constituted himself sole judge. There was trouble about the appointment of a clerk of the provost court. Martinière questioned the probity of Vaudreuil. He was so independent, in fact, that Raudot proposed to the minister the abolition of the local court of Quebec. The minister thought the proposal impracticable.[2] Martinière was retained in his post and was raised to be

[1] Raudot wrote that Auteuil boasted of his omnipotence with the King, and of having caused the recall of Frontenac; that his son had thrown a stone at a soldier inflicting a wound from which the man died, nobody venturing to lay a complaint so great was the fear of the resentment of the family. He concluded with the declaration that one or the other of them must be dismissed. *Sup. Can. Archives Report*, 1899, p. 213.

[2] *Ibid.*, pp. 112, 113, 118, 392.

First Councillor in 1710.[1] The activity of Raudot, separately and with the Council, in enacting police regulations, was followed by a period of inaction in that respect during Begon's early years of service. Whether it was in a spirit of independence or of sincere belief in the need of measures of this nature that Martiniere acted, is impossible to determine. It is sufficient that he produced a most illuminating report upon the condition of the country and the need of breaking the grain monopoly by police ordinances.[2] Although the Governor and Inten-

[1] *Jugements et Délib.*, vol. vi, p. 114.

[2] The writing of Martinière, presented to the Council on July 17, 1714, ran as follows: Since the King has withdrawn the country from the hands of the old Company, and has rendered the authority of the Council more sovereign than it formerly was, that assembly has striven to reform abuses in the administration of justice with a diligence worthy of its position. It has made the people obey previously neglected laws and ordinances; it has abolished lengthy and formless trials, and regulated procedure according to usage and the special needs of the country. It has enacted, registered, promulgated and executed great numbers of police regulations, necessary as well for the towns as the country. New Governors Intendants and Councillors have found these ordinances to be exceedingly wise and just. Now one speaks only of them to blame those who have made them, not because they dislike the regulations, but because these measures are not executed. This failure to execute them has encouraged a feeling of disrespect towards Councillors. They are not content with speaking scornfully of the Council in private but must express it in public, on the street, and even in the houses of Council members. They may say with impunity that it seems that all their power is suppressed, since they cannot have even one minot of wheat delivered to a multitude (*Infinité*) of poor families, who are refused it at 7 or 8 livres a minot cash (*l'argent à la main*), and consequently are starving at a time when the abundance of wheat should reduce the price to 4 livres. Far from selling it, they keep wheat and flour hidden until a chance for shipping it out of the colony occurs, which is so much the more dangerous as the colony sees itself threatened with famine. The people anticipated it when they saw the considerable number of vessels in the roadstead, those that departed laden with grain and those that are yet to come. As the interests of God, of His Church, of the King, of the public, of widows and orphans, are placed in the hands of the King's

dant were absent, the Council took action upon this report and instructed the Attorney-General to draw up relief measures and report at the first meeting when Vaudreuil and Begon should be present.

On July 30, 1714, Governor and Intendant submitted their joint opinion of what had happened. Instruction to the Attorney-General to draw up police regulations was the initial step in ordinance-making. As such the action of the Council was surprising, since by his decree of March 10, 1685, His Majesty had expressly forbidden the Council from making any regulations relating to the general police in the absence of Governor and Intendant. The Intendant claimed that this power could be executed by him separately; because the King, while annulling the ordinances of August 16, 1684, of the Sovereign Council, confirmed those of Intendant Meules of August 22 regulating the same matter. If Governor and Intendant agreed to allow the flour to be shipped away, it belonged to the Governor alone to give passports. They therefore considered the memoir of July 16 as an attempt against their authority. This opinion was spread upon the Minutes and the objectionable decree was left unexecuted.

None of the Councillors disputed the reasoning in this document. A d'Auteuil or a Villeray would have questioned the claim of an Intendant to make general police ordinances on his own responsibility, or the presumption that the instruction to the Attorney-General to present certain propositions designed to remedy certain evils constituted a contravention of the King's decree of March 10, 1685. But now the Council accepted the rebuke and

officials, it seemed to M. de la Martinière that provision should be made now or never, etc., etc. *Jugements et Délib.*, vol. vi, pp. 794-797.

it was perhaps as well, for the combination of Governor and Intendant was very powerful. The Council lost no ground, for it participated with the Intendant in making the next general police ordinances.[1]

It was probable that the action of M. de la Martinière was prompted not by any intention of exalting the political position of the Council, but by a genuine desire to relieve the economic situation. Less than a month later an armed mob collected just outside of Quebec as a protest against the misery of the people and the high cost of merchandise. Upon the rumor of approaching troops the people dispersed. No energetic prosecution followed. A year later two of the ringleaders were arrested by the Council, but were delivered from prison upon promising to appear when wanted. One lived with the Lieutenant General while the other lived with a notary. They were apparently not of the lower class.[2] When such men led men with arms in their hands there must have been grievances such as Martinière described in his report.

The successors of Vaudreuil and Begon did not work so harmoniously together. In fact it was through hostility towards each other that Charles Marquis de Beauharnais and Claude-Thomas Dupuy involved Canada in her greatest constitutional struggle during the eighteenth century. The atmosphere was rendered electric by several minor flashes of temper and obstinacy. Among the first was the episode of the drummer in 1727. In January Dupuy had occasion to issue a summons against a certain fugitive from justice. It was the custom to promulgate such writs accompanied to the roll of the drum. In this

[1] December 2, 1715. *Ibid.*, p. 1056.

[2] For a summary of this case, see *ibid.*, p. 997.

instance the Intendant asked the Governor for a drummer from the troops. The Governor refused the request and the Intendant made shift with a civilian drummer. On March 1 he appointed the Sieur Pierre Duranceau to be city drummer of Quebec, with instructions to assist the bailiffs on special occasions. Dupuy communicated this order to Governor Beauharnais, who summoned the Intendant to repair at once to his house upon important business. Dupuy refused to respond to this summons until his order was returned. This the Governor refused to do. At length upon the intervention of Bishop St. Vallier the order was returned, but the irritation was considerable.[1] Towards the end of the year a series of events began that made this estrangement of the greatest significance. Upon Christmas night Bishop St. Vallier breathed his last within the walls of the General Hospital, which he had founded and honored with his presence of late years. The Cathedral chapter of canons decided that the episcopal chair was vacant, although M. Louis-Francois de Mornay had performed the functions of coadjutor since 1713, and in that capacity governed Louisiana. The chapter assumed the duty of providing for the government of the diocese until another Bishop should be appointed. Lotbinière, canon and archdeacon, was the highest dignitary in Canada. For various reasons he was unpopular with the majority of the chapter, which elected three Grand Vicars to conduct the ceremony of the obsequies of the Bishop, to the exclusion of Lotbinière.

The archdeacon appealed to the Intendant during the Christmas recess of the Superior Council, asking that the question of title be settled by that body. The Intendant

[1] *Supplement Can. Arch. Report*, 1899, pp. 130–131.

promised to have the canons cited before the court at its next meeting. He ordered them meanwhile to appear before him on Friday, January 2, 1728, which was the eve of the day set for the burial of the Bishop. Lotbinière alone appeared; his opponents sent a paper which stated that the canons of Quebec recognized no judge in Canada capable of passing on their dispute with Lotbinière, not even the Superior Council; that they appealed from the ordinance of the Intendant to the Council of State of the King.[1] The third day of January witnessed a tumultuous scene. The body of the late Bishop was to have been viewed in all the churches of Quebec, ending with the Cathedral, whence it was to be carried to the parish church of the General Hospital for burial. The chapter, so the Intendant alleged, projected a plan to retain possession of the body, mitre, cross and other pontifical ornaments at the Cathedral. To avoid this scandal he had the hospitallers, the inmates of the hospital, and several of the clergy and laity summoned, and with full funeral service laid the remains of the Bishop away in the vault of the special chapel built for that purpose. The chapter, upon learning of this service, claimed that the body had been hidden rather than buried. They had the Cathedral bell rung on pretence that a fire had burst out at the General Hospital. Thither they ran followed by a crowd of people; they burst into the hospital, thence into the church, only to find the chapel heavily draped in mourning, the tomb closed and candles burning on the altar. In their chagrin they laid a temporary interdict upon the Superior and the church.

[1] This narrative is taken from the introductory part of an ordinance issued January 4 by the Intendant. *Edits et Ord.*, vol. ii, pp. 322 323.

On January 4, the Intendant issued an order forbidding them from holding any solemn service until the Council should determine who should conduct it as temporary head of the parish. The Superior Council assembled on Monday, January 5, and decreed that the episcopal chair was not vacant in view of the existence of Duplessis de Mornay, Bishop of Eumenia in Phrygia. It forbade Boullard or any one else from taking the title of Vicar General or from using the seals or performing any act of jurisdiction.[1] After vespers the next day Canon Tonnancour read a mandate explaining the attitude of the chapter.[2] It was the first official order of Boullard and the other Vicars General, issued in direct contravention of the decree of the Council. Without waiting for the bailiffs to summon the Councillors for an extraordinary session, Dupuy undertook to uphold the authority of the Council by an ordinance in which he forbade the Vicars General to issue further mandates or parish priests to publish them.[3] The Vicars General ignored this order, issued a defiant mandate and sent out canons to urge the priests in the surrounding parishes to publish it and to refuse obedience to the Council. The canons proposed to send one of their number to France via New England. The Intendant forbade it as an action aimed at the Superior Council.[4]

[1] *Edits et Ord.*, vol. ii, p. 327.

[2] "Considerant de plus que c'étoit une injustice et un affront au Chapitre, qui se tenait prêt pour aller, lever solenneilement ce vénérable depôt, et lui faire des obsequies avec la décençe et la forme convenables, et le réporter ensuite avec la même pompe funébre au dit hôpital général." *Mandements des Evêques de Québec*, vol. i, pp. 522-523.

[3] Ordinance of January 6, 1728. *Edits et Ord.*, vol. ii, pp. 327-329.

[4] "C'est dans de pareilles circonstances qu'il est de notre devoir d'empêcher toutes demarches indirectes et suspectes, étant aussi peu convenable que Sa Majesté soit informé par dautre quie par son Conseil

The ecclesiastics must have been assured of the passive support of Beauharnais. Otherwise they would hardly have dared to take such a bold stand. In March the Governor actively entered the field as their champion. Usually in questions involving ecclesiastics the Intendant took their side, but in this instance the situation was reversed. On March 8, Beauharnais entered the Council with his secretary and read an order to the Council to enact no further decree in the "Boullard affair"; and to prosecute the case no farther by receiving petitions or responses from witnesses already cited. At the same time he suspended all ordinances already passed on the ground that they were passed without his participation.[1] He forbade the bailiffs from executing summonses or promulgating orders not sanctioned by him. He ordered the Grand Provost to take his four constables or tipstaffs unarmed to the Chateau St. Louis, thus seeking to make the Superior Council helpless. The Intendant as head of the police enjoined the Grand Provost to disregard any orders of the Governor pertaining to justice or to the decrees of the Superior Council.[2] The order of Beauharnais, aiming to destroy the jurisdiction of the Council over the "Boullard affair," was promulgated at the head of the troops to the roll of the drums and the cry of "*Vive le Roi! et Beauharnais!*"

This order was followed by another forbidding the authorities throughout the country to receive the decrees of the Superior Council. On March 27 it called

Superieur même des motifs de ses Arrêts, qu'il serait peu àpropos et même dangereux que ses subjets . . . aller en France, la voie détournée de la Nouvelle-Angleterre." Doutre et Lareau, *L'Histoire du Droit du Canada*, vol. i, p. 272.

[1] *Ibid.*, p. 273.

[2] *Edits et Ord.*, vol. ii, pp. 330–331.

out a masterly ordinance from Dupuy ordering the reception and publication of such decrees. He maintained that the attempted attack upon the Council had developed into an attack upon the authority of the King, which was eminently resident in his Superior Council, charged as well as other parlements and superior councils with the most precious part of the Majesty of kings, *i. e.* the administration of their sovereign justice; that a rebellious clergy had been protected and the troops had been forced to disobey the decrees of the Superior Council; that the action taken subsequently to a disagreement between authorities depended upon the department of government concerned; that therefore if the Superior Council disagreed with the Governor in a matter which concerned the administration of justice, the decree of the Council should be executed; that similarly if a diversity arose between Governor and Intendant relating to matters of common interest, the decision of the former was paramount whenever war and military discipline were involved; that except in those matters the Governor had no right to make an ordinance independently or to interfere with the officers of justice;[1] that there was no one who could wrest the guilty from the hands of the judges without betraying his duty; and that still less could any one excuse the people from the obedience which they owed to the King and consequently to the orders of his justice.[2]

[1] "Le Gouverneur et lieutenant général dans le Canada n'a aucune autorité sur les cases d'amirauté, et nulle direction sur les officiers qui rendent la justice" (Règlement de 1684, signé du roi et de Colbert, et nombre d'autres règlements rendus depuis dans le même sens). Garneau, vol. ii, p. 118.

[2] The whole ordinance is very interesting. See *Edits et Ord.*, vol. ii, pp. 333-336.

In the weeks following, scenes of tumultuous and outrageous character occurred. On March 30 the garrison of the Fort cut to pieces the ordinances of the Council and the decrees of His Majesty. On April 9 the prisons were opened and the prisoners were set free, and on May 6 the Château St. Louis was offered by the Governor as an asylum for the liberated prisoners. Meanwhile the Governor imprisoned four officers who had disapproved of his course of action.[1] On May 13 he instituted "lettres de cachet" in Canada, by which he ordered the Sieur Gaillard to Beaupré and the Sieur d'Artigny to Beaumont.[2]

The Council wavered; Crispin, who had voted with the others upon measures to be taken, now refused to perform certain functions delegated to him in the struggle. The Council suspended him. The Intendant, on May 29, issued an order to the Councillors to remain at their posts, notwithstanding the *lettre de cachet* of Beauharnais. He cited his commission and his position as president of the Council as reasons that Councillors should have regard for his ordinance and he affirmed that the Governor had no power over the officers of justice.

During the summer, however, the defection of several Councillors decided the Intendant to hand in his resignation. This decision was strengthened by the failure of the Minister to support him. Cardinal Fleury, who had replaced Cardinal Dubois as prime minister, was in the midst of the acrimonius controversy over the papal bull Unigenitus, which disturbed France during more than half of the eighteenth century. This bull which was a

[1] Narrative by the Intendant in his ordinance of May 29. Doutre et Lareau, vol. ii, p. 279. This is confirmed in detail by a letter from him to Elie Faure, under date of May 28.

[2] For this *lettre de cachet*, see *ibid.*, p. 278.

sweeping condemnation of Jansenism was extremely unpopular in France and thereiore when fn 1727 the provincial convocation of Embrun condemned the Bishop of Senez, who with other bishops had refused to accept the bull and had demanded a general council, the Parlement and bar of Paris rose against the decision and later refused to register the bull. Thus defeated in his policy at home, it is not strange that the Cardinal Minister was glad to support the ecclesiastical against the secular power in the French dependencies over seas. Accordingly in this case Dupuy was recalled, and on June 1, the Comte de Maurepas, minister and secretary of State, wrote to Beauharnais that the King desired the Superior Council to restore the ecclesiastical property taken from the canons of the cathedral, Vicar General Boullard, and the Recollets by the decrees of January 5, 12, and 26, February 3 and 16 and the first and eighth of the previous month. At a meeting held September 17 attended by the Governor and nine of the Councillors, action was taken upon this letter. As evidence of the most profound submission to His Majesty's wishes, the Council voted the restoration of the disseised ecclesiastics and the anulment or repayment of the fines laid during the dispute.[1]

At the time, this action promised ill for the Superior Council; but with M. Dupuy, hopeless of success, making his peace with the King, and other Council members banished from the city, this recession from their position

[1] "Vu au Conseil l'extrait de la lettre de Monsieur le Comte de Maurepas, etc., le Conseil pour donner à Sa Majesté des preuves de sa profonde soumission, fait dès à présent main-levée des dites saisies prononcées par les dits Arrêts; décharge des dites amendes, ordonne la restitution d'icelles, si aucune, en tout ou en partie, ont été exigées; déclare ceux entre les mains de qui les dites saisies auront été faites, bien et valablement déchargés, en payant aux parties saisies ce qui leur est dû sur l'expédition du présent Arrêt." *Ibid.*, pp. 281–282.

was perhaps natural. Still the Councillors could not but have felt the defeat and the disgrace of this moment of surrender. This feeling must have been increased when on October 4 the banished Councillors d'Artigny and Gaillard returned to the Council. Instead of receiving them as heroes, that assembly voted that they should refrain from taking their seats until the order given by the Governor to retire to Beaumont and Beaupré should be rescinded.[1] The Councillors saw that submission even to the exclusion of their former leaders was the only course to pursue. Such men as Councillor Hazeur even sought by abject letters to regain the favor of the Minister.[2]

The cloud had a silver lining, however. The restoration of property and fines to rebellious clergy, which meant the annulling of certain ordinances of the Superior Council, was indeed humiliating, but the principle of episcopal succession as laid down in its decree of January 5 was maintained by the home Government. Mgr. de

[1] Garneau, vol. ii, p. 120; *Supplement Can. Archives Report*, 1899, p. 135.

[2] "... la lettre qui a esté envoyée a Sa Majesté et que jay signé sur lespressantes solicitations et raisons démonstratives que M. Dupuy m'a fait, me representant qu'il estoit de la dernière importance d'en agir ainsy affin de soutenir avec honneur l'authorité de Sa Majesté les droits et privileges du Conseil. Prevenu à la verité que jetois monsieur, de l'erudition de M. Dupuy et estant très peu experimenté dans ces sortes d'affaires n'estant au surplus arrivé nulle exemple en ce pays de cette sorte, il m'etoit tres difficile de ne pas donner dans un sentiment qui m'etoit exposé avec autant de probabilité en d'apparence de verité. J'ay reconnus depuis, mais à la verité trop tard combien et jusqu'a quel point j'avois esté abuzé en le voile epais qu'il m'avoit mis devant les yeux. Je me voyois, Monsieur, sans ressource lorsque j'ay fait reflections a vostre équité et a vostre justice et je me suis flatte que vous voudries bien avoir égard a mon innocence et croire qu'en suivant le party de M. Dupuy, j'ay cru estre dans le vrai chemin de la justice," etc. *Corres. Gen.*, series C xi, vol. 1, p. 135 *et seq*.

Mornay as next in dignity in the diocese succeeded Bishop St. Vallier as Bishop of Quebec. Lotbinière as Mornay's attorney, after annoying attempts at hindrance from the canons, performed the act of taking possession, which was sustained by a decree of the Council of State dated March 2, 1729.[1] Meanwhile the canons had ordered a Te Deum to be sung in gratitude for the appointment of Mornay as their Bishop.

The next thirty years produced few situations of interest for the historian of the Superior Council. The personnel shifted somewhat rapidly. It will be sufficient here to indicate these changes in a general way. Martinière was succeeded by Delino as First Councillor. François-Etienne Cugnet, an able man and a scholar, served in this position until his death in 1751, when he was succeeded by François Foucalt, who generally presided over the Council during the rest of its existence.

Undoubtedly there were many honest Councillors, but some wolves in sheep's clothing sat about the Council board. Still of the fifty-five persons who were charged with defrauding the King there were but four whose names were in any way connected with the Superior Council. Varin had departed early with his loot and Estèbe sailed for France in 1758 with a large fortune. Intendant Bigot desired to follow a like course of action, but the demands for his services in the critical part of the war kept him in Canada until the English conquest

[1] After securing two long adjournments the canons contrived by cunning means to avoid meeting with Lotbinière to perform the necessary ceremonies. They absented themselves from the chapter house, ordered the beadle not to ring the cathedral bell to summon them, and removed the rope from the chapter-house bell. When Lotbinière took possession without them, they claimed the action was illegal because clandestine. It was this dispute that the Council of State decided. *Supplement Can. Archives Report*, 1899, pp. 235–236.

was complete. Although the great majority of Councillors cast no dishonor upon that institution, as the eighteenth century advanced the Council failed to attract the most intelligent and enterprising Canadians. In a letter dated January 8, 1759, the Minister observed that the educated class in Canada appeared to prefer trade to law and public service. He was surprised that none offered themselves to fill the vacant offices of Councillor.[1]

There remains only the sad story of the end. By November 24, 1759, the situation of the Superior Council had become pitiful. Upon the surrender of Quebec it had begun its sessions in Montreal. It was forced to borrow a bailiff from the local court of that city, as its own bailiffs were too poor to follow the court. Its business had so fallen off that the Attorney-General proposed to substitute a regular monthly session for the weekly Saturday meeting, which was then the rule.[2] The Council made a formal announcement concerning place of residence and meeting. It said that it continued its service in Montreal because there Governor, Bishop and Intendant resided and that in order to conform most closely to the King's intention, it would hold all its sessions in the "Palace" in which the Intendant lived. The proclamation ended by setting December 17 as the next day of meeting, providing for the widespread announcement of this session. When it was thought to be advisable to fix a date nearly four weeks later as the meeting-time of the Superior Council, it is evident that

[1] *Coll. Moreau St. Méry*, series F iii, vol. xiii, p. 174.

[2] ". . il seroit inutile de s'assembler, suivant l'usage ordinaire du Conseil, tous les samedis de chaque semaine, n'y ayant aucune affaire; il estime qu'il suffiroit que le conseil voulût indiquer un jour certain dans le cours du mois prochain où sera fixée la rendrée ordinaire du dit Conseil," etc. *Edits et Ord.*, vol. ii, p. 254.

the Councillors realized the moribund condition of the Court. Let us leave it planning no farther ahead than one more meeting, content if only the seventeenth of December might be reached. Let us leave it protesting its loyalty to a King,[1] who so unwisely wasted his resources in fighting Austria's battles in Germany, instead of supplanting Bigot and his parasites by honest men and French troops.

[1] ". . que le conseil superieur, toujours conduit par le desir qu'il a de donner à Sa Majesté, des preuves de son zèle en rendant sans interruption la justice à ses sujets," etc. *Ibid.*

CHAPTER IV

Membership and Organization

Personnel

The membership of the Conseil Supérieur (*né* Souverain) was repeatedly increased. As we have seen, the first Council was composed of the Governor General, the Bishop, five Councillors, an Attorney-General, a clerk, and an attendant called an usher or bailiff. A special commissioner of the King sat in the first Council for several weeks.[1] He had no official title, but the Council permitted him the title of Intendant in its minutes. The first official to exercise the powers of Intendant and to enjoy the title also, took his seat in the Council on July 6, 1665. With the exception of the three years following Talon's administration and a few months following the departure of Dupuy in 1728, the Intendant was continuously a member of the Council until the English conquest.[2]

In 1674, two ordinary Councillors were added. The King's declaration of June 5, 1675, confirmed these appointments and provided that there should henceforth be seven ordinary Councillors.[3] In 1703, the number was

[1] Gaudais is not spoken of as Intendant in either his commission or his instructions. *Edits et Ordonnances*, vol. iii, pp. 22-27. The Council record of November 28, 1665, speaks of him as "*Monsieur le Gouverneur*". *Jugements et Délibérations*, vol. i, p. 67.

[2] Agremont served as *de facto* Intendant but without commission until Hocquart arrived.

[3] *Edits et Ord.*, vol. i, pp. 83-84.

raised to twelve and such it remained. The normal composition of the Council in later times consisted of the Governor General, the Bishop, the Intendant, twelve Councillors, the Attorney-General, the secretary or chief clerk, and the bailiffs.

There were, however, many extraordinary members sitting at different times in the Council. While the colonial government was nominally under the control of the Company of the West Indies, the general agent of that Company had the right to sit and to vote in the Sovereign Council meetings.[1] While Tracy, the King's Viceroy in all the Americas, was in Quebec, he presided over the Council. During 1665 and 1666 a preponderance of great officials was noticeable in its composition: Lieutenant General of all America, Governor General of Canada, Bishop of Petraea (later to be Bishop of Quebec), Intendant, General Agent of the Company of the West Indies—such were the most dignified members of the Council. In 1679 the provost of the Maréchaussée was permitted to serve as Councillor in cases that concerned breach of the peace.[2] In 1733 the Commissioner of Marine serving at Montreal was granted admission to the Superior Council with the right to a seat and deliberative voice.[3]

In 1742 assistant judges (*assesseurs au conseil*) were

[1] Le Barrois, Basire and La Chesnaye, successively held this post. There is evidence of the great activity of the first and third. *Edits et Ord.*, vol. i, pp. 51-60, and *Collection de Manuscrits de Nouvelle France*, vol. i, pp. 245-61.

[2] Until the King had created the proper number of judges for the court of the provost of the Maréchaussée, the Provost "aura séance et voix délibérative en notre dit conseil de Québec, apres le dernier conseiller, sans ce que sur ce prétexte il y puisse prendre séance ni avoir voix délibérative dans les autres affaires." *Ibid.*, p. 238.

[3] Royal Letters Patent of April 7, 1733. *Collection Moreau St. Méry*, Series F iii, vol. xii, p. 137.

added to the number of active Councillors. The Governor and Intendant might appoint as many as four assistant judges,[1] who should eventually become Councillors. Until 1703 the Bishop was allowed to be represented by a substitute, who was usually the Grand Vicar. The increase of the Council in that year included a clerical Councillor, and since after his admission there was no longer need that the Bishop should have the right to send a representative, that privilege was withdrawn.[2]

In theory the privilege of voting by proxy belonged to Councillors, but in practice it was rarely used. Several commissions were granted providing that sons should represent their fathers in their absence and become full Councillors upon their deaths, but no son actually sat in the Council during his father's lifetime, with the exception of the younger Raudot, who performed the financial duties of Intendant and presided over the Council during his father's absence.[3] Representation of the Bishop by proxy until 1703 and of Raudot during the years 1705 to 1712, were the only instances of the kind.

Beginning with the second decade of the eighteenth century, demands were made upon the King to appoint honorary Councillors. On June 4, 1711, the minister responded that His Majesty would not appoint any person as honor-

[1] *Edits et Ord.*, vol. i, pp. 561-563.

[2] The Declaration of 1675 says: "l'evêque de Québec, ou en son absence du dit pays et lorsquil passera en ce royaume seulement. de son grand vicaire"; the Declaration of 1703 provides for the Bishop's attendance alone and proceeds to say, "et au moyen de la création du dit conseiller-clerc le dit grand-vicaire ne pourra dorénavant prendre place au dit conseil sous prétexte d'absence du dit sieur évêque ou autrement". *Ibid.*, p. 300.

[3] The commission of Raudot *fils*, provides: "nous vous avons commis, ordonné, et députê, etc. pour en l'absence, maladie ou autre légitime empêchement, même à son defaut, nous servir en la dite qualité d'intendant." *Ibid.*, vol. iii, p. 62.

ary Councillor who had not first served as Councillor. In pursuance of this rule, the King named Estèbe honorary Councillor. Estèbe had been Councillor and Commissioner of Marine, had amassed a large fortune (ironically enough, at the expense of the government), and had now resigned from the Council as a step preparatory to his departure for France. "As a mark of satisfaction for M. Estèbe's long services," the King, on February 1, 1758, gave him the necessary commission, providing for the enjoyment of all the honors, privileges, and franchises of active Councillors, and for the right to attend any meeting. Estèbe was, however, not to receive any salary or emolument.[1] This appointment, the only one of which I have any knowledge, was not a particularly happy one.

The greatest possible membership, to which the Council could attain during the forty years it was called the Sovereign Council, was twelve, including the Attorney-General and the chief clerk. The average actual attendance was about seven. In the later period the greatest possible number, including two assistant judges (four assistant judges never held office at once), the provost of the Maréchaussée, the Commissioner of Marine, and honorary Councillor, was twenty-two; the average attendance was between nine and ten. It appears therefore that these special members attended Council sessions but rarely. The assistant judges were, however, valuable additions, and were faithful in their attendance.

Appointment

In regard to the appointment of Councillors, the King tried various experiments. By the Edict of Establishment he entrusted appointments to the Governor and Bishop jointly. The illegal dismissal of Villeray, Auteuil and

[1] *Edits et Ord.*, vol. i, p. 116.

Bourdon by Governor Mésy and the appointment of Lotbinière upon his own responsibility,[1] followed at the end of the year by the appointment of his five friends, proved that joint action in making appointments was almost an impossibility.

When the Company of the West Indies was organized in 1664, the appointment of Councillors was one of the broad powers granted to it.[2] Before the Company had a chance to use the power, the King authorized Tracy, Courcelles, and Talon to reconstruct the Council as they chose.[3] They did so, but the general agent of the Company, anxious to save something for the future, proposed that the Governor and Intendant should grant commissions in the King's name to the nominees of the Company.[4] The Bishop was thus deprived of participation in the process of making new Councillors. Between 1665 and 1674 there is no evidence that the Company used its power, which was in fact appropriated by the Governor, who on January 16 and August 21, 1673, appointed Vitré and Peiras to fill certain vacancies.[5] In his annual speech Frontenac gently reminded Councillors of his ability to retain or dismiss them.[6] The

[1] *Jugements et Délib.*, vol. i, pp. 121 and 129.

[2] "et où il sera besoin d'établir des conseils souverains, les officiers dont ils seront composés, nous seront nommés et présentés par les directeurs généreux de la dite Compagnie; et sur les dites nominations les provisions seront expédiées." Article xxxi, *Edits et Ord.*, vol. i, p. 46.

[3] *Lettres, Instructions, et Mémoires de Colbert*, vol. iii, pt. ii, p. 389.

[4] "Que . . . les officiers du Conseil Souverain soit nommés par la dite Compagnie sur leurs nominations, les provisions leur en être par vous expédiées au nom de Sa Majesté," Article ii of M. Barroys' Propositions to MM. de Tracy, de Courcelles, and Talon. *Edits et Ord.*, vol. i, p. 53.

[5] *Jugements et Délib.*, vol. i, pp. 709, 763.

[6] "j'ay cru ne devoir aporter cette année d'autre changement dans le Conseil Souverain, que celuy de remplir la charge qui y estoit vaccante,

Councillors were undoubtedly uneasy concerning this tenure —"during pleasure" of the Governor—and welcomed the introduction of royal commissions.

In 1674, the Company of the West Indies employed its power of appointment for the first time, but not according to the agreement of 1665. Instead of applying to the Governor (the post of Intendant was vacant at the time) for commissions for their appointees, Auteuil and Villeray, they applied to the King.[1] After this, royal commissions were held to be superior titles to office. Holders of them claimed precedence over Councillors who had none. Lotbinière, who had also been given a commission by the King, claimed that he should be given a place of honor at the Council board,[2] and the other Councillors asked the Governor to obtain royal commissions for them.[3] The Governor consented and in September, 1675, all the Councillors were provided with royal commissions. Henceforth, except in rare cases,[4] appointments were made and commissions issued, directly by the King.[5]

d'une personne qui se conformant sur vos exemples essayera sans doute a ne me pas donner lieu de me repentir de l'avoir choisie, pour l'occuper." *Ibid.*, pp. 707-708.

[1] *Ibid.*, pp. 859 *et seq.*

[2] "Et luy ayant esté indiqué une place apres celuy de la Compagnie qui estoit le dernier en reception, Le dict sieur De Lotbinnière a dict qu'il pretendoit avoir une autre place atendu qu'aucun de la Compagnie n'est pourvu du Roy comme luy." *Ibid.*, p. 857.

[3] In his annual speech of January 1675 Frontenac refers to "La commission que j'ay bien voulu prendre a vos prieres en me chargeant d'escrire a la Cour pour vous faire obtenir de Sa Majesté des provisions de vos charges." *Ibid.*, p. 889.

[4] The Intendant practically appointed Auteuil to succeed his father. *Ibid.*, vol. ii, p. 342.

[5] Says the Declaration of 1675: "vacation avenant, nous pourvoirons à l'avenir de plein droit." *Edits et Ord.*, vol. i, p. 84. Reference has been made to the blank commission filled out by the Intendant in 1679.

In later times there were four ways by which an aspirant might become a Councillor. First, he might impress either the Governor or the Intendant with a sense of his fitness for the office. Correspondence between these officials and the minister was filled with a discussion of the qualifications of different candidates for office. For instance, in 1709, Raudot wrote that Martinière asked for the office of First Councillor; that he would have been senior Councillor had he remained in the Council; that Sieur Delino asked for the office of Martinière, if he were promoted; and that Gaillard and Vincelotte would be suitable persons to fill the two vacancies.[1] The King followed no set rule. In many cases, however, he appointed according to the recommendations of the highest officials.

Secondly, a man might petition the King directly to consider him for an appointment.

In the third place, the office might come in reversion. Although positions were not hereditary as in the Parlement of Paris, in a number of instances Councillors obtained commissions providing for the reversion of their offices to their sons upon their deaths.[2] The King did not desire that the office of Councillor should pass from father to son as an inheritance,[3] but nevertheless recognized that the family of a Councillor had some claim upon the office. For example, in 1698, he gave the position of Councillor, which Damours de Freneuse found impossible to fill, to Riverin, only upon condition that he pay 1,000 livres to the Damours family.[4] This provision for compensation and the grant of commis-

[1] MM. Raudot, father and son, to Pontchartrain, October 28, 1709. Extract from *Supplement Canadian Archives Report* for 1899, p. 221.

[2] Tilly, Damours, Auteuil, Lotbinière, Guillemin, and Dupuy, are mentioned in this connection.

[3] Minister to Auteuil, May 28, 1702. *Ibid.*, p. 362.

[4] Minister to the Bishop of Quebec, May 21. *Ibid.*, p. 332.

sions by reversion marked the limits of the King's concession to occasional demands that the office of Councillor should be made hereditary. Each ambitious father was compelled to seek a commission for his son not as a right but as a favor.[1]

The fourth way of entering the Council was by promotion from the position of assistant judge or assesseur. About 1740 the King decided that candidates who had obtained a knowledge of jurisprudence should take precedence of all others. The Attorney-General gave Cugnet and Guillemin lessons in law. On September 20, 1741, Governor and Intendant gave a commission to the latter, appointing him to the office of Assistant Councillor of the Superior Council. In the spring of 1742 the King wrote Beauharnais and Hocquart assuring them that Guillemin would be appointed Councillor if they reported that they were satisfied with his ability and services.[2] In August of the same year the King definitely provided for such a system of promotion. The office of assesseur was created as an encouragement to persons to make themselves capable of filling the post of Councillor.[3] Guillemin, Perthius, Nouchet, Cugnet the younger, and others, entered the Council in consequence of such preparatory service.[4]

[1] The family of Lotbinière was the only one that held office beyond the second generation: the old families seemed to die out.

[2] *Coll. Moreau St. Méry*, vol. ii, F folios 33, 69, in *Ibid.*, pp. 190-191.

[3] "L'Attention continuelle que nous donnons à l'administration de la justice dans nos colonies, nous a porté, depuis quelques années, à autoriser les Gouverneurs et entendans à établir des assesseurs dans nos conseils supérieurs, non-seulement pour y accélérer l'expédition des affaires, mais encore pour mettre ces assesseurs à portée de se rendre de plus en plus capables de remplir les charges de conseillers, etc.; nous avons la satisfaction de reconnoitre par l'experience que cet établissement répond à nos vues et qu'il est tems de lui donner une forme stable et authentique." *Edits et Ord.*, vol. i, p. 561.

[4] The custom was to grant the assessor a commission as Councillor

Election to office was almost unknown. No case of permanent occupancy of an office in the Council upon such a title exists. Temporary appointments were, however, made by the Council.[1] For example, the Council on December 13, 1700, elected Dupont to succeed Villeray, deceased, in the office of First Councillor. Dupont held office by authority of this election until 1703, when the King commissioned Lotbinière as First Councillor.[2] explaining to Dupont his satisfaction with his conduct, but expressing the necessity of rewarding Lotbinière for certain services. The King did not question the title of Dupont; his action was based upon the ground of expediency.

Qualifications

Long service in the King's business, some knowledge of jurisprudence, and orthodoxy in religious matters, were qualifications most necessary for appointment to the Council. Many of the Councillors had shown some ability in places of trust, in business of a judicial or administrative or commercial or military character. For example, Villeray had been assistant judge of the court of Quebec, and Lotbinière had been its lieutenant general; Tesserie had been president of "*l'ancien conseil*" in the absence of Avaugour; Monseignat had been controller of marine and fortifications, and Mazé, captain of the garrison of Fort Saint Louis. The King appointed Reverin because he was pleased with his management of the fur business and Sarrazin because of his efficiency as a surgeon and physician.

towards the close of his third year of service. For example, Cugnet the younger was appointed assesseur on October 4, 1754, and Councillor on April 24, 1757. *Ibid.*, vol. iii, pp. 114-115.

[1] Macart commissioned by the Council to be substitute Attorney-General, November 22, 1706. *Coll. Moreau St. Méry*, series F, vol. ix, pt. i, p. 68.

[2] *Jugements et Délib.*, vol. iv, pp. 513, 902.

Later, legal knowledge was seen to be a desirable qualification,[1] but this requirement it was difficult to fulfil. To be sure, the Attorney-General offered to give lectures on law to any who chose to present themselves, while the King sent over law books, and the Intendant placed books at the disposition of the judges. Moreover, only a knowledge of the ordinances and the elements of French law was expected. But even so, it was difficult to get young men to study law without hope of employment. Accordingly, in order to encourage legal study, the King, in 1741, declared that he would fill the next vacancy with a person who had applied himself to jurisprudence,[2] and in the next year he definitely established the office of assessor to train men for the Superior Council.

Religious orthodoxy in a country where there were but few heretics was a purely nominal qualification. There is no record of exclusion from office on this score. Nevertheless, the form of directing an investigation into " the life, manners and religion, Catholic, Apostolic and Roman ", of the candidate was punctiliously followed. The certificate of a man's religious fitness was at first obtained from the Bishop or in his absence from the Vicar General.[3] Later, this inquiry was made by the Attorney-General, who was bound to receive depositions from three witnesses, one of whom must be an ecclesiastic, and to report to the dean (*doyen*) of the Council.[4] The formality possibly impressed

[1] *Correspondance Générale*, series C xi, vol. lvii, pt. i, p. 5.

[2] Minister to Beauharnais April 26, 1741. *Supplement Canadian Archives Report* for 1899, p. 149.

[3] Thus in 1674: "Certifficat de venerable et discrette personne Mre Henry de Bernieres viccaire general de Mre François Delaval, Evesque etc., de la religion Catholique apostolique et romaine du dict sieur D'auteuil." *Jugements et Délib.*, vol. i, p. 858.

[4] For example in 1703: "il seroit Informé de la Req^te^ dud. pro-

the candidate, but hardly worried him as to his eventual reception into office.

Another nominal qualification was that a Councillor must be twenty-five years of age. Auteuil the younger, was given a commission and received into the Council despite the Governor's objections, when he was only twenty-two and he served in the important office of Attorney-General for two years before the letter dispensing with the age qualification in his case arrived. It was probably because of the violent protests of Frontenac that less laxity was afterwards shown concerning the age of candidates and the immediate necessity of letters of dispensation, since in 1703, "*aage competent*" and "*conversation*" were added to the other subjects to be investigated. In 1711, Lotbinière was not received into the Council until he had obtained letters of dispensation from the King.[1]

Tenure of Office

During the first decade of the Council's history, tenure of office was nominally for one year; in practice it was during good behavior. At the end of their term of one year, Mésy had dispensed with the services of five members of the Council. During the succeeding years Auteuil and Villeray were supplanted. In 1674 and 1675 royal commissions introduced tenure during the King's pleasure, which in practice meant tenure for life. While Frontenac and Beauharnais suspended certain Councillors from their functions, they did not dismiss them from office. They might have done so with the royal consent, but lacking that consent they were powerless to end the term of Councillors;

cureur general par devant Mre Nicolas du Pont de neuville des vie, moeurs, aage competent, conversation, religion catholique apostolique et Romaine dud Sr Lotbinière." *Ibid.*, vol. iv, p. 905.

[1] *Jugements et Délib.*, vol. vi, p. 267.

the King alone could cancel a royal commission. Tenure for life resulted in long periods of service. Damours and Tilly were in office for thirty-three years; Lotbinière for thirty-five years; Dupont for forty-two years. Villeray ended his official career as president of the Council just one week before his death in 1700, having served as First Councillor for a period of thirty years, counting out the seven years that he was excluded from the Council. Several Councillors of the eighteenth century could show almost as long records of service. Assistant Councillors held office for three years and might be reappointed for an additional term of three years.[1]

Emoluments

The office of Councillor was not very remunerative. Its value depended as much upon the privileges and dignity of the office as upon the salary attached thereto. Salaries were not large in New France. The Governor received 20,000 livres, from which sum he was obliged to maintain and pay the wages of his company of guards. The Intendant received 12,000 livres. Of his obligations I am ignorant. Neither Governor, Bishop, nor Intendant received additional sums for attendance at Council meetings. In 1675 the personal stipend of the Governor amounted to but 3,000 livres. At the same time the First Councillor received 500 livres, the six ordinary Councillors 300 livres each, the Attorney-General 500 livres, the clerk of the court as much, plus fees for his assistants, the bailiff 100

[1] "les commissions... ne soient que pour trois années à compter du jour de leur réception aux dits conseils superieurs, et à l'expiration des dites trois années, nous permettons aux dits gouverneurs et intendans . . . de donner de pareilles commissions d'assesseurs à d'autres sujets, ou d'en accorder de nouvelles, s'ils jugent à propos, à ceux dont le tems sera expiré." Article v, Letters Patent 1742, *Edits et Ord.*, vol. i, p. 562.

livres, and the executioner 300 livres and 30 livres for his lodging.[1]

When the Council was enlarged in 1703, the King was unwilling to increase the expenses of government by providing salaries for the additional members. To be sure, the Declaration of Augmentation provided that these new members should have all the wages and emoluments of Councillors of the court of the Parlement of Paris,[2] but the King explained that the new members should receive salaries only when they succeeded to the old offices in the Council left vacant by death or promotion. Furthermore the representative of the clergy was never to receive a salary.[3] In 1734, however, in consquence of repeated representations, the four lay Councillors added by the Declaration of Augmentation were granted salaries of 300 livres.[4]

Councillors were probably envious of the prominent position and larger salary of the First Councillor for, after the death of Villeray in 1700, they petitioned the King to abolish the office.[5] The King refused but raised the salary of the second and third Councillors to 450 livres, while reducing that of the First Councillor from 500 to 450 livres. This increase in salary was the result of an interesting letter written by the Sovereign Council in 1702. After asking to be retained in office, they thus described the salary situation: "We have, Monseigneur, a second favor to ask of your Highness; that is, that he should increase our sal-

[1] *Coll. de Man. de Nouv. Fr.*, vol. i, pp. 233-235.

[2] *Edits et Ord.*, vol. i, pp. 299-301.

[3] "Ces cinq derniers n'auront point de gages; mais ils monteront à la place des autres qui viendront à vacquer à la reserve du Sr de la Colombière qui sera toujours sans gages." *Coll. Moreau St. Méry*, series F iii, vol. viii, pt. iii, p. 391.

[4] *Canadian Archives Report* for 1904, Appendix K, p. 199.

[5] Minister to Beauharnais June 20, 1703. Supplement *Canadian Archives Report* for 1899, p. 106.

aries, which are so modest that they reflect scorn upon the offices with which we have the honor to be vested. The cost and maintenance of carriages necessary to convey us to the court house, the difficulty of traveling through the snows, and other expenses, so eat into our salaries as to leave us nothing. As the country grows and business increases, it no longer comports with our dignity to supplement our salaries with petty trade. There is not in the country an officer, however unimportant, who does not receive a larger salary. M. the Governor and M. the Intendant are kind enough to join their prayers with ours in this regard." [1]

In 1752 the King raised the salaries of the first three Councillors from 450 to 600 livres and the salaries of the other Councillors from 300 to 450 livres.[2] These salaries for the last four Councillors in 1734 and increases in the salaries of all the Councillors in 1752 were obtained only as a result of repeated requests from Governor, Intendant, and Councillors.

For example, the meagerness of the salaries and the need of making the office financially more attractive are set forth in a letter of Beauharnais (Governor) and Hocquart (Intendant), written under date of October 1, 1732: "We last year gave His Majesty some account of the qualifications of the officers of justice who compose the tribunals of this colony, and we hope that after having been informed of the necessity which exists of filling the Superior Council with capable persons, he will be pleased to provide for it. We cannot excuse ourselves from representing to him anew the lack of resources we have in persons of any rank in this colony from which to choose judges, capable of filling the desires of His Majesty in the administration of justice.

[1] *Corres. Gen.*, series C xi, vol. xx, pt. i.

[2] Supplement *Canadian Archives Report* for 1899, p. 162.

"On account of the meagerness or total lack of resources that they find in judicial employments, the majority of those who might have a disposition to become adept in the law, hold themselves aloof, and this is an insurmountable obstacle to finding suitable persons to fill the vacant places. At present there is not a person except the Sieur Gaillard who has solicited a position as Councillor since there have been vacancies. Of his qualification we speak in another despatch.

"In general, in a country as poor as this, little value is set upon an honorary position to which no profit is attached. The Attorney-General, the Sieur Verrier, will gladly present himself to give lessons in French law, but he will have no listeners at all unless they are flattered by the hope that their work will lead to some profitable employment. We cannot leave His Majesty in ignorance of all these circumstances." [1]

In the previous year, these officials had proposed that two decrepit old Councillors be retired with honors and salary and that two young men of family be sent to Canada to serve as Councillors with salaries of 600 livres each. It was only upon the King's refusal that they pushed the alternative of training young men in Canada with a view to becoming Councillors. It took ten years to convince the King that no one would study law without such a prospect.

In addition to regular salaries Councillors voted themselves good pay for special commission work. For example, Damours was allowed a rate of two sous for every pound of beaver skin inspected by him. In 1680 the rate of a commissioner was raised from 10 to 15 livres a day and that of the clerk from 7 to 10 livres a day.[2] Furthermore, the King occasionally added small pensions to the

[1] *Corres. Gen.*, series C xi, vol. lvii, pt. i, p. 5, *et seq.*

[2] *Jugements et Délib.*, vol. ii, p. 452.

salaries of officials. In 1676 Tilly and Damours received a double pension " in consideration of their services and of the number of their children, at the rate of 61 livres for each child ".[1] In 1700 Auteuil was given a pension of 300 livres,[2] and Lotbinière received the same sum.

In the seventeenth century the Councillors were generally farmers, taking recesses for the annual sowing and harvesting. Probably they depended as much upon the fruits of the soil as upon their salaries. Sometimes they traded, perhaps sold meat in their houses as did Villeray.[3] In fact the business of huckstering yielded an income for more than one Councillor. Frontenac said that there was no use in establishing a market in Quebec when people were scouring the country to buy up cattle. Auteuil, feeling the shoe pinch, retorted by saying that he could do as much for his family as the chefs of the Governor and the Intendant did for their tables. Auteuil's enemy Cadillac accuses him of being the most persistent of hucksterers.[4]

In the eighteenth century such small traffic gave way to larger enterprises. The provision of the Edict of Establishment, prohibiting Councillors from enjoying other wages, etc.,[5] which was enforced during the seventeenth century,

[1] *Archives des Col.*, series B, vol. vii, pp. 1676-1678.

[2] Minister to Auteuil May 5, 1700. *Ibid.*, vol. xxii, pt. i, p. 336.

[3] The King wrote La Barre in 1684 that he was surprised to hear that the Governor permitted Councillors to absent themselves for the purpose of trading. *Canadian Archives Report* for 1899, p. 268. Cadillac relates how Villeray, the wealthiest man in the colony, turned his house into a butcher's shop in which his servant sold the meat and his wife collected the money. *Corres. Gen.*, series C xi, vol. xiii, pt. i, pp. 256-257.

[4] " . . . il n'y a qua s'informer s'ily a dans le pays un plus grand regratier que luy s'il ne fait pas revendre et burre et viande et pain apres avoir couru les costes pour l'achapter." *Ibid.*

[5] " . . . sans que les officiers du dit Conseil souverain puissent exercer autres offices, avoir gages ni recevoir présents, ou pensions de qui que ce soit que ceux qui leur seront par nous ordonnés, sans notre permission." *Edits et Ord.*, vol. i, p. 39.

became a dead letter. In 1685 Martinière had been ordered to resign from the position of Councillor because he had entered the employ of the Hudson Bay Trading Company.[1] Later he was allowed to make his choice and he preferred to retain his seat in the Council. But in the eighteenth century the King felt the need of making the position of Councillor attractive. He listened favorably to Auteuil's request that the Governor grant hunting licenses to Councillors,[2] and his minister approved of the election of Councillors as directors of the Company of the Colony of Canada, and congratulated Auteuil upon his election as manager.[3] In 1733 the Commissioner of Marine was admitted to a seat in the Council.[4] In 1738 the minister declared that Lotbinière should have his revenues as canon in addition to his salary as Councillor.[5] It is apparent, therefore, that a member of the Council was not limited to his official salary.

The honors and privileges pertaining to the office were almost as desirable as the stipend attached to it. The dignified and prominent position which Councillors enjoyed called forth covert gibes from envious neighbors and enemies.[6] The exaltation of Councillors was due in part

[1] Decree of Council of State March 10, 1685. *Coll. Moreau St. Méry*, series F iii, vol. vi, p. 297.

[2] "...qu'il leur fasse part des avantages qu'il accorde par les congez d'envoyer aux Outuoux, et ausquels cependant ils n'ont peu pas participer jusqu'a present." *Corres. Gen.*, series C xi, vol. xiii, pp. 144-50.

[3] Minister to Auteuil May 31, 1701. *Archives des Col.*, series B, vol. xxii, pt. ii, p. 236.

[4] Supplement *Can. Arch. Report* for 1899, p. 142.

[5] *Ibid.*, p. 147.

[6] La Hontan tells us that a Gascon title of Capa y de Spada was given to them because they walked very gravely wearing neither robe nor sword but leaning upon canes. *Voyages*, vol. i, p. 402.

to the position assigned them in church ceremonies. An elaborate order of march was developed during the first half century. In 1716 the King determined its ultimate form. Thenceforth processions were to be headed by the Governor and the Intendant, the latter on the left of the former. The Governor was preceded by his guard and upon his right marched the Captain of the guard. In advance of the Intendant were the bailiffs including the first usher and the chief clerk. Behind Governor and Intendant marched the Councillors two abreast, led by the First Councillor and Dean of the Council, and followed by the Attorney-General. Third in the procession came the Lieutenant General of the provost court of Quebec, the royal attorney and clerk.[1]

Inside the church, the Council occupied a pew immediately behind that of the Governor and Intendant, and in the same order the *pain benît,* or eulogiae, the pax (*le paix*), the incense, the tapers (*les cierges*), and the palm branches (*les rameaux*), were presented to them by the officiating priest, before the church wardens themselves.[2] Frontenac realized the value of such ceremonies. In 1675 he replied to some discontented church wardens that His Majesty intended these honors to be shown his officers of justice in order to teach the people to respect their persons, ordinances and judgments, and that there was no more effective means of holding the people to the service of His Majesty than by impressing upon their minds some respect for the magis-

[1] See *Edits et Ord.*, vol. i, p. 352, article vi, supplemented by a description of earlier customs found for example in *Jugements et Délib.*, vol. v, pp. 167-168.

[2] *Edits et Ord.*, vol. i, pp. 65, 67; *Jugements et Délib.*, vol. i, p. 904. Note the interesting reason advanced: "qu'il n'est pas de sa dignité de recevoir de la main d'un bedeau, les rameaux et cierges benits, comme aussi d'aller a l'adoration de la Croix en la manière que faict le commun peuple." *Ibid.*, vol. i, p. 922.

trates.[1] For these reasons the most honorable places in all the churches were on occasion reserved for the Councillors. They celebrated His Majesty's victories in the cathedral church; they sang Te Deum in Notre Dame des Victoires when in 1711 the English fleet was wrecked;[2] they honored the memory of Frontenac in the church of the Récollets.[3]

Councillors were perfectly ready to add to the privileges they enjoyed. In 1676 they passed a provisional ordinance that henceforth the members of the court, and the widows of those officers who died while in office, should, if litigants, plead in first instance before one of their number appointed for the month. From this individual Councillor there was to be appeal to the Sovereign Council.[3] The King, however, considered that such an arrangement compromised impartial justice and in June, 1679, ordered causes involving Councillors to be tried before the lieutenant general of the provost court of Quebec. Appeals were to be tried by the

[1] Frontenac wished no jot or title of the ceremonies of procession to be abated. Formerly the government had given to the cathedral a stretch of land all about the church to be used as a route for grand processions. The churchwardens had enclosed this land, leaving two large gates which were used only to admit firewood. The Governor complained that this was a misappropriation of the gift and that the accustomed processions were thereby prevented. *Ibid.*, vol. i, p. 909.

[2] *Ibid.*, vol. iv, p. 526; vol. vi, p. 246. After Sir William Phipp's expedition, it was called Notre Dame de la Victoire. After the second English *débac e* in 1711 the name was changed to Notre Dame des Victoires. It is to-day the most interesting church in Quebec. Such ceremonies occasionally palled upon the Councillors. For example, on July 17, 1689, the King's victories were to be glorified by the singing of a Te Deum at the cathedral, to be attended by the Council. Villeray and Martinière were the only Councillors present at the rendezvous. After waiting more than an hour and having learned from a bailiff that the service had finally begun, the two faithful Councillors retired in disgust. *Ibid.*, vol. iii, p. 346.

[3] *Ibid.*, vol. ii, p. 97.

Intendant and six judges chosen by him.[1] In 1781 Tilly thought it not in accordance with his dignity as a Councillor to wait upon the lieutenant general to give his testimony in a case on trial before that judge. The Council decreed that when the testimony of Councillors was desired, the lieutenant general must wait upon his witnesses in the Council chamber.[2] Again, the Council sought to exempt its members from the obligation of appearing in lawsuits as witnesses or as defendants. As early as 1663 ushers were forbidden to serve a summons upon a Councillor.[3]

Honors and privileges added to the prestige of Councillors. Undue criticism detracted from it and therefore was not allowed. Freedom of speech was not at that period an established principle and no government could afford to submit to criticism. The earliest display of disrespect towards the Governor, Intendant, or Council, was checked as dangerous. Among the nine or ten cases of punishment for disrespect the following are interesting. In 1664 the Council condemned Jean and François Pelletier to an hour's imprisonment for having retorted when under trial that Councillor Auteuil was guilty like themselves of selling liquor to the Indians. Later, it refused to entertain the written charges which they subsequently brought.[4] In 1669 the Council condemned Giles Rageot to tear up a memoir containing terms injurious to Councillors Damours and La Tesserie, and to beg their pardon.[5] In 1675 it commissioned Dupont to ferret out the authors of certain

[1] Declaration of the King June 1680. *Corres. Gen.*, series C xi, vol. v, pp. 217-219.

[2] *Jugements et Délib.*, vol. ii, p. 516.

[3] *Ibid.*, vol. i, p. 68.

[4] *Ibid.*, vol i, p. 115.

[5] *Ibid.*, vol. i, p. 556.

scandalous placards, defamatory and insulting to the honor of the Sovereign Council, following upon the banishment of prostitutes from Quebec.[1] It commissioned Tilly to investigate insolent and disrespectful remarks made at the house of one Parent. Insolence to Denonville by Genaple, *père* and *fils,* was followed by condemnation of the father to ask pardon on his knees and condemnation of the son to two months' imprisonment.[2] During Frontenac's administration a certain Madame Fournier in conducting a suit for her husband addressed a petition to Frontenac, a part of which was couched in an unknown gibberish in prose and verse. The Governor, who plumed himself upon his wit, employed like terms in his reply. Madame Fournier, contrary to the Governor's expectations, used his answer as a document in her suit. Frontenac thereupon handed over her unusual petition to the Council and asked that she be fined for irreverence. The Council fined her 10 livres, which was applied by the Governor to the needs of her children "because of their great necessity", and the rejected petition was returned to the Governor, "although," affirmed the Council, "it ought to be torn up".

The institution of royalty was defended against criticism. In 1671, Pierre Dupuy had said among other things that there was nothing like executing your own justice, that the English had done well in killing their king. On February 4th the Council condemned him, clothed only in his shirt with a torch in his hand and with a rope around his neck, to be led by the hangman to the great gate of the Château St. Louis, there to ask pardon of the King. Thence the procession was to move to the stocks where the delinquent was to be branded with a fleur-de-lis upon the cheek.[3]

[1] *Jugements et Délib.*, vol. i, pp. 978, 985.

[2] *Ibid.*, vol. iii, p. 24.

[3] *Ibid.*, vol. i, p. 644.

Great Officials

The peculiar organization of the Sovereign Council did not foster uninterrupted application to business. We have seen disputes of a fundamental character interrupt business during the court terms of 1664, 1680-81, and 1728. When the few months during which the Council was thus incommoded are compared, however, with the century during which it administered justice, one is inclined to deprecate its critics[1] and admire its operation. Nevertheless there were faults in its organization—notable faults that experience partially repaired. The very composition of the Council was vicious. To give three co-ordinate officials such as the Governor General, the Bishop and the Intendant, seats and large powers in a court of justice and administration was to court dissension. They represented different classes with different interests—classes that were without clear distinctive marks and that freely intermingled, but, nevertheless, representing broadly the noblesse who sought the army and more dignified offices, the ecclesiastics and the most pious of their followers, and the merchant class, the most enterprising class in Canada. Of course a noble might be very devout and, therefore, an upholder of the clergy; or he might enter upon a business career, the King having opened trade to the noblesse in Canada. Moreover, successful business men in the colony obtained letters of nobility: the Tillys, the Damours, the Duponts, the Villerays, and many others bestrode trade and a title. Persistent rumor

[1] In La Hontan's account of the government of Canada that author writes: "But the most important alteration would consist in keeping the Governor, the Intendant, the Sovereign Council, the Bishops and the Jesuits from splitting into factions, and intriguing one against the other; for the consequence of such Divisions can not but thwart His Majesty's Service and the Peace of the Publick." *Voyages*, Thwaites' edition, vol. i, p. 268.

had it that the Jesuits traded with the Indians, and such business men as Auteuil the elder were undoubtedly under ecclesiastical influence. Therefore there was no hard and fast line between these classes, and groups from each of them might be relied upon to support the Governor, the Bishop, and the Intendant, respectively, whenever disputes arose.

The Governor

These officials might have worked well together from the start had the King clearly defined their functions and position in the Council. Even on the points where he was clear he delegated overlapping powers to his officials. The first instance of definition of power occurred in 1663. It concerned the appointment of Councillors and was prolonged in a mild way until 1675. The Governor was given the power jointly with the Bishop to remove and appoint Councillors. His commission however provided that he should have supreme power over the officers of the Sovereign Council.[1] When therefore the Bishop refused to co-operate with him to replace objectionable members at the end of their term of office, Governor Mésy violated the Edict of Establishment, relying upon the broader powers designated to him in his commission. The Bishop's friends had control in the Council and by refusing to make "joint action" possible, Laval planned to retain that majority until Mésy was replaced.

As we have seen this question was by no means settled by the advent of the West Indies Company administration. The Edict of Establishment was not abrogated. The Council retained the organization authorized by this Edict and

[1] "Nous donnons plein pouvoir, puissance, autorité, commission, et mandement spécial de commander dorénavant . . . à tous nos officiers, ministres et sujets d'icelui." *Edits et Ord.*, vol. iii, p. 21.

functioned as before. The Bishop was theoretically able to participate in making nominations, but the general agent succeeded in formulating a process of nomination that excluded the Bishop; Governor and Intendant were to grant commissions to nominees of the Company. But Governor Frontenac, depending upon the broad powers of his commission, assumed the sole right of both appointment and commission.[1] Both Edict and agreement with the Company were thus superseded by a third method, based solely upon the Governor's commission. This indefiniteness was remedied in 1675 by the provision that the King should fill vacancies in the Council.[2]

The same overlapping of powers was responsible also for the dispute concerning the title of president of the Council. The commission of the Intendant provided that he should preside only in the absence of the Governor.[3] The Declaration of 1675 stipulated that although he should be third in point of dignity, the Intendant should serve as president of the Council.[4] The long and dreary dispute that arose from these contradictory provisions was terminated only in 1680 with the royal regulation that neither Governor nor Intendant should have the title of president but that the Intendant should perform all the functions of president.[5] In 1681 the privilege of presiding in the Intendant's absence,

[1] Frontenac's commission provides that he is to "avoir commandement sur tous les officiers du Conseil souverain." *Ibid.*, vol. iii, p. 40.

[2] "auxquelles charges, vacation avenant, nous pourvoirons à l'avenir de plein droit." Declaration of 1675, *ibid.*, vol. i, p. 84. Confirmed in 1703, *ibid.*, p. 300.

[3] "presider au Conseil souverain en l'absence du dit sieur de Frontenac." *Ibid.*, vol. iii, p. 42.

[4] "l'intendant . . . lequel dans l'order ci-dessus aura la troisième place comme président du dit conseil demande les avis, recueille les voix," etc. *Ibid.*, vol. i, p. 84.

[5] *Ibid.*, vol. i, p. 238.

even though the Governor was present, was secured to the dean of the Council, who was usually the First Councillor.

However, even without the power to fill vacancies in the Council, to address the assembly, to administer the oath of office annually to the Councillors, or to preside either as actual or honorary president, the Governor was the most powerful member of the Sovereign Council. He controlled the military forces and the terms of his commission might warrant using soldiers to carry out his wishes in the Council. The clause "*avoir commandement sur les officiers du Conseil souverain*", was the authority of Frontenac, when in 1694 he delivered Mareuil from prison by force; when in 1679 he banished several members of the Council from Quebec; when he forced the Councillors to continue a session until the noon bell sounded although not a word was uttered; when he stood before the door of the Council chamber barring egress to Councillors and Intendant until the latter had promised to sign the minutes in his office. It was this same power that Beauharnais employed in 1728 to suspend the execution of the Council's decrees, to forbid further proceedings against the chapter of the cathedral, and, later, to banish two of the Councillors from Quebec. In all these cases the power was successfully exercised. We may conclude therefore that if the Governor thought himself justified in making use of his supreme authority, no one in the Council could resist him.

He was the most powerful of the members of the Council, but only when he adopted arbitrary methods. Upon ordinary occasions after 1679-81 he was no more powerful than the most prominent of the Councillors, except that he was supposed to be consulted by the Intendant as to the advisability of calling special sessions.[1] In fact, in 1679,

[1] This is the position of Frontenac, but he failed to sustain it. *Jugements et Délib.*, vol. ii, p. 293.

the Intendant maintained in the Council chamber, that the Governor was only an honorary member, as was the Bishop or his substitute, the Grand Vicar.[1] and that their only prerogatives were to sit above him at the Council board. In theory this was true, but in practice the Governor voted, he expressed his opinion, and that opinion had great weight in Council deliberations. Moreover Councillors who had relatives that aspired to conciliar appointment, could not forget that the Governor enjoyed great influence with the King. Still the period of the Governor's greatest influence in the Sovereign Council was in 1674, while he exercised the appointing function, presided over the sessions, made his annual speeches to Councillors and administered each year the oath of office.[2] What power the Governor later lost was resumed by the King, who made the appointments; or was exercised by the Intendant or First Councillor; or passed away as an outworn or objectionable custom.[3]

[1] Frontenac said that the Intendant "luy a dit en particulier et en plein Conseil qu'il n'y estoit que Conseiller honoraire et n'y avoit d'autres prerogatives que celles d'estre assis au dessus de luy Intendant, comme Monsieur Levesque, et en son absence son grand vicaire." *Ibid.*, vol. ii, p. 292.

[2] The oath may be of some interest. Councillors raised their right hands and swore: "et promis a Dieu chacun a son esgard, de bien et fidellement servir le Roy dans la fonction de leur charges, sous l'authorité de celle qu'il a plu a Sa Majesté luy donner dans ces provinces Et de rendre la justice a tous esgalement, sans distinction niy acceptation de personnes, conformement aux ordonnances Royaux avec toute l'integrité de Juges incorruptibles, Et la celerité que demande le bien des peuples, comme aussi s'il venoit quelque chose a leur cognoissance contre le service de Sa Majesté, d'en advertir aussitost le dict Seigneur Gouverneur, Et s'il n'y estoit par luy remedié d'en donner advis a Sa dicte Majesté." *Ibid.*, vol. i, p. 709.

[3] Thus the escort of honor, consisting of two Councillors sent each day to meet the Governor at the head of the staircase in the Palais de Justice, was abolished after the death of Frontenac in 1699. The annual speech was discontinued with the abolition in 1675 of the one-year term of office.

The Intendant

It has been increasingly evident that the Intendant was acquiring a position of the greatest importance in the Council. Of the three great officials he was most intimately connected with the Councillors, and in that position might seek like Duchesneau and Dupuy to exalt the Council or like Bégon to abase it. In any case his opportunities to influence its proceedings were many.

Until 1675, his title to a seat rested upon no edict but only upon his commission and instructions. The Royal Declaration of 1675 empowered him to act as president of the Council, to take the opinions, to collect the votes, to pronounce the decrees and to enjoy the same advantages as the first president of the King's courts.[1] His position was further strengthened in 1680 when the Governor was forbidden to take the title of chief and president of the Council.[2] As president he decided when special sessions were to be called, often without consultation with the Governor, and he despatched bailiffs to summon the Councillors. He determined a quorum and deputed the clerk or a special committee to invite the Governor to be present. During the meeting he served as president and at the close he signed the minutes. He might easily use his position as president to introduce or suppress the consideration of business. For example, in 1727, the Attorney-General complained that he had presented three requisitions to the Council which had never been considered because the Intendant had put them into his pocket.[3] He might use the office of "reporter" so often assigned him to give what color he chose to the cases he investigated.

[1] *Edits et Ord.*, vol. i, p. 84.

[2] *Ibid.*, vol. i, p. 238.

[3] Beauharnais to the Minister April 24, 1727. *Corres. Gen.*, series C xi, vol. xlix.

By virtue of his instructions he obtained the appointing power in conjunction with other officials.[1] In the case of Auteuil the younger, he filled out a commission without consulting the Governor. Although the King assumed the appointing function in 1675, the Intendant was compensated for a time by permission to name several lesser officers of justice.[2] Although subsequently deprived of this right, which properly belonged to the Council, the Intendant, according to Auteuil, usurped the nomination of judges, royal attorneys, clerks, notaries, and bailiffs.[3] Thenceforth his influence over Councillors was largely due to a desire on their part to win a favorable report or recommendation in his letters to the King.

For a few years he possessed the legal right to determine in what jurisdiction cases of first instance were to be tried. He thus received all petitions and distributed them at his discretion.[4] Although this function was ostensibly taken away in 1671 by Colbert, there is much evidence that the Intendant continued to exercise it. For example, in 1684, Auteuil complained that Meulles took cognizance of all cases by sending his secretary to summon the litigants, whereupon he judged them orally, making use of prisons

[1] Instructions of Talon: "suivant le pouvoir que lui est donné et au dit Sieur de Tracy et de Coucelles, ils auront ou licencié le Conseil Souverain pour le composer d'autres personnes, en cas qu'ils aient rémarqué qu'ils n'aient pas fait leur devoir, ou se seroit contentés d'en ôter quelquesuns, ou enfin les auront confirmés, si effectivement ils auront reconnu qu'ils ont de bonnes intentions." *Lettres, Instructions, et Memoires de Colbert*, vol. iii, pt. ii, p. 389, *et seq.*

[2] On May 29, 1680, the King empowered Duchesneau to appoint the usher of the Council and clerk of the Maréchaussée. But other Intendants did not possess this power. Supplement *Canadian Archives Report* for 1899, p. 129.

[3] *Corres. Gen.*, series C xi, vol. xxii, pt. i, pp. 363, *et seq.*

[4] January 16, 1668. *Jugements et Délib.*, vol. i, p. 469.

and fines to execute his judgments; that he was thus depriving the local judge of Quebec of all business, and was reducing him to a life of laziness. About forty years later, the same activity of the Intendant brought forth an opinion of the Attorney-General that the Intendant could not judge a case alone nor evoke to his jurisdiction causes, except those at Montreal, because at Quebec, when there were causes to be tried, he had only to summon the Council in extraordinary session.[1] Thus it appears that accordingly as the Intendant was pleased or displeased with the Council, he gave or withheld judicial business. He possessed a further hold over Councillors in that he judged with six of his nominees causes involving them.

In administrative business, Intendant and Councillors were intimately associated, for the great fundamental ordinances that governed New France were for the most part made by them jointly.[2]

In brief, a vigorous, industrious Intendant occupied a constitutional position of great strength in the Council. Upon ordinary occasions, he was the most powerful of its members; but upon extraordinary occasions where the Governor chose to "*avoir commandement sur les officiers du Conseil souverain*", he was no match for that official. That occasions of this kind were few, was fortunate for the routine work of the court. That Councillors obtained com-

[1] Beauharnais to the Minister April 24, 1727. *Corres. Gen.*, series C xi, pt. i, vol. xlvii.

[2] The way in which the Governor was dropped from participation in making police ordinances is shown by the following documents: Talon's Instructions provide: "il pourra par la participation du Gouverneur et du Conseil Souverain en dresser un reglement," but the commissions of later Intendants provide that they "faire avec le dit Conseil Souverain les reglemens que vous estimerez necessaires pour la police générale du dits pays." *Edits et Ord.*, vol. iii, pp. 5, 10, 25, 31, 48.

missions from the King and that the Intendant became the undisputed president of the Council made for the independence and effectiveness of that assembly. As a member of the *gens de robe*, trained in the French courts, the Intendant was specially fitted to participate widely in the labors of the highest court.

The Bishop

The constitutional position of the Bishop was inferior to that either of the Intendant or of the Governor. From the status of a creator of Councillors he became only an honorary member. His power in coöperation with the Governor to continue Councillors in office, to remove and replace them—a power provided by the Edict of Establishment—was enjoyed only in the selection of the first Councillors. His right to be represented by an ecclesiastic was abolished in 1703 when a clerical Councillor was appointed to be the permanent representative of clerical interests. His right to sign the minutes was not exercised after 1668,[1] and, in fact, lapsed when that act of responsibility was made one of the Intendant's duties in 1675. There is no evidence that he ever voted in the deliberations of the Council, nor is his opinion ever spread upon the minutes like those of Governor, Intendant, and Councillors.[2] He was in fact an honorary member, whose chief prerogative was to sit at the head of the Council board.

Honors certainly were shown him. In 1685, a deputation of Councillors escorted Bishop St. Vallier into the

[1] November 3, 1668. *Jugements et Délib.*, vol. i, p. 528.

[2] In March 1664 he protested in writing that his signature to acts of the deputy Attorney-General who had been placed in Bourdon's place should by no means prejudice the claims of Bourdon. *Ibid.*, vol. i, 129. This was, however, not an opinion, in the sense of a reason for a vote or proposition.

Council chamber. In 1688, another deputation was delegated to congratulate him upon his return from France.[1]

The influence of the Bishop was not exerted upon Councillors in the Council chamber. He seldom participated in the disputes of the Council. In those exciting scenes others carried the episcopal banner. In 1664 it was Father Charney who led in opposition to Governor Mésy and it was Villeray and Auteuil, notoriously under clerical influence. who aided and abetted this priest. It was Duchesneau and Auteuil the younger, men chidden by the King for partiality towards the Bishop,[2] who showed some clerical influence in the measures they proposed to the Council in 1680-81. For example, it was the Bishop's idea that the coureurs de bois should be vigorously dealt with. Frontenac favored milder measures. The Council adopted the policy of the former. During the prosecution of Mareuil in 1694, constant communication was maintained between Auteuil and Villeray and Bishop St. Vallier. They three were jointly responsible for the methods of delay, bribery, and intimidation by close imprisonment, which were designed to cover over the *faux pas* of the Bishop. Like a modern general the Bishop could on occasion direct the course of his forces from his bureau. The routine work of the court did not concern him and matters of interest could be watched over by his friends in the Council. It is not surprising that the attendance of both Bishop Laval and his successor dropped off after a few years. Nevertheless the former began to attend the Council again, when the friendly Duchesneau came to Canada in 1675. Apparently he took such a prominent part in Council proceedings that the minister became

[1] *Jugements et Délib.*, vol. ii, p. 1012; vol. iii, p. 242.

[2] Minister to Duchesneau May 15, 1678. Supplement *Can. Archives* for 1899, p. 262.

alarmed. On May 1, 1677, he wrote to Duchesneau that as the Bishop was evidently assuming too independent an authority, it would perhaps be wise that he should not have a seat in the Council; that the Intendant must seek every opportunity, and on all occasions take every means practicable, to wean him from the craving for attending the Council. He must however act in this matter with great discretion, taking care that what the minister wrote be not divulged.[1]

The fact that Councillors would not pass judgment and punish the offenders in the Rolland, Callières, Mareuil, and Gosselin cases, proves that they shared the minister's dislike to appear as the Bishop's critics. They sent the papers of these suits to the King, glad to transfer to him the responsibility of a decision. La Motte Cadillac, however, stung by conciliar action beyond the bounds of caution, declared that since the foundation of the colony it had never been possible to secure a decree against a single ecclesiastic, but that on the contrary the Council had aided the ecclesiastical power in oppressing the people.[2]

But although the Council never had the courage to array itself against the Bishop, it occasionally dealt fearlessly with subordinate ecclesiastics, in spite of Cadillac's assertion. When Rolland sought justice against his priest, the latter had had a petition testifying to the bad character of the trader passed about in the church among the faithful. The Council decreed the abolition of such practices.[3] In 1705 two parish priests attempted to make produce, cattle, etc., tithable. The tithe was one twenty-sixth of the grain

[1] Minister to Duchesneau, *op. cit.*, p. 70.

[2] *Corres. Gen.*, series C xi, vol. xiii, pt. i, p. 255.

[3] *Jugements et Délib.*, vol. ii, pp. 132-33.

alone and the Council forbade parish priests to make any innovation.[1]

In 1677 the Council temporarily deprived church wardens of all honors because they had contravened the regulations for precedence in church.[2] In 1713, the Council declared that the Vicar General had judged a case ill and sent the petition before the ecclesiastical judge of the Officialty of Quebec,[3] and in the next year, it instructed the Bishop to appoint another official or judge and another promoter or attorney, for a certain trial, because the former had been challenged and the latter had contravened the ordinance of 1667.[4] Later, it several times reversed the decisions of the ecclesiastical court. These examples simply illustrate that the Council was able and for the most part willing to administer justice whether the offence was committed by clerical or lay brethren. The hesitation therefore and the refusal to judge cases involving the Bishop serves to illustrate the strength of his position in the Council.

The First Councillor

Upon ordinary occasions the First Councillor and the Attorney General shared the most prominent positions in the Council. The office of First Councillor became the reward of long service. Its possessor was usually the dean or eldest member of the Council. As such he presided in the absence of the Intendant; he investigated into the habits, religion and age of prospective Councillors; he conducted the preliminary investigations of many cases, thereby serving as reporter (*rapporteur*) to the Council.

[1] *Jugements et Déib.*, vol. v, pp. 184-186.

[2] *Ibid.*, vol. ii, p. 166.

[3] *Ibid.*, vol. vi, p. 665.

[4] *Edits et Ord.*, vol ii, p. 165.

The Attorney-General

The Attorney-General combined a knowledge of past ordinances and decrees of the Council and the laws and ordinances of France with considerable political discretion. Upon every important step in a trial, he was consulted. He stated the conditions of the case with the laws that bore upon it. His discretionary power lay in his interpretation of those laws as regards the case (*conclusions*) and in the course which he proposed as the legal remedy (*requisitoire*).[1] The Council usually acted in conformity with his proposals. Thus his power of steering its policy was tremendous. His obstructive ability was just as great as his constructive. If a proposed measure were obnoxious to him or his friends, he would demand the submittal of the written proposition for his conclusions, and could then easily delay his report upon it for an indefinite period. Sending a paper to a hostile Attorney-General usually meant tabling the matter indefinitely. The Attorney-General introduced a great deal of business into the Council. It was upon his representation that relieving ordinances were made and that suits were prosecuted. He supervised the royal attorneys of the local courts, who met him at first on Saturday mornings in his house, and later in the antechamber of the Council. Lastly, he was responsible for the promulgation of royal and conciliar measures.

The strengthening of these offices depended upon the tact

[1] In 1679, for example, the Attorney-General after summing up the documentary authorities concerning the Governor's right to the title of president, decides that the despatches which are the basis of the Governor's claim are not so authentic as the Declaration of 1675, which speaks of the Intendant as president. His view was accepted by the Council. Another typical case of this use of political discretion was in 1681, when the Attorney-General decided that the Governor could not ask for written opinions of Councillors. *Jugements et Délib.*, vol. ii, pp. 313-317.

and energy of the occupants. Villeray, twice banished from Quebec, nevertheless raised the office of First Councillor to its highest point. During his life the presidency of the Council was secured to the dean in the absence of the Intendant. Following him Lotbinière was said to dominate Governor de Vaudreuil.[1] In spite of the vigorous attempt of Martinière in 1714 to prevent decadence in the position of the Council by enacting relieving ordinances and seeing that they were enforced, we have seen that his efforts failed. Delino and Cugnet were both good men for the office.

Bourbon rather set the pace for succeeding Attorneys-General. He had assumed an attitude of independence towards Mésy. Upon receiving his dismissal at the end of the year 1664, instead of accepting it philosophically with the others, he declared defiantly that he did not consider himself dispossessed of his office, whereupon he was chastised and sent over to France. Auteuil the elder endangered the prestige of his office in 1675 on behalf of his friends the ecclesiastics. In the case of Father Morel, who refused to be tried by the Council and sought to be tried in the ecclesiastical court of Quebec, Auteuil agreed with the priest's reasons and those of the Grand Vicar. On June 10, 1675, the Council disregarded his conclusions, and when he persisted, it bestowed a stinging rebuke upon him, claiming that he was acting in league with the ecclesiastics and not in the service of the King.[2] Later, however, he

[1] Minister to Lotbinière June 9. 1706, supplement *Can. Archives Report* for 1899, p. 392.

[2] "...il a paru qu'il ne s'acquittoit pas du devoir de sa charge, Et atendu l'uniformité qui paroist Entre ses conclusions Et les reponses des Ecclesiastiques, qu'il soit adverty par le Conseil qu'a l'advenir Il aye a considerer de plus prez ce qui regarde le service du Roy Et l'autorite du Conseil pour le soutien de ses arrêts." *Jugements et Délib.*, vol. i, p. 940.

regained the favor of the majority in the Council, stood against its intimidation by the Governor, and was one of those banished from Quebec in 1679. In fact, the Intendant painted Auteuil as a martyr to the cause of consiliar independence, claiming that he died because of the exposure to the weather and excitement caused by his banishment.[1]

Auteuil the younger entered the Council under the auspices of Duchesneau. In the exciting scenes of the next two years (1679-81), he played a rôle second only to the Governor and Intendant. He, like his father, was alert against enterprises directed as he thought at the independence of the Council, but only if they emanated from the Governor. He was however content to be the right hand of Duchesneau, because he thought that the Intendant was aiming at conciliar independence. Throughout the great cases of 1694 he was under the influence of Bishop St. Vallier, but later became more independent. In 1706 he frustrated the designs of the parish priests in the matter of the tithes. The dispute turned in great measure upon the regulation, real or alleged, of August 23, 1667, on which Fathers Boullard and Fournel relied. The Attorney-General replied that the regulation upon this matter was of date September 4, 1667, that the letter was duly signed, executed and registered in the office of the recorder of the Council, whereas the other was unknown until that day, and being neither registered nor published, could be nothing more than the draft of a regulation.[2] Auteuil's view was sustained by the decision of the King. Later, in the month of January, Auteuil was found to have assisted Madame de la Forest in her attempt to prevent the trial of her suit before the Superior Council. Furthermore, he

[1] *Jugements et Délib.*, vol. ii, p. 342.

[2] *Supplement Can. Archives Report* for 1899, p. 198.

charged the Intendant at this time with maltreating the Council. The rebuke which followed indicated his loss of influence in that body. He appealed to France in a letter exposing grave abuses in the system of justice in Canada, and was met by the request to prove his charge on pain of being treated as a libeler. Auteuil assembled evidence against the Governor and Intendant and went to France. Pontchartrain received him with displeasure, kept him waiting for six weeks, and then dismissed him from office.[1] For a number of years after his return to Canada, he continued to address memoirs to the King, in which he pointed out the preponderating influence of the Governor and Intendant in the deliberations of the Council, and the consequently bad administration of justice. His criticism included even the King's minister. In one memoir he proposed that Pontchartrain's power over Canada be limited; in another, that three Councillors of State be named to receive the complaints of the Canadians. He further proposed that the Governor be maintained in office not more than six years, reminding the King of his Declaration of 1698 which provided for a three-year term. These documents, written after he was out of office, indicate that he had the welfare of the country at heart. As Attorney-General he had consistently opposed the intimidation of the Council by the Governor. When the Intendant stood with the Governor, Auteuil attacked them both.[2] Although personal ambition

[1] Memoir to the King written in 1712. *Corres. Gen.*, series C xi, vol. xxxiii, pt. i, pp. 429-437.

[2] *Ibid.*, vol. xxii, pt. i, pp. 363, *et seq.* and vol. xxxiv, pt. i, pp. 530, *et seq.* In his memoirs he poses as the champion of justice. For example, Vaudreuil desired some unjust decision, to which the Raudots assented in an attempt to keep on good terms with him, as did also Lotbinière, his uncle, Monseignet, Lotbinière's son-in-law, and Delino, his protegé. Of the other Councillors the greater part feared to offend the Governor, or knew no better, and consequently Auteuil had been exposed to a thousand disagreeable things because he wished to do his duty.

was probably responsible for some of his acts, the chief motive was the desire to defend the independence of the Council.

Later Attorneys-General also attempted to maintain the position of the Council. In 1720 Collet complained that quarrels between citizens and soldiers invariably resulted in the imprisonment of the former, although the latter were always the aggressors, and that such citizens were kept in prison by the Governor because the judges did not dare to bring them to trial. Collet recommended that the Governor be limited in his power over civilians to persons charged with infractions of his own ordinances, and persons guilty of disrespect to his person.[1] It is evident, therefore, from this sketch of the acts of various Attorneys-General that they consistently opposed encroachments upon the jurisdiction and independence of the Council.

Other Officers

Besides the officials described above and the ordinary Councillors there were numerous other officers attached to the Council. The clerical Councillor added in 1703 served as a permanent representative of ecclesiastical interests;[2] the assistant Councillors first commissioned in 1741 completed the quorum and served as reporters.[3] Clerks, bailiffs and executioner complete the list. The tale of the

[1] *Corres. Gen.*, series C xi, vol. xlii, pt. i, p. 182, *et seq.*

[2] "...lequel étant toujours en fonction sera plus instruit et plus a portée de veille à la conservation des droits de l'Eglise." *Edits et Ord.*, vol. i, p. 300.

[3] The functions of the assesseurs are thus described in the Letters Patent of 1742: "il n'y auront voix deliberative que dans le jugement des affaires dont ils seront rapporteurs, à moins que les autres dont ils ne seront pas rapporteurs, il ne se trouvât pas un nombre, suffisant de juges auquel cas ils auront pareillement voix delibérative comme aussi dans le cas de partage d'opinions entre les autres juges." *Ibid.*, vol. i, p. 562.

latter is curious enough to relate. The office of executioner was in such ill repute that it could be filled for the most part only with condemned criminals whose death penalty was remitted. It was in this way that Jacques Elie was made executioner, only to meet a violent death in 1710 because of his office. Thereafter it was more difficult than ever to fill the post. Finally, the King sent over a man who was so stricken with madness and given to drunkenness and so furious in his cups, that it was impossible with the most severe chastisement to get him to do his duty as executioner. He was sent back to France in 1730. His successor was a feeble old man much given to wine, and so weak, in fact, that he found it difficult even to burn in effigy three criminals who had escaped. It was later agreed that a negro was a more suitable person for executioner in Canada. One was secured, and also a negress to comfort his idle moments. In 1744 Hocquart was instructed to sell her since the negro hangman had died and was succeeded by a white man.[1]

[1] *Jugements et Délib.*, vol. v, p. 191; vol. vi, p. 74. *Corres. Gen.*, series C xi, vol. lii, pt. i, pp. 52, 70, 115.

CHAPTER V

Methods of Procedure

Time of Sessions

The meetings of the Council of Quebec were held continuously throughout the year with the exception of four recesses. The Council discontinued its meetings during the Christmas season until the first Monday after Twelfth Night. In the spring it declared a recess of from six to ten weeks to allow Councillors to sow their crops. It reconvened on the first Monday after the Feast of St. John the Baptist, which falls upon June 24. The autumn recess for harvesting the crops occurred during September and the first or second week of October. Towards the close of the latter month Councillors voted a recess to enable them to write their letters in time for the vessels returning to France. Time and length of recesses became fixed only in the early "eighties".

During the greater part of the Council's history, the regular sessions occurred on Monday of each week. During the latter years of the French dominion Saturday was the day for regular sessions, and, finally, the Council met at monthly intervals.[1] Special sessions, called by

[1] "...il seroit inutile de s'assembler, suivant l'usage ordinaire du conseil, tous les samedis de chaque semaine, n'y ayant aucune affaire; il estime qu'il suffiroit que e conseil voulût indiquer un jour certain dans le cours du mois prochain où sera fixée la rentrée ordinaire du dit conseil." The Council acted upon this suggestion and appointed a future date for the next session. *Edits et Ordonnances*, vol. ii, p. 254.

the Intendant for the consideration of important business,[1] fell upon other week-days during both term and recess time. Sometimes a recess was filled with as many meetings as the regular term time.

Regular sessions began at nine o'clock in the morning and closed at half after one. Any afternoon session began at three o'clock.[2] Special sessions might be called for eight o'clock in the morning,[3] in which case they were adjourned at noon.

Place of Sessions

The early meeting places of the Sovereign Council were unpretentious in character. The Council was a new and untried institution in a frontier community. It is not surprising then that its surroundings were mean and unimpressive, nor that its prestige and sphere of usefulness quickly outstripped the dignity of its place of meeting.

Governor Mézy held the first few meetings in the Château St. Louis and summoned the Council thither upon various occasions,[4] but routine court was held

[1] Both Governor and Intendant were empowered to call special sessions, but the latter assumed the sole exercise of the power. In 1729 the King legalized this assumption. The litigant desiring to rush his suit appealed to the Intendant, who summoned the Councillors through the agency of the bailiff of hearings (*huissier audiencier*). Supplement *Canadian Archives* for 1899, p. 136.

[2] For examples, see *Jugements et Délibérations*, vol. ii, pp. 659, 754, 501.

[3] *Ibid.*, p. 756. They were occasionally called for seven o'clock. *Ibid.* p. 507.

[4] I should judge that the hall in which the election of the Mayor was held was in the Château rather than in a small house: "se sont presentez en la Chambre du Conseil, en presence du dict Conseil assemblé nombre des plus considerables habitans de cette dicte ville et banlieue et ressort d'Icelle, etc." *Ibid.*, vol. i, p. 15.

in the house of Jean le Vasseur, the court usher.[1] The Council had meantime called upon Péronne du Mesnil to vacate a house belonging to the King, which they destined for public uses.[2] This house was probably the hall of justice (Palais) mentioned in 1664. Here, after two months' residence with the usher, the Council held its sessions. The anticipated arrival of Tracy caused the Council to vacate the "*palais*" that it might be fitted up for his reception. Therefore in June, 1665, the Council resumed its sessions in the house of the usher.[3]

A month later Tracy summoned the Council to meet in the Château, where later the Governor's antechamber was definitely assigned to it.[4] During the controversies of 1679 to 1681 this situation became embarrassing. The addition of two new officers in 1674 added overcrowding to the annoyances caused by the Governor's soldiers. The Attorney-General had no room where he could confer with his subordinates, the royal attorneys, and had

[1] December 5, 1663, Le Vasseur is paid 250 livres annual salary for services "et pour la chambre du Conseil par lui fournie." *Ibid.*, p. 77.

[2] September 20, 1663, *ibid.*, p. 4.

[3] "Le Conseil, attendu que le pallais est reservé et qu'on y travaille incessamment pour y loger Monseigneur de Tracy, a ordonné qu'affiches seront mises pour faire savoir a tous que le Conseil se tiendra aux jours ordinaires dans le maison de la vigne [nickname for Le Vasseur] huissier ou il se tenoit ce devant." *Ibid.*, p. 362. October 17, 1667, he brings in a bill "pour l'occupation de sa maison par le Conseil." *Ibid.*, p. 456.

[4] He held his first Council on July 6, 1665, "en la première Salle du Chasteau Sainct Louis," his second in "son hostel," and succeeding ones likewise. Therefore, during 1665, 1666, 1667, the Council met in the house of the usher, the former *palais*, now M. de Tracy's *hostel*, and occasionally in the Château. The usher is not paid after 1667, and there is this record for November 3, 1668: "Prononcé aux dicts Chamot et Tolomy mandez *en la chambre du Conseil Souverain au Chasteau St. Louis* present." By 1668 I conclude that the Council was assigned a room in the Château. *Ibid.*, p. 530.

to receive them in his house.[1] There was no room where judges who had been challenged might wait until another case should be called.

Agitation for the erection of a Palais de Justice was started as early as 1679[2] and was kept up until the royal government purchased and remodeled the building, which had been constructed by Jean Talon as a brewery.[3] On November 29, 1688, the Council indicated its intention of removing into the new Palais de Justice on the first Monday after the Fête des Rois of the approaching year.[4] For the first few years the Council occupied a smaller room in the new building, the Council chamber not yet being finished. On January 7, 1692, however, the Council was finally installed in a suitable hall, abandoning its old room to the provost court of Quebec.[5]

On the night of January 5, 1713, this building was de-

[1] The royal attorney of Quebec did not wish to wait upon the Attorney-General, whose reply is illuminating as to conditions in the Château; "icy a Quebec où le Conseil tient sa seance dans l'une des salles du Chasteau ou il n'y a aucun lieu designé pour les gens du Roy, il semble que le dit sieur boulduc par derision ou pour avillir son ministere veuille luy designer *la porte* de cette salle pour *parquet*, Et que la en presence des gardes de Monsieur le Gouverneur des officiers et des soldats de la garnison, et des partyes qui s'y trouvent ordinairement, il y entende les avis que le dit procureur du Roy a luy donner concernant les interests du Roy ou du public," etc. *Ibid.*, vol. ii, p. 272.

[2] "... jusques a ce qu'il ayt plû a Sa Majesté de faire bastir un Pallais pour la justice," *ibid.*, p. 272.

[3] On March 10, 1685, the King orders the Council to move into the new Palais de Justice as soon as it shall be finished: "qu'il soit transferé dans le palais, qu'elle a ordonné être bâti à cet effet en la dit ville, en lieu presentement appelé la Brasserie." *Edits et Ord.*, vol. i, p. 254.

[4] Epiphany, twelve days after Christmas.

[5] "Aujourd'huy le Conseil sest assemblé dans sa Chambre, Et a l'aissé a la prevosté celle ou Il avoit continue de tenir au Pallais." *Jugements et Délib.*, vol. iii, p. 597.

stroyed by fire.[1] Plans were at once drawn up to replace it while the foundations were still in a condition to be utilized. The new Palais de Justice contained the chapel and prison, besides the Intendant's dwelling, the bolting-room, the armory, the Council chamber and the provost courtroom.[2] Pending this reconstruction the Sovereign Council assembled in one of the rooms of the Bishop's palace. There being but one hall available for such purposes, the Council and the court of the Provost occupied it on different days.[3] The second Palais de Justice was "incomparably more beautiful," says a contemporary.[4]

During the Christmas season of 1725 this building burned, leaving only the walls, the vaults and the chimney. Bégon for the second time took measures to rebuild the palace, in order, he wrote, to make use of the walls before they became impaired.[5] In this building the Council sat until 1759, when it removed to Montreal,

[1] Letter from Bégon to the Minister February 11, 1713: He could not imagine the cause of the fire. He had spent the day at the Governor's with Madame Bégon. His valet and two maids lost their lives in the fire. His secretary, found half-frozen in the garden, died two days later. He has lost property to the value of 3,000 livres, besides 1,500 livres in card-money. He asks for indemnity. *Collection Moreau St. Méry*, Memorials 1540-1759.

[2] Minister to Engineer Beaucours, July 1, 1713. Supplement *Canadian Archives Report* for 1899, p. 471.

[3] The Council met each Tuesday and the Provost Court sat each Wednesday. *Jugements et Délib.*, vol. vi, p. 550.

[4] Soeur Juchereau, *Histoire de l'Hôtel-Dieu*, quoted in the introduction to *Jugements et Délib.*, vol. i, p. xl.

[5] "Dec. 25, 1725, Le Palais brulé, il y a 13 ans et rebâti par les soins de M. Bégon a brûlé une seconde fois, Le feu a pris par un poele dans la chambre de Monsr. d'Aigremont commissaire à 7 h. du Soir." *Canadian Missions*, Parkman Collection, "Extraits du Journal des Jésuites, 1710-1759." A letter of June 30, 1726, gives the time as nine o'clock of December 28. *Canadian Archives Report* for 1904, Appendix K, p. 76.

thereafter to meet in the "palace" of the Intendant.[1] The second building constructed by the efforts of Bégon was destroyed in the siege of 1775.[2] Thus the Palais de Justice did not long survive the Conseil Supérieur of New France itself.

Quorum

A quorum in the Council varied with the nature of the judicial business. The King's Declaration of 1685 provided that suits in which members of the Council were involved should be tried by the Intendant and six judges, chosen by him from among the unchallenged Councillors or from outside; that three Councillors should constitute a quorum to pass upon objections of suitors to certain judges; that if three Councillors did not remain unchallenged, judges of the lower court should be summoned to complete the quorum of three; and that five judges should give judgment in criminal suits. If five Councillors did not remain unchallenged in a criminal suit, the presiding officer was to choose other officers even of the lower courts, except the court from the judgment of which the appeal was made.[3] In civil suits but three judges were necessary.

It was sometimes difficult to obtain a quorum of three judges for the settlement of ordinary affairs. On October 31, 1689, Peuvret, chief clerk, was summoned to give the pen to the usher and sit as Councillor, in order to make a quorum.[4] On June 27, 1701, but three Councillors, the Attorney-General and the clerk, being present, it was asked if two of those Councillors could call a third

[1] *Edits et Ord.*, vol. ii, p. 253.

[2] *Jugements et Délib.*, vol. i, introd., p. xli.

[3] *Edits et Ord.*, vol. i, pp. 253-254.

[4] *Jugements et Délib.*, vol. iii, p. 362.

judge, should one of them be challenged or interested in the case. It was decided for ordinary justice two judges had the right to nominate a third.[1]

Even with a nominal membership of twelve after 1703, a similar method of obtaining a quorum was instituted in 1710. On January 20 of that year the Provost of the Maréchaussée and the practitioner Gaillard were summoned to complete a quorum. At this meeting the presence of but two Councillors, one of whom had to act as Attorney-General, made these appointments necessary.[2] The new judges served during the greater part of the year. On December 14, 1711, a case in which six of the Councillors were interested was tried by the other two members present and three persons drawn from outside.[3] In such cases as these, provisions of the Declaration of 1685 were followed in order to avoid delays in the administration of justice.

Ceremonial

The elaborate ceremonies and etiquette of the Parlement of Paris were either not practiced at all or were greatly modified in New France. There were times when the Sovereign Council, even in earlier years, administered justice in an impressive and ceremonious manner, but there were factors that worked against producing such an effect. Councillors attended court sessions in ordinary clothes, some with swords, others without them.[4] The removal of the hat being an ac-

[1] *Jugements et Délib.*, vol. iii, p. 585.

[2] The reasons for the scanty attendance are thus given: "qu'attendu l'absence de plusieurs de Messieurs dont les uns Sont en france, d'autres a montreal, d'autres sur leurs terres, et d'autres qui par leurs Infirmitez ne peuvent assister regulierement au Con^el^." *Ibid.*, vol. vi, p. 7.

[3] *Ibid.*, p. 285.

[4] Mention of Councillors as wearing robes is made in only one place.

knowledgment of inferiority or deference, Councillors sat covered, while suitors pleaded their causes, sometimes with swords at their sides but with hat in hand.[1] Because of the intimacy existing between members of a frontier community, the aloofness of French Parlementaires was impossible. Councillors rose early, went to the tavern for breakfast perhaps, and hurried over in a group to be in time for a seven o'clock session.[2] Each one having taken his place, the Intendant determined the presence of a quorum. During the second administration of Frontenac it was the custom to despatch an usher to invite the Governor to "come and take his place in the Council." When the usher or the clerk announced the approach of that dignitary, two Councillors were deputed to escort him from the stairway to his seat. Considerable ceremony probably attended the meetings of the Council when Tracy, Courcelles, Laval and Talon participated, and again when Vaudreuil and the Raudots, father and son, were at the head of the Council board; but in no case does the picture of a Council meeting approach the splendor of a session of the Parlement of Paris.[3]

Precedence at the Council board was highly prized,

Minister to Meulles, May 31, 1686, *Supplement Canadian Archives Report* for 1899, p. 274.

[1] In 1732 the King decided that gentlemen could plead their causes without laying aside their side arms, since Councillors sat with swords at their sides. *Coll. Moreau St. Méry*, series Fiii, vol. xii, p. 12.

[2] Account of the preliminaries to the session of March 16, 1681, by Villeray: "Il auroit esté à la buvette trouver let dit procureur general (sur les sept heures). . . . Et dans le moment la Compagnie ayant quitté la buvette pour entrer [la chambre du Conseil], Et estant entrée Et chacun des Messieurs ayant pris sa place, etc." *Jugements et Délib.*, vol. ii, p. 507.

[3] See Desmaze, *Le Parlement de Paris*, pp. 307-309.

and was the subject of several royal and conciliar orders. The usual arrangement around the long rectangular Council table was as follows. The Governor sat at the head of the table with the Bishop on his right hand and the Intendant on his left. Before him on either side of the table sat the Councillors according to rank and length of service, the more honorable places being those nearest the three great dignitaries. Nearest the Bishop sat the Dean, on his right the next oldest of the Councillors. Opposite them was the First Councillor, and at the foot of the table the Attorney-General and the chief clerk.

The addition of new officials somewhat disarranged this plan of seating. During the existence of the Company of the West Indies the General Agent was privileged to take precedence over the First Councillor.[1] In 1730 the clerical Councillor, who like the other Councillors had previously sat according to seniority, was given a seat upon the right hand of the Dean, or, in his absence, upon the right hand of the eldest Councillor.[2] He was thus always separated from the Bishop by one Councillor. In later times the occasional presence of the Provost of the Maréchausée,[3] or of the Commissioner of the Marine,[4] or of one or two of the assistant Councillors,[5] increased the number at the lower end of the table. These men sat below the last Councillor. At the first session of each term, all notaries, ushers, and bailiffs, reported in the

[1] "Voix délibérative au dit Conseil souverain . . . et seance audessus du premie conseiller." *Edits et Ord.*, vol. iii, p. 37.

[2] *Ibid.*, vol. i, p. 521. See also the Abbé de la Tour, *Histoire de la vie de M. de Laval*, book vii, for the way in which La Tour obtained the same rights that the clerical Councillors in the French courts enjoyed.

[3] *Edits et Ord.*, vol. i, p. 238.

[4] Doutre et Lareau, *Histoire du Droit Canadien*, vol. i, p. 287.

[5] *Edits et Ord.*, vol. i, p. 562, articles iii and v.

chamber to respond to any complaints made against them.[1] Towards the close of our period, the ushers became so remiss in their attendance that, upon complaint of the first usher, the Council ordered all the ushers to be present during the entire time that the court should be in session.[2]

Judicial Procedure

During the first forty years there are few cases of any litigant being represented by another. During that time each person pleaded his own cause. When he appeared before the Council he probably spoke to the broad backs of a third of its members, since they sat around a table. It is probable that there was a particular portion of the hall enclosed with a railing, upon which the witness leaned.[3] The witness was at liberty to object to any Councillors whom he deemed to be prejudiced against him. The grounds of his objection were judged without appeal by the other Councillors. If they were decided to be frivolous, he was occasionally fined for contempt of court.[4] Relationship to the fourth and fifth degree with any Councillor[5] on the part of either of the

[1] *Jugements et Délib.*, vol. i, p. 788.

[2] *Edits et Ord.*, vol. ii, p. 225.

[3] The evidence at my command is scanty and conflicting. On October 17, 1667, the usher asks compensation for "travaux de menuiserie par luy faictz au pallais tant en portes chassis qu'en la facture d'un barreau et autres ouvrages, etc." *Jugements et Délib.*, vol. i, p. 456. On the other hand, there seemed to be no particular place for Abbé Fénelon in 1674. He walked up and down the room. He sat down at the Council table. They gave him a chair in the corner. There is no mention of a space railed off where the accused might stand.

[4] *Edits et Ord.*, vol. i, p. 237. He was never fined the sum named in the Ordinance of 1667, title xxiv, article xxix.

See title xxiv, articles i and ii, Ordinance of 1667, *Edits et Ord.*, vol. i, p. 177.

litigants was considered sufficient ground for disqualifying him, and even religious connections (*les alliances spirituelles*), that is, the relationship of godfather to the families of litigants, was a disqualification up to 1708.[1]

Upon an appeal from one of the lower courts, the clerk of that court filed all papers with the clerk of the Sovereign Council. These documents were accessible to either party, and were submitted to the Councillor, who was deputed to investigate the case, and who, after his investigation, handed them over to the Attorney-General. Usually a case involving written evidence was reported upon by Attorney-General and Councillor reporter in writing, although in cases of a grave character the former was allowed to give his conclusions *viva voce*. The earlier form of procedure was for the Attorney-General to leave the chamber after giving his conclusions, if the case were a criminal or important civil suit.[2] Even in the suits in which he remained in the hall, he interfered with the unbiased deliberations of the Councillors to such an extent[3] that he and all persons except the judges were finally excluded from the chamber in all cases, oral or written, trivial or grave, returning only when a new

[1] The Decree of 1708 provides: "que dorénavent les dits juges seront tenus de demeurer en causes de ceux avec qui ils auront des dites alliances sans qu'il leur soit libre de se retirer, ni aux parties de les récuser," etc. *Ibid.*, vol. ii, p. 153. This action on the King's part was due to the complaints of Raudot, that three Councillors had been excluded in an important case because they were godfathers of Madame de la Forest's children, and that this exclusion meant the summons of inexperienced outsiders to complete the quorum. *Correspondance Générale*, series C xi, vol. xxvi, pt. i, pp. 21, *et seq.*

[2] See the Royal Order of 1704, *Edits et Ord.*, vol. i, p. 301.

[3] Frontenac claimed that the Attorney-General interrupted the deliberations of Councillors on the pretence of throwing new light upon each point, and that he argued with the judges to change their opinions. *Corres. Gen.*, series C xi, vol. xiii, pt. i, p. 257.

cause was called—a very inconvenient process, according to the Abbé de la Tour.[1]

When the case came to deliberation, the President called upon the Councillor last installed for his opinion, then upon his seniors, pronouncing his own opinion last. This method had the advantage of restraining Councillors from concurring with Governor or Intendant. On the other hand, it sometimes led to a blind following of the Attorney-General's conclusions or of the report of the Councillor reporter, on the part of less experienced members.[2] Delino, on this account, proposed that senior and junior members give their opinions alternately, but the old method was adhered to.[3] Opinions of Councillors were not spread upon the minutes except in a few cases

[1] *Vie de M. de Laval*, book vii.

[2] Attorney-General d'Auteuil confirmed his enemy's memoir when he wrote that hitherto he had given his conclusion orally upon every subject, upon which expositions of law Councillors had formed their conclusions, and that justice would greatly suffer because of the meagre experience and study of the Councillors, of whom the eldest had hardly been three years in office. *Corres. Gen.*, series C xi, vol. xii, pt. i, pp. 363, *et seq.*

[3] "L'on observe au Conseil de prendre l'advis du dernier Conseiller Ensuitte de celuy qui le precede et cela jusqu'au President.

"Cette manière peut quelquefois estre tres prejudiciable aux parties En ce que naturellement les derniers Conseillers n'ont pas l'experience des anciens dans le fait du droit, sont très souvent obliges d'estre de l'advis des conclusions du Procureur General ou de l'advis du Conseiller raporteur. Et comme il y a peu de voix au Conseil il le rencontre assez souvent qu'il y aura quatre ou cinq Voix de l'advis de Monsieur qui rendent par la inutiles les voix de deux ou trois anciens qui restent a parler. C'est pourquoi pour obvier un si grand mal je croirois qu'il seroit bon d'ordonner qu'apres que le procureur General auroit parlé Celuy qui presideroit prendroit l'advis d'un ancien qui seroit à la teste du Conseil. Ensuitte un de la [dernière] puis un de la teste observant cet ordre jusqu'au qu'il eut pris toutes les voix." *Corres. Gen.*, series C xi, vol. xi, pt. i, p. 600.

of a somewhat political nature;[1] and the dislike to this publication of the secret workings of the court was evident. The Attorney-General expressed the view of the Council when he said in answer to Governor Frontenac's demand for the inscribing of opinions upon the minutes, that recorded opinions could only serve to embarrass Councillors and intimidate them in the execution of justice.[2]

A judgment usually expressed the view of the majority of the judges, but sometimes was only arrived at by a compromise. When opinions were equally divided, the less servere punishment was meted out. Whereas the Council usually followed the advice of the Attorney General as to law, it invariably determined the fact for itself.

In criminal cases the Councillor reporter and the clerk went immediately after the session to read the decision to the prisoner, and sentence was executed the same day. In civil cases, the expenses of the suit as well as the damages, allowed by the court upon estimates made by the Councillor reporter, were collected, if necessary, through imprisonment. Refusal to pay damages was also met by the sale of property, starting with the personal property of the defeated litigant. If this person opposed such action, he was summoned before the Council, and unless he could show just cause why execution of the decree should be stayed, he was subjected to a fine of 12 livres. At different times, varying sums were charged appellants who did not win their causes. This was to prevent foolish appeals.

Although appeal might be made to the King from a judgment or decree of the Council, the execution of it

[1] *Jugements et Délib.*, vol. i, pp. 940-941; vol. ii, pp. 308-309.

[2] *Ibid.*, vol. iii, p. 892.

could not be stopped, but the party who received judgment had to give surety for restitution, in case the Council of State should annul the action of the Sovereign Council and commit the trial of the case to another court.[1]

The procedure in some trials was complicated, consisting, for example, of examination of witnesses, with whom the prisoner was confronted, of re-examinations and re-confrontations, of deposition of the accused, of interrogation of the same in the Council chamber, of conclusions of the Attorney-General upon the objections of the prisoner to certain judges, of decisions of the Council upon the grounds of challenge, of inquisitions of the prisoner, of the summary of the case by the Attorney-General, of the report of the Councillor Commissioner, and of deliberations of the Council.[2] Failure to conduct the trial according to the laws of procedure sometimes resulted in a conciliar vote of censure upon the Attorney-General or his substitute.[3]

Committee System

It is evident that the Council was forced to delegate considerable power to individual members who should

[1] For an excellent account which I have verified from the records, see *Corres. Gen.*, series C xi, vol. xv, pt. i, pp. 124-137.

[2] A moderately short trial is here summarized. *Jugements et Délib.*, vol. iii, p. 44.

[3] In 1678 the Council condemned the acting Attorney-General because (1), he had not presented to the Council for its judgment, the claim of the Provost to take cognizance of the Leclerc case, (2) the papers of accusation furnished by the Provost had been assumed to be valid, without presenting them to the Lieutenant-General of the provost court of Quebec, and (3) in an affair which had concerned the murder of a woman with child, he had advised sentencing the murderer merely to a fine of 10 livres and six years additional service in the King's regiment. *Jugements et Délib.*, vol. ii, p. 209.

conduct most of the preliminary steps in a trial or a civil suit. This committee system began on October 27, 1663, with the assignment of certain cases to Villeray to investigate and report upon at the end of November. The Attorney-General assigned as a reason for the Council being unable to settle them, that it did not know whom to address, and that its sessions were limited to certain days and hours.[1] The committee system, which was begun thus as a judicial expedient, was rapidly extended by the Council to administrative functions. It entrusted to its individual members the expenditure of funds voted by it.[2] It sent commissioners to the vessels to ascertain the truth of their invoices and reports. It sent commissioners into the shops to mark the goods and see that they were sold at the price marked, and to see that the bread was of the proper weight and quality. It despatched members to supervise the unloading of merchandise and provisions from the King's ships, and the subsequent distribution.

As a judicial expedient this system was considered to possess the following advantages: First, it enabled the Council to gain complete information without going through the preliminary hearings. Second, it saved witnesses time and the parties involved expense, for the commissioner was sent to the scene of the crime or dispute, where by taking testimony he enabled the witnesses to remain at their farming.[3] In the third place, it en-

[1] *Jugements et Délib.*, vol. i, p. 42.

[2] In 1665 Damours accounted for 10,000 livres 6 sous 6 deniers spent by him upon order of the Council. *Ibid.*, p. 324. During the same year he was paid 35 livres for inspecting beaver skins and fixing the price. Thereafter he received 2 sous per pound for this service. *Ibid.*, p. 353.

[3] For an interesting example, see *ibid.*, vol. iii, p. 39.

abled the Council to perform functions through its individual members that it could not readily perform as an assembly. Lastly, it enabled the Council to reach a tremendous number of decisions in their weekly sessions.

The system had counterbalancing disadvantages, however. In the first place, objection was raised to the rates of 15 and 10 livres a day granted to the commissioner and clerk respectively. This objection loses force when one considers that such expenditure saved witnesses and litigants the payment of traveling expenses to Quebec and board and lodging there, as well as the damages they might sustain by prolonged absence from their business.

Secondly, the system entrusted arbitrary authority to individual Councillors.[1] Fortunately there were comparatively few cases of abuse. Two of these cases involved Villeray, that is, the Mareuil case in 1694 and the case of Jean Péronne Dumesnil in 1663. The latter shows the system at its worst, for it was here used to attain an unworthy end. Dumesnil had come out to Canada as the agent of the "Hundred Associates," to investigate cases of reputed fraud. Every obstacle had been put in his way. Before the creation of the Sovereign Council he had asked and been refused a seat in the *ancien conseil.* His objections to the appointment of Villeray and

[1] For instance, when in 1665 the officers of justice at Three Rivers and Cap de la Magdeleine quarreled with each other, connived at breaches of conciliar ordinances and maltreated the local judge who sought to enforce the law, the Sovereign Council sent Louis Péronne, Sieur de Mazé, to the scene of the trouble as its commissioner, giving him full powers to imprison there or to send to its prisons in Quebec those he might be convinced were guilty of either seditious, threatening menaces, or dealing in liquor with the Indians. The commissioner was accompanied by a file of soldiers lent by Potherie, the acting Governor. *Ibid.*, vol. i, p. 353.

other alleged defrauders of his Company to positions in the new Council had been ignored, and one of the first acts of the Sovereign Council was to depute Villeray to enter Dumesnil's dwelling, to take those papers which concerned the service of the King, to enclose them in a box and give the key to the Governor.[1] The commission was violently executed, and Dumesnil appealed to the Council for justice. The appeal was referred to Gaudais, special agent of His Majesty, who suppressed it. A month later the box containing his papers was produced in a suit in which Dumesnil required certain documents as proof. The box was unlocked but the desired papers were not there.[2] If Dumesnil spoke the truth he had been rifled of more than the public papers in his possession, and the suspicion rests upon the commissioner, who had collected and sorted the papers. Villeray had been under suspicion of defrauding the Company: its agent claimed to have sufficient evidence to warrant an inquiry by Mésy and the new royal government. Villeray had every incentive to seize or destroy evidence which might damage him or his *confrères*. Under such conditions the appointment of Villeray as commissioner to make the seizure was a very questionable one, and the use he probably made of this office would condemn the committee system if this case were typical. There were other cases of abuse of power by commissioners, but the small proportion of them to the thousands of cases in which committee work passed unchallenged by the parties concerned, prove the effectiveness of the system.

[1] *Ibid.*, p. 4.

[2] "...qu'il a fait recherche dans ses papiers et qu'il n'a trouvé en iceux aucune quictance du dict Sieur Bazile," etc. *Ibid.*, p. 36.

Records

The records of the Sovereign Council were kept with increasing care as the importance of their preservation became better appreciated. As copies of the minutes were constantly sent to the King, the correctness of each record was essential: they served in lieu of letters to His Majesty, who knew his Councillors through their deeds thus recorded. It is not surprising that the Governor, Intendant, First Councillor, Attorney General, and others, thought it important to have their opinions spread upon the minutes, that the King might learn of their respective attitudes towards each important question.

The minutes were at first written upon loose leaves. On February 8, 1664, the Council ordered the clerk of the court to keep a minute-book in which the *arrêts* and *ordonnances* of each session should be written, and signed by both president and reporter (*rapporteur*). These minutes were to be transferred to a register, which should be signed by the Councillors every month.[1] The minutes of each session were duly signed, but the Attorney-General reported on July 30, 1667, that the records on the register had not always been signed. A committee was appointed to compare the decrees and judgments in the minutes with those in the register and to report upon the accuracy of the unsigned copies.[2]

When the system of judicial records was fully developed, there were no less than six registers: (1) a record of the names of litigants; (2) a record of that part of the judgment which formed the judges' decision, together with the pleas of the litigants; (3) a record of the decree *in extenso* with signature of the Intendant and the bailiffs,

[1] *Edits et Ord.*, vol. ii, p. 15.

[2] *Jugements et Délib.*, vol. i, p. 433.

deputed to execute it; (4) a record of edicts, decrees, and declarations of the King, commissions of officers of justice, and titles to land; (5) a record of bequests, etc.; and (6) a record of declarations, and affirmations of each litigant. All these registers were verified and initialed by a Councillor elected by the Council.

The value of these records was recognized by retiring officers of the court. Once or twice, clerks embarrassed proceedings by their reluctance to deliver their minute books to their successors,[1] and Governors and Intendants on retiring from office kept the originals of the edicts, decrees and regulations sent them for registration and promulgation. To remedy this abuse, the King in 1699 ordered that in future these documents should be filed with the secretary of the Council.[2]

In 1706 it was ordered that a catalogue of the documents and registers of the Council should be made. The records were again arranged and catalogued in 1745 at the instance of Bigot.[3] This action received the approval of the King.[4] At the same time he refused to accede to the proposal of Galissonnière to establish a printing office for the publication of ordinances, police regulations, etc.[5] Thus, to the end of the French rule, copies of minutes and all official documents were made by hand.

From the time of Frontenac and Duchesneau there had been trouble as to who should have charge of the records. The clerk had for some months lived with the

[1] See, for example, *ibid.*, vol. i, p. 287.

[2] Memoir from the King to Callières and Champigny May 27, 1699, *Collection Moreau St. Méry*, series F iii, vol. viii, pt. i, p. 255.

[3] *Edits et Ord.*, vol. ii, p. 223.

[4] Minister to Bigot, April 11, 1749, supplement *Can. Archives Report* for 1899, p. 159.

[5] Minister to Jourquière May 4, 1749, *ibid.*

Intendant, who, according to the Governor, changed the records as he thought best. Although it was evident that the records ought to be kept in a place where they could not be tampered with, the erection of an archives building was not proposed until 1731. It was at the instance of Intendant Hocquart that two contiguous chambers on the second floor of the Palace of Justice were in 1735 prepared to receive the registers and public documents.[1] This was the humble origin of the present handsome building that adorns the Canadian capital.

All these collections and catalogues indicate unusual care to preserve the records. Members of the Council realized that what went into the record was a lasting justification or condemnation of themselves, and there were several cases of expunging from the records. For instance, when, in April, 1664, Governor Mésy became temporarily reconciled to certain members of the Council he erased parts of the minutes pertaining to his proclamation of February 13.[2] In 1665 Tracy had certain acts which had been registered during the controversy between Mésy and Bishop Laval expunged from the register.[3] Frontenac erased damaging words and phrases, and a scandalous record for which Talon was responsible was erased with his consent.[4]

Decrees, ordinances and judgments were sealed, dated and countersigned by one of the Councillors, who held

[1] *Corres. Gen.*, series C xi, vol. lxiv, pt. i.

[2] *Jugements et Délib.*, vol. i, p. 170.

[3] Doutre et Lareau, vol. i, p. 152.

[4] Talon proposed an investigation into scandals and disorders which were alleged to have been committed in assemblies of pious women and girls convoked by Bishop Laval under the name of the Holy Family. The Council acted upon the proposal and appointed an investigating committee. The record was later erased with Talon's consent. *Jugements et Délib.*, vol. i, p. 384.

the office of Keeper of the Seal.[1] In 1663 this office was created at the suggestion of the Attorney-General. At first it was held from month to month by successive Councillors, but by 1703 the tenure of the office was made permanent. When the King wished to recompense Dupont for his services he gave him this office.[2] Later, Delino held it, and in 1733 Sarrazin was granted a royal commission as Keeper of the Seals.[3]

Promulgation of Decrees

Manuscripts, thus signed, countersigned and sealed, were published by the bailiffs (or ushers) of the Council and lower courts under the orders of the Attorney-General. These officers were usually sent only to the chief settlements, but in 1676 and 1681 they were obliged to promulgate royal edicts in the most distant frontier communities. The Edict of Amnesty of 1681 was promulgated by an usher at Nipissing, Sainte-Marie du Sault, Saint Ignace, Lake Huron, Saint François-Xavier, and in the Bay des Puants (Green Bay). He was given eleven months in which to perform his task.[4] The Attorney-General was usually allowed two months in which to accomplish the promulgation and receive satisfactory reports from bailiffs and royal attorneys.[5] Sixty days was usually an ample allowance of time. A royal regulation, for example, was registered in the Sovereign Council on March 4, 1675, was published in Quebec on

[1] "...qui mettra son 'visa' à coté avec la date du jour et mois, et signera." *Edits et Ord.*, vol. ii, p. 11.

[2] Minister to Dupont, June 14, 1704, supplement *Can. Arch. Report* for 1899, p. 378.

[3] *Edits et Ord.*, vol. iii, p. 101.

[4] *Jugements et Délib.*, vol. ii, pp. 652, 655.

[5] *Ibid.*, pp. 1020-22.

March 10 by Bailiff Roger, on March 17 in Three Rivers by Bailiff Aneau, on the same day in Cap de Magdeleine by Cusson, on March 18 in Champlain by Adhemar, and towards the end of the month at Montreal by Bailiff Bailly.[1]

Where promulgation was more widespread it was entrusted to the royal attorneys of the courts of Quebec, Montreal and Three Rivers, under the direction of the Attorney-General. These officers sent their bailiffs to the judges of seignorial courts, or in default of such courts, to the captains of the militia of the districts, with orders to read, publish and post the transmitted order.[2] This process of promulgation, ending with the posting of manuscript copies of edicts, decrees, ordinances, etc. in the most frequented places, generally on the doors of churches, was often done to the roll of the drum or the blare of the trumpet in order to draw a crowd. The Attorney-General was responsible for transmitting the orders of the Government to the public, so that ignorance might not reasonably be offered as an excuse for lawbreaking.

[1] *Jugements et Délib.*, vol. i, p. 904.

[2] One of the most detailed orders for promulgation through the agency of the royal attorneys (the Attorney-General's deputies) and their bailiffs is the following: "Et que le tout sera leû, publié et affiché dans les lieux ordinaires; et registré tant en la Prevosté de cette Ville, qu'aux Sieges royaux de Montreal et des trois Rivieres a la dilligence des substitûsts du Procureur General du Roy qui tiendront la main, a ce que lesd. articles Soient executtez Selon leur forme et teneur, Et en envoyeront des copes collationnées par les Greffiers aux juges des seigneurs, Et ou il n'y aura point de juges, aux Capitaines de milice de leur ressort, pour estre pareillement Leû, publié et affiché . . . Desquelles Lectures, publications et affiches les dits substitûts Seront tenûs chacun en droit soy de faire certiffier au ledit Procureur General du Roy dans les delays ordinaires. *Ibid.*, p. 994.

There is but one startling case in which this official did not perform his duty. After the withdrawal of Auteuil, junior, in consequence of his questionable part in the Madame de la Forest affair of 1706, the deputy Attorney-General pushed forward a suit that had hung fire since 1704. In doing this he discovered that although a decree of the Council of State ordering seigniors to build grist mills within one year from the publication of the decree had been registered on October 21, 1686, it had never been promulgated. With the registration went the usual order to the Attorney-General and his deputies to promulgate the act and to report performance of the duty within two months.[1] Such a report could not have been avoided without the connivance of the Councillors, who themselves objected to building grist mills on their estates. Had the case of Duplessis *vs.* Charest not arisen, had a deputy Attorney-General not brought this scandal to light, the royal decree might have been evaded for an indefinite time. On December 20, 1706, the decree was again registered and ordered to be promulgated.[2]

[1] *Jugements et Délib.*, vol. iii, p. 87.

[2] For an admirable summary of this interesting case, see *ibid.*, vol. v, pp. 480-488.

CHAPTER VI

THE FUNCTIONS OF THE COUNCIL

ALTHOUGH the division of the powers of government into the legislative, the executive, and the judicial is as old as Aristotle, it was not in practice in the France of the seventeenth century, where all the powers were gathered into the hands of the monarch. In theory the King made the laws, executed them and was the fountain of justice. Though in practice he shared the routine work of government with various institutions and officials, nevertheless he remained all powerful. Although he might share the legislative power with the Parlement of Paris, he could bend it to his will by means of a "lit de justice" or by banishment from Paris. Although he might delegate the judicial power to this same Parlement of Paris and other courts, he could force his will upon the judges when the importance of the case prompted his interference.

As the King and as the Parlement of Paris exercised the various powers of government, so we see the Governor, the Intendant and the Sovereign Council in Canada serving in a judicial capacity, in an administrative capacity or in a legislative capacity. The King might delegate more or less power to any one of these agents, but he did not limit any one to the exercise of one exclusive function. The Intendant, for example, was given power to issue ordinances, to execute them by means of his bailiffs and the Provost of the Maréchaussée with his six archers, and to judge any infractions of those ordinances and determine the penalty to be paid. Similarly the Council performed the three functions of government; but it is evident that it could make no claim to the exclusive exercise of any of them. Nevertheless the King recognized that his executive representative, the Governor of New France, should be separated from the judicial department of government; and eighteenth-century Canadians had some idea of the separate exercise of administrative and judicial powers.[1] Their Soverign court, however, while emphasizing the business of justice, passed detailed special acts that savored of the executive, and broad ordinances that resembled statutes.

Registration

The legislative power of the Council, which we shall first treat, consisted in the registration of royal measures and in broad ordinance powers. Concerning the function of registration a controversy has raged among scholars for some time, one side maintaining that without this process no royal measure nor colonial ordinance had the force of law; the other that no royal measure required such action to validate it. The question cannot be settled by *a priori* arguments or by analogy with the procedure of the Parlement of Paris or other councils, but only by the evidence of Canadian records. In consulting the archives I find that the question is more complex than either side seems to realize, for in some cases unregistered measures are accorded the force of law, while in others registration and publication have been necessary.

During the seventeenth century French law was codified into five great codes. These codes did not require

[1] *Edits et Ordonnances*, vol. ii, pp. 333-336.

registration in Canada, but were there accepted as law from the beginning. Other royal measures for the most part did not go into effect in that colony unless registered. Registration was likewise necessary to validate letters patent of nobility, land titles, commissions, etc. It happened that the measures which did not require registration were of seventeenth-century origin, and that those which did are dated principally in the eighteenth century. No single statement can therefore be made concerning the whole period of the Council's history.

The Great Ordinances

The idea that the five great ordinances, which covered reams of manuscript, were copied and posted in public places for the edification of the reading public, is unreasonable. If the attorneys-general, councillors, and subordinate judges had access to them, that was sufficient to ensure their being used as the basis for judgments in Canada; they became the law of the land without promulgation and without the preparatory process of registration. They did not exist therefore in the Council registers but as separate law codes.

It is claimed that the civil code of 1667 was registered and that this act of the Council indicates the need of legalizing such royal measures in Canada. But the truth is that this ordinance never was registered *in extenso*. Owing to the great distances in New France and the poverty of the people, it was found necessary to make some changes in the delays accorded to litigants, fines, etc. Accordingly in 1678, the King instructed Duchesneau to make any needful changes, these amendments to go into effect provisionally until the royal assent should be obtained. Villeray and Peiras were commissioned to revise it, and on November 7, 1678, the final draft was agreed upon.[1] Some of the modifications thus adopted by the Sovereign Council were accepted by the King and were addressed in the form of letters patent to the Council for registration.[2] Only the amendments, which were accepted by the King, were actually registered on October 23, 1679, by the Sovereign Council and subsequently promulgated.[3] The Council never passed an act to register the civil ordinance in its original form or as amended but only to register the amendments. "This registration was without precedent," says Attorney-General Auteuil, "and was ordered that the amendments might be inviolably followed."[4] Publication of the few provisions, which peculiarly affected Canadians, was a reasonable matter. Publication of the whole civil ordinance would have been useless.

There are two further reasons why registration and publication of the great French ordinances were regarded as unnecessary: first, because of their textual form; second, because of their actual enforcement without such preliminaries. The opening clauses demanded immediate enforcement. While offering an opportunity for amendment, the civil code stipulated that its provisions be executed without interruption.[5] The four other codes

[1] *Ibid.*, vol. i, pp. 106-107; *Jugements et Délib.*, vol. ii, p. 262.

[2] "Les dites patentes addresées en cette Cour pour estre registrées, gardées," etc. *Ibid.*, pp. 322-324.

[3] The amendments may be seen both in *ibid.*, p. 322 and *Corres. Gen.*, June 1679.

[4] *Ibid.*, series C xi, vol. x, pt. i, p. 593.

[5] Civil Code, article vii: "N'entendons toutefois empêcher que par la suite du temps, usage et experience aucuns articles de la présente ordonnance se trouveroient contre l'utilité ou commodité publique ou être sujets à interpretation, declaration ou moderation, nos cours ne puissent en tous tems nous représenter ce qu'elles jugeront à propos sans que sous ce prétexte, l'execution en puisse être sursise." *Edits et Ord.*, vol. i, p. 108.

provided that they should be observed throughout the kingdom after a certain day.[1] The records of the Council show that they were known and were in use. In 1712, for example, a case arose in which the plaintiff alleged the contravention of the Marine Ordinance of 1681.[2] It was this ordinance which the courts of admiralty, erected in 1717, were to interpret,[3] and according to this ordinance the Superior Council was to confirm or disavow the decisions of the admiralty courts.[4] Even without these instructions the Marine Ordinance would have been the law used in the admiralty courts.

The Criminal Ordinance of 1670, although unregistered, was enforced in like manner. The Council not only applied it but several times rebuked the lower courts for failure to observe all its forms.[5] The Civil Ordinance of 1667 also played its part long before it was amended. For example, when Frontenac asserted that he could not be made a party to a suit, the Council voted to ask the King whether or not article 16 of

[1] The Criminal Ordinance is typical: "Voulons que la présente ordonnance soit gardée et observée dans tout notre royaume, terres et pays de notre obéissance, à commencer au premier jour de janvier de l'année prochaine 1671; abrogeons toutes ordonnances, etc." Isambert, *Recueil des Anciennes Lois Françaises Depuis L'an 420, Jusqu'à la Revolution* de 1789," vol. xviii, p. 423.

[2] "Et speciellement contre l'ordonnance de la Marine, qui Veut que les Capitaines rendent compte des merchandises, etc." *Jugements et Délib.*, vol. vi, p. 504.

[3] Titre premier: "Il y aura à l'avenir dans tous les ports des isles et colonies françaises en quelque partie du monde qu'elles soient situées, des juges pour connoitre des causes maritimes . . . et pour être par eux les dites causes jugées suivant l'ordonnance de 1681, et autres ordonnances et reglements touchant la Marine." *Edits et Ord.*, vol. i, p. 358.

[4] Titre troisième, *ibid.*, p. 360.

[5] *Jugements et Délib.*, vol. vi, pp. 823-24, 1069-70.

chapter 24 of the ordinance of 1667, which forbade any president from presiding in any suit in which he was challenged, should apply to his Lieutenant-Governor of New France.[1]

If one turns from the great codes to less general laws he sees that registration was really a necessary legislative act. To be sure certain old laws were enforced and were only treated to a belated registration and promulgation in order that the people might know their provisions;[2] but as a rule the royal edicts and declarations were not enforced in Canada unless registered upon the King's order in the Sovereign Council of Quebec. One act was not enforced until its registration thirteen years after its passage; another providing that the King get cargoes of vessels cast away upon his coasts was ignored until at his command it was registered twenty-one years after passage.[3] The Canadians themselves were quick to recognize the advantages of having some share in law-making. For example, when protesting against taxation by Governor and Intendant, the inhabitants held that the only legal way to tax them consisted of a royal order duly registered in the Council, "since His Majesty," they explained, "wishes that this be done concerning his Edicts and Declarations."[4] Delino, having pointed out a fault in the ordinance of 1669, was answered that it was not followed in Canada for two reasons: 1) because it was not *sent out* and *registered there*, and 2) because

[1] *Jugements et Délib.*, vol. i, p. 843.

[2] A law of Henry II which provided the death penalty for women who concealed their pregnancy and were guilty of abortion was registered and published at the request of Talon. *Coll. Moreau St. Méry*, series F iii, vol. xiii, p. 345.

[3] *Jugements et Délib.*, vol. vi, p. 522.

[4] *Coll. Moreau St. Méry*, series F iii, vol. xiv, p. 12.

the ordinance of 1667 as amended in 1678 had superseded it.[1]

Royal and Canadian Acts and Titles

As to regulations and ordinances, made in Canada, registration was necessary to their validity. In 1706 the Attorney-General set aside a so-called regulation of August 23, 1667, upon which one party to a suit relied, in favor of a regulation of September 4, 1667, because the latter alone had been duly signed, registered and executed. The King supported this opinion, writing that no reliance could be placed in the alleged regulation of August 23, 1667, because it was not presented in an authentic form, being only a copy of a copy, and since it was not registered in the office of the Recorder of the Sovereign Council.[2] Canadians knew the value of the process. For example, certain regulations had been made by those inhabitants, who proposed to enter the "Cie de la Colonie." These were confirmed by the Council of State on October 15, 1700; but their registration was also sought from the Sovereign Council. The urgent desire of the Ursulines of the convent of Three Rivers that their property be assured by the record of their letters patent was only typical of the eagerness with which holders of commissions, land deeds, and letters of naturalization sought their registration. How else could a man's title to land and nobility be assured?[3]

[1] "Reponce—L'Ordonnance de mois d'aoust 1669 n'est point suivie en ce pays par deux raisons: La Ier par ce qu'elle n'y a point esté envoyée n'y registree, etc." *Corres. Gen.*, series C xi, vol. ii, pt. i, p. 595.

[2] *Ibid.*, abstract in *Supplement Canadian Archives Report* for 1899, pp. 198, 199.

[3] There were privileges attached to a clear title. In 1732 it was specified that only those whose titles of nobility were or should be recorded in the Council, or should immediately give evidence of nobility, should be allowed to plead in the Council wearing their swords. *Coll. Moreau St. Méry*, series F iii, vol. xii, p. 12.

Royal View of Registration

The King of France knew the efficacy of registration. It was because he recognized that a registered measure would be enforced, and a registered title would ensure possession, that he ordered extreme care in exercising the function. Perhaps the Council had not scrutinized letters of nobility, commissions, etc., sufficiently before thus legalizing them. Whatever the reasons, the king issued two letters in 1744 and 1746, the first of which runs as follows:

"M. the Marquis de Beauharnois and M. Hochquart, although I have already explained what you ought to observe regarding registration in my Sovereign Council of New France of my edicts, etc., I write this letter to warn you to take care, that no edicts, decrees, and ordinances, other than those which are addressed to you by my Secretary of State for the Department of the Marine, shall be registered, nor pardons, commissions, letters of nobility and naturalization bearing my seal or that of my Council of State, until my Secretary of State has notified you that you may proceed with the registration."[1] Two years later the king addressed the Superior Council in a similar letter.[2] The Council should wait for special authorization to register, for such registration meant validation of the act recorded. We may infer the converse: that no unregistered act was legal in the eighteenth century in Canada. If this be true, registration by the Superior Council was a necessary process. When applied to edicts, declarations, decrees, and ordinances, it put them into effect; it made them the law of the land to be interpreted in the courts; it was a legislative function.

[1] *Edits et Ord.*, vol. ii, p. 224.

[2] *Ibid.*, p. 588.

In conclusion there are three points to remember about registration by the Council: (1) It was unnecessary in the case of the ordinances of the seventeenth century, while essential for other acts royal and provincial. The former were elaborate and incomprehensible to the people at large, fit only to be interpreted by men of legal training. It would have been useless to post them on the parish church doors. On the other hand, specific prohibitions or other acts comprehensible to all, and requiring the highest degree of publicity, needed to be recorded in the Council register and published throughout the country. Common sense determined that the great laws should not receive the same registration and promulgation that simple laws, titles, commissions, etc., required. (2) When, however, the body of Canadian law had been formed by seventeenth-century royal edicts and ordinances, and no more elaborate codes were formed, registration and promulgation became the rule for all measures—from admiralty courts to letters of naturalization. The old measures continued to be executed without registration, while the new ones appear to have required it to make them the law of Canada. (3) If these conclusions be true, and the absolute need of conciliar action to validate a measure be once established for the eighteenth century, the importance of the Council as a legislative body is apparent. I believe that in this one particular the eighteenth-century Superior Council was more powerful than the seventeenth-century Sovereign Council.

Administrative Power

Still registration of royal acts was only the shadow of a legislative power. Although Councillors went through the formality of deliberating upon the legality and expediency of the measures to be registered, they invariably ordered registration. Holding office during the King's pleasure, they could not do otherwise. Yet the Council possessed more substantial powers, that gave it wide scope for legislative and administrative action. The Edict of Establishment enumerated five such powers: In the first place it authorized the Council to expend the public funds. In the second place it had the right to regulate the fur trade with the Indians. Thirdly, it might regulate the trade between the inhabitants of Canada and French merchants. Fourthly, it was empowered to make general and special police measures for the whole country. Finally, it was authorized to create courts of justice in Quebec, Montreal, Three Rivers, or whatever other place it might choose, and to appoint the necessary judges, clerks, bailiffs, notaries, etc.[1] All of these powers were exercised by the Council during the first years of its existence. Most of them were later transferred to the Intendant, quite in accordance with the contemporary centralizing tendency in France.

It is our purpose to trace this process. We must

[1] "Voulons, entendons et nous plait, que dans le dit Conseil, il soit ordonné de la dépense des deniers publics, et disposer de la traite des pelleries avec les sauvages, ensemble de tout le trafic que les habitants pourront faire avec les Marchands de ce Royaume; même qu'il y soit réglé de toutes les affaires de Police, publiques et particulières de tout le pays, au lieu, jour et heure qui seront designés à cet effet: en outre donnons pouvoir au dit Conseil de commettre à Québec, à Montreal. aux Trois Rivieres, et en tous autres lieux, au tems et en la maniere qu'ils jugeront nécessaire, des personnes qui jugent en premiere instance, sans chicane et longueur de procédures, des différents procès, qui y pourront survenir entre les particuliers; de nommer les Greffiers, Notaires, Tabellions, sergents, autres officiers de Justice qu'ils jugeront à propos, notre désir étant d'ôter autant qu'il le pourra toute chicane dans le dit pays de la Nouvelle France afin que prompte et breve justice y soit rendue."

turn from the Edict of Establishment, which granted power to the Council, to commissions, instructions and royal legislation, which took it away, resumed it or granted it elsewhere. All these acts mark the changing constitution of the Council. The alteration of name from Sovereign to Superior Council is simply indicative of the real constitutional position to which that institution was rapidly sinking.

I. The power to order how the public funds should be expended was never expressly abrogated but fell into disuse. By "public funds" the Edict of Establishment meant the tax of one-fourth the beaver skins and one-tenth the Canadian elk skins, the revenue derived from leasing out the trade of Tadoussac, and a ten per cent import duty on merchandise. The first two sources of income had been leased in 1648 for an annual sum of 35,000 livres. Subsequently the sum granted the government had been larger. In 1664–65 the Council had had the expenditure of 46,500 livres from this source, besides 30,000 to 40,000 livres sent out by the King.[1] It had determined what sum should be granted to the Governor for himself and bodyguard; it had voted sums of money to pay government debts, and had even deputed the Governor and Bishop to superintend the distribution of the stores sent out by the King.

The Council had less discretion in determining how the duties on merchandise should be spent. In 1660 Canadians had guaranteed to pay the expenses of government. They had fallen into debt. French and Canadian creditors insisted upon payment. Therefore, the 10 per cent import duty on merchandise had been laid to

[1] Talon to the minister, November 13, 1666.

liquidate this debt.[1] To this purpose the Council assigned the duties; and, when the people complained in 1670, it shifted the 10 per cent ad valorem tax upon merchandise to a specific duty of 10 livres per cask on wine, 25 livres per cask on brandy and 5 sous per pound on tobacco.

In 1674, the Council's connection with import taxes ceased, when the King took over the whole debt.[2] Villeray and others who had collected the duties under authority of the Council, were ordered to give account to the Intendant of receipts and expenditures and to turn the balance over to Bazir, the farmer of the peltries, for advances to the Government.[3] This concluded the Council's connection with the import tax.

In 1665 Talon arrived, bearing a commission authorizing him to direct the management and distribution of the royal funds.[4] Later commissions provided that the Intendant should have charge also of the distribution of the revenues raised from the sources we have been describing.[5] These grants of power do not in theory conflict with the right of the Council to determine how the public funds were to be spent.[6] The Intendant was to execute what the Council ordered. But in practice, the Intendant absorbed the Council's power. Even the 10 per cent duties, which the Council had set apart for the liquidation of the public debt, were diverted by Talon to

[1] For an excellent account of income and expenditure in seventeenth century Canada, see Chapais, *Jean Talon, Intendant*, chap. xii.

[2] *Ibid.*, p. 264.

[3] *Coll. Moreau St. Méry*, series F iii, vol. iv, pt. ii, p. 759.

[4] "Voulons aussi que vous ayez la direction du maniement et distribution de nos deniers."

[5] "Voulant de plus que vous connaissez de la distribution des deniers provenus de la levée des dits Droits."

[6] "... dans le dit Conseil il soit ordonné de la dépense des deniers publics."

pay government expenses. In 1666, Talon wrote to the minister: "I have found it necessary to employ the same sum from the product of the "farm" (that is, beaver and elk tax, and trade of Tadoussac), which the Council employed during the preceding years, as well for paying salaries aud indispensable debts of the country as for other expenses contracted in the service of the King and for the preservation of the colony. I have even been obliged to employ for this purpose whatever revenues have accrued from the 10 per cent duties."[1]

Not only did the Intendant assume the management of the ordinary fund, but he also administered the extraordinary fund which consisted of the comparatively large sums sent out to Canada by the King. Had the Council continued to determine how these sums should be spent, and been able to resist the temptation to corruption offered by the disposal of them, the history of Canada might have been different. In 1865-66 the Intendant disposed of 358,000 livres.[2] In the eighteenth century the colony cost the King about a million a year. From the beginning of the war the Intendant administered about 6,000,000 in 1755 and 11,000,000 in 1756. In 1757 the expenditure reached the staggering sum of 19,000,000, only to increase in 1758 to 24,000,000 and in 1759 to 36,000,000.[3]

II. The Edict of Establishment deprived the Governor of the right to regulate trade with the Indians and granted it to the Sovereign Council.[4] To ordain concerning,

[1] Talon to the minister November 1666. *Corres. Gen.*, vol. ii.

[2] Chapais, *Jean Talon, Intendant*, chap. xii.

[3] From 1755 to 1760 the government expended 104,000,000 for Canada. *Coll. de Man. de Nouv. Fr.*, vol. iv, p. 226, Montcalm to the minister, April 12, 1759. See also, Beaudouin de Guémadeuc, *L'Espion devalisé*, p. 128.

[4] "... disposer de la traite des pelleries avec les sauvages."

or dispose of, the trade in peltries with the Indians meant (1) awarding the lease for the farm of Tadoussac and for the collection of the duties on peltries; (2) attempting to keep the traffic in the towns by measures against those who went to the Indian villages, and (3) regulating the nature of the commodities traded for Indian furs. The first function was exercised once.[1] Then the Company of the West Indies assumed it, and after 1674 it was taken over by the King. The second duty involved the determination of the government's policy towards the coureurs de bois. Here the Council's power was cut in upon by royal action. The King granted the Governor the right to issue annually twenty-five licenses to traders to go to the Indian villages, or he ordained that the trade should be open to every one.[2] Furthermore, in 1676, he authorized the Intendant to render decrees against intractable coureurs de bois by virtue of his jurisdiction over causes involving farming of the furs.[3] Duchesneau, however, did not make use of this authorization, but encouraged the Council to prosecute the coureurs de bois vigorously. Whenever the Governor was granted the disposal of the trading licenses, he naturally assumed the responsibility of keeping persons who did not hold such licenses in the towns. He governed the Montreal fair. Still the Council occasionally exercised its unabrogated power of regulating the trade with the Indians, enacting as late as January, 1707, an ordinance forbidding all traders to traffic with the Indians except in Quebec, Montreal and Three Rivers.

[1] In 1665 the duties and the farm of Tadoussac were leased by the Council to Aubert de la Chesnaye, *Jugements et Délib.*, vol. i, pp. 9-12.

[2] The history of the uncertain policy of the Crown between the years 1675 and 1696 is well told in Lorin, *Comte de Frontenac*, pt. i, chap. vii and pt. iii, chap. v.

[3] *Ibid.*, p. 175.

The decision as to whether or not liquor should be given to the Indians in exchange for peltries remained with the Sovereign Council during the first decade of its history. Thereafter the policy was determined by His Majesty. When the Council had no right to decide who should trade with the Indians, who should have the farm of Tadoussac, or what should be the goods (wet or dry) to be given for skins, its constitutional power to "disposer de la traite des pelleries avec les sauvages" was merely a dead letter.

III. Furthermore, the Council was granted the right to regulate commercial relations between Canadians and French merchants.[1] It was under authority of this clause that the Council regulated the import duties, the rate at which French money should pass in New France, the amount of profits which foreign merchants might make, the time during which they might do business in Quebec and Montreal, the rate at which merchandise should be carried overseas, etc.

IV. A power closely connected with the above was the regulation of internal commerce and the preservation of good order, public health and safety. These were among the police functions authorized by the Council's charter.[2] The power to make police ordinances was never formally abrogated, but the position of the Council was undermined by the grant of wide police powers to the Intendant. It was only gradually, however, that the Intendant assumed the exercise of the powers of his commission. By it he was authorized to make all regu-

[1] "...de disposer...ensemble de tout le trafic que les habitants pourront faire avec les marchands de ce Royaume."

[2] "...même qu'il y soit reglé de toutes les affaires de Police, publiques et particulieres de tout le pays, au lieu, jour et heure qui seront designés à cet effet . . ."

lations he might deem necessary for the general police of the country, acting in conjunction with the Sovereign Council if possible, but without that body if the case demanded expeditious treatment.[1] Under authority of this clause Intendant Meulles issued an ordinance on August 22, 1664, annulling that of the Council made six days before during his absence. The King sustained the Intendant, validated his ordinance and annulled that of the Council. Bégon went beyond Meulles. He claimed that the ordinary procedure was for him to make police ordinances alone, the extraordinary method to make them, with the Council. He was to enact them with the Council only when he chose, that is, in exceptional cases.[2] No remonstrance was made by the Council to this interpretation, more especially as the Intendant chose soon afterwards to work with that body in forming the necessary regulations.

In the seventeenth century the Intendant aimed to gain the support of the Council to his measures. As its president, he could get his measures incorporated as conciliar ordinances. He therefore made very few ordinances alone. Thus were Talon's great ordinances adopted by the Council on January 24, 1667. In this way regulations were made in 1676, which formed the backbone of Canadian police law until the conquest.[3] At a later date, Duchesneau was careful to inform the Council that it was enacting a regulation, not simply registering a measure previously decided upon by Governor and Intendant. He intimated that he had refrained from

[1] "In case you deem it necessary for the good of our service, either by the difficulty or delay of making police regulations with the Council, you may make them alone." *Edits et Ord.*, vol. iii, p. 50.

[2] *Jugements et Délib.*, vol. vi, p. 804 *et seq.*

[3] Cugnet, *Loix de Police.*

previous consultation with the Governor in order that the Council might really participate in determining the measure.[1] But the framing of a measure by Governor and Intendant to the exclusion of the Council became rather a common practice in the eighteenth century.

The attitude of the French government was responsible for this assumption of power by Governor and Intendant. Jealousy of the colonial Governor had disappeared since the days when Frontenac had been prevented from encroaching upon the ordinance-making power of the Council. At that time the home government had been anxious to assure the exercise of the power to the Council. When in 1673 the Governor had made police ordinances upon his sole responsibility, Colbert had written: "His Majesty orders me to tell you that you have, in that particular, gone beyond the limits of the power given you, inasmuch as police regulations ought to be made by the Sovereign Council, over which you preside, rather than by yourself alone . . . You have sole command of the armies, but in regard to all that concerns justice, what authority you have consists in your presidency of the Sovereign Council, established in that country by his Majesty. Furthermore, his intention is that you have matters of police discussed and examined in the said Council, where you will take the opinions of those who constitute it; in order that it may be the Council, which shall pronounce on all matters concerning the police. His Majesty thinks this course not only in accordance with the power granted you, but also absolutely necessary to raise the spirits of those who compose the Sovereign Council." [2]

During the next forty years the French government

[1] *Jugements et Délib.*, vol. ii, p. 752.

[2] *Coll. Moreau St. Méry*, series F iii, vol. iv, pt. i, p. 385.

ceased to insist upon even the participation of the Governor.[1] The Intendant however was to be present when police ordinances were made, but the Governor's presence was merely desirable. In March 1685, the King ruled that the ordinance made by the Council in the absence of these officials was invalid. In 1710 the commission of the Intendant contained several additional powers, and thenceforth, it appears that the King intended to deprive the Council of its administrative functions. On May 14, 1726, the minister wrote that the Council ought not to mix directly or indirectly in what concerned the government. His Majesty had delegated to his Council a part of his authority, to render justice to his subjects; wherefore those that constituted that tribunal ought to apply themselves exclusively to their judicial functions.[2]

In a letter written three years later the minister shows that he considered the Superior Council to be no longer a coördinate part of the government, but merely the ward of the Intendant. As supervisor of justice, the latter was instructed among other things to prevent officers of justice from using their position to avoid paying their debts, and to stop them from preying upon their neighbors. The general police power was explicitly granted to the governor and Intendant, and the Superior Council was mentioned only to repeat the warning against its mixing either directly or indirectly in what concerned the government.[3]

[1] For example, the King wrote Callières that the Intendant and the Sovereign Council ought to work together with great application at everything that concerned the police, which, he said, was the most solid basis of new colonies. *Coll. de Man. de Nouv. Fr.*, vol. ii, p. 326.

[2] "... en faire toute leur attention." *Coll. Moreau St. Méry*, series F iii, vol. xii, p. 61.

[3] "Ce Conseil ne doit se mesler ni directement ou indirectement de ce qui regarde le Gouvernement." *Ibid.*, vol. xi, p. 320, *et seq.*

The eviction of the Council from the field of administration naturally left Governor and Intendant either as rivals or as allies. Dupuy and Beauharnais were the former, their successors the latter. The French government no longer feared the power of the Canadian Governor. It consented when Governor and Intendant jointly constructed police regulations. It even went so far as to confirm an ordinance made in 1750 by Governor Jonquière and Intendant Bigot, levying a tax upon the citizens of Quebec for the maintenance of barracks in that town.[1]

The ordinance power of the Council was thus undermined by the power given to the Intendant and by the attitude of the home government. The activity of the Council as an ordinance-making body did not long survive the opening of the seventeenth century, while its most lasting work in that line was done in 1676.

V. The fifth administrative power granted to the Sovereign Council by the Edict of Establishment implied the right to erect courts, by authorizing as it did the appointment of judges by the Council. These judges might be appointed to hold courts of first instance in Quebec, Montreal. Three Rivers or any other places where the Council might see the necessity for such courts. The Council was, furthermore, to appoint all clerks, bailiffs, notaries, etc., for these new courts. The Council immediately created royal jurisdictions at Montreal and Three Rivers. Then followed the transfer of the country to the Company of the West Indies. To it was also delegated this power; and, under authority of such a grant, the provost court of Quebec was erected in 1666. When Canada reverted to the King, the Intendant was given the right to name the judges in places where the

[1] *Coll. Moreau St. Mary*, series vol. xiv, p. 8.

Company of the Indies had not established them.[1] The Intendant accordingly appointed three officers for the royal court of Three Rivers.[2] In 1680 the Intendant was given the power to appoint various inferior officials about the courts,[3] and the appointment of the more important ones was reserved to the King. No man was to be considered a bona-fide judge without a royal commission. Thus, very early in its history, the Council lost its power of creating courts and nominating their officials.

Derived from the charter power of appointment, but even more from the Council's position as head of the hierarchy of courts, was the right to supervise the lower courts and regulate their procedure. In 1664, the Council forbade the inferior judges and attorneys throughout the country from asking fees, threatening to give their places to those who exposed them.[4] In 1714, in 1715, and again in 1748, the Council outlined the procedure of the lower courts in regard to appeals, in accordance with the criminal ordinance of 1670.[5] In 1747, in order to determine that the ordinance of Henry II had been made known to the offenders before the commission of their crime, the Coun-

[1] *Edits et Ord.*, vol. i, p. 72.

[2] Chapais, *Jean Talon, Intendant*, p. 441.

[3] *Jugements et Délib.*, vol. v, p. 5.

[4] *Ibid.*, vol. i, p. 297.

[5] The Ordinance of 1670 provided that sentences pronounced by the court should be executed on the same day. The Council, however, pointed out that the same ordinance "y a prévu par l'article six du titre des appellations qui porte que si le sentence rendue par le juge des lieux porte condemnation de peine corporalle, de galeres, de banissement à perpetuité ou d'amende honorable, soit qu'il y en ait appel ou non à l'accusé et son procès seront envoiés surement aux cours supérieures." *Coll. Moreau St. Méry*, series F iii, vol. ix, pt. ii, p. 474; *ibid.*, vol. xiii, pp. 431-432.

cil ordered that a statement of the last publication of the ordinance should be attached to each judgment meted out.[1]

Moreover, there are interesting examples of regulation in specific cases. For example, the Council stipulated that the Seminary of Quebec, seignior of Château-Richer, should provide for court sessions to be held there regularly each fortnight, in a definite and advertised place, with a capable secretary living and keeping the records in the place, and that no judgments should be given elsewhere.[2] While correcting mistakes in procedure made in the lower courts, the Council sometimes extended its condemnation to the court officers. In 1712, the judge of the royal court of Three Rivers was condemned to pay the expenses of a case, which, although not within his jurisdiction, he had judged.[3] In 1729, several unjust practices in the provost court of Quebec were condemned by the Council, and the judge and prosecuting attorney were fined respectively two-thirds and one-third of the costs of suits tried by such procedure, as well as the costs of appeal to the Superior Council.[4] Again, in 1740, the Council forbade this local judge to proceed with the investigation of civil causes based upon "frivolous" or unsupported evidence. The failure of some of the judges of the lower courts, from the beginning of the eighteenth century, to follow the forms of procedure laid down in the ordinances, thus invited the interference of the Council.[5]

[1] ". . . ordonne aussi à tous autres juges de ce pais en semblables cas de joindre en leur jugement leur certificat de la dernière publication . . de ladite Ordonnance." *Ibid.*, p. 345.

[2] *Edits et Ord.*, vol. ii, p. 226.

[3] *Jugements et Délib.*, vol. vi, p. 629.

[4] *Coll. Moreau St. Méry*, series F iii, vol. xi, p. 382. Should perhaps be printed *in extenso*.

[5] For example, the minister wrote to Raudot as early as June 13,

Apparently, however, the King disapproved of the efforts of the Council to regulate the lower courts, thinking it was too aggressive or that the Intendant could better perform the function. Whatever his reason, the King placed the lower courts under the protection of the Intendant. Until 1710, that official's commission had instructed him to see to it that all judges and other officers of justice be maintained in their functions without molestation, and then proceeded to indicate his relations with the Sovereign Council. Bégon's commission, however, ordered him to prevent inferior judges and officers of justice from being disturbed in their functions *by the Superior Council.*[1] This new power might have enabled the Intendant to encroach upon the supervisory function of the Council, but there is no evidence that it was so used. Certainly the Council continued to regulate the lower courts throughout the period of French rule.

Having concluded our history of the five great administrative functions originally given to the Council by the Edict of Establishment in 1663, let us consider what means the Council had to enforce its measures. The Edict of Establishment authorized Councillors to *see to the execution*

1708. "J'ai vu avec beaucoup de peine le peu de règle que l'on a observée dans tout ce qui s'est fait jusqu'à présent," etc. *Coll. Moreau St. Méry,* series F iii, vol. ix, pt. i, p. 150.

[1] The commission of Duchesneau, June 5, 1675, runs: "présider au Conseil Souverain en l'absence du dit Sieur de Frontenac, tenir la main à ce que tous les Juges inférieurs de notre dits pays, et tous autres Officiers de Justice soient maintenus en leurs fonctions, sans y être troublés, que le Conseil Souverain auquel vous présiderez ainsi que dit est, juge toutes matieres civiles et criminelles, conformément à nos Edits et Ordonnances et à la coutume de notre bonne ville de Paris." The Commission of Bégon, March 31, 1710, runs: "tenir la main à ce que tous les Juges infériers du pays et tous autres nos officiers de Justice soient maintenus en leurs fonctions, *sans y être troublés par le Conseil Superieur.*"

of their measures; and that they might act advisedly, they *were to investigate* matters which ought to come up before the Council. Furthermore, they should give ready ear to complaints and accusations or other matters brought forward by the syndics of the various towns, by the *habitants*, by strangers, travelers, and others, and should report them to the Council. Thus the institution was provided in part with authority for learning what decrees were necessary, and for executing them when passed.[1]

In addition, the Council enjoyed the right to enforce its ordinances in its own court. Infractions were there judged severely and without appeal except to the King. A few exemplary punishments meted out may be as effective as an army. As an executive body the Council passed such detailed measures as to provide conclusively for their execution, specifically placing the responsibility upon certain of its own members, other officials, or certain citizens. The Attorney-General and his subordinates in the lower courts, that is, the royal attorneys, were its servants. The marshal and his six "archers" were at its disposal. In its early history at least it held the whip hand over the officers of the lower courts. Since under ordinary circumstances the Council did not need to apply to other institutions of government for the execution of its measures, and since those measures were often in the nature of executive orders, we may think of it as an executive body.

Yet the powers of the Council were chiefly legislative and judicial. In extraordinary crises, when pitted against

[1] "Voulons de plus que les cinq Conseillers . . . avoir l'oeil et tenir la main à l'exécution des choses jugées au dit Conseil, afin que les dits Commissaires prennent une connoissance plus particuliere des affaires qui devront être proposées en celui, en y rapportant celles dont ils pourroit être chargés par les Syndics des habitations du dit Pays; habitans d'icelui, étrangers, passages et autres auxquels nous voulons et entendons que prompte et breve justice soit rendue."

the real executive department of the government, it was helpless. To the Governor the King delegated the chief executive power. His was the command of the military forces and the control of Indian and colonial policies. With the troops at his back he might and did prevent the execution of Council measures that were objectionable to him. His soldiers might with impunity cut to pieces the decrees of the Council and the executive officers of the court might be ordered under arrest to the Château St. Louis. In the face of the Governor's resistance, the Council could not enforce its ordinances and judgments. Interference by the Governor in the execution of Council measures was, however, exceptional, and in the administration of justice he the more seldom interfered because he was specially warned against it.

Judicial Power of the Council

It was as a court that the Sovereign Council differed from its predecessors in New France, and it was as a law court that it functioned throughout the whole period of French rule. A sketch of the developing court system will reveal its constitutional position. The old councils of 1647 and 1648 had been administrative in character. The judicial power belonged to the Governor until 1663, although in 1651 the office of Grand Sénéchal was created to supervise the execution of justice in Canada. Courts of first instance were established in Quebec and Three Rivers, presided over by lieutenants of the Grand Sénéchal. Yet from them appeal was carried not to their superior but to the Governor. These courts were created when the country was under the control of the Company of New France. The Island of Montreal remained outside its jurisdiction, and there justice was rendered for the Sulpitians by a bailiff. In 1663, royal justice replaced proprietary justice except in the bailiwick of Montreal. The Governor's council became a Sovereign Council and to it was transferred his judicial function.[1] In addition it exercised the function of a court of first instance in Quebec,[2] while creating under authority of its charter royal jurisdictions at Three Rivers and Montreal.[3]

For a time there were two rival jurisdictions in Montreal, but in 1666 Talon recognized the court of the Sulpitians, thereby abolishing the royal justice. In the same year the Council ceased to try petty cases, for the Company of the West Indies, the new proprietors of New France, created a local court in Quebec.[4] It was argued that the Sovereign Council ought not to sit upon appeals from its own judgments. With the re-establishment of the royal government in 1674, this provost court was abolished and the Council was again made to serve as court both of appeal and of first instance.[5] As such the tribunal was called upon to decide twenty to twenty-five causes in a single session. The King was gradually convinced that a local court in Quebec

[1] Edict of Establishment: "donnons et attribuons le pouvoir de connoitre de toutes causes civiles et criminelles, pour y juger souverainement et en dernier ressort selon les Loix et Ordonnancs de notre Royaume."

[2] *Ibid.*, "Voulons de plus que le cinq Conseillers choises par dits Gouverneur, Evêque, ou premier Ecclésiastique, soient commis de terminer les procès et affaires de peu de consequence."

[3] The Edict reads: "donnons pouvoir au dit Conseil de commettre à Québec, à Montréal, aux Trois Rivieres, et en tous autres lieux, des personnes qui jugent en premiere instance."

[4] For authorization, see articles xx, xxiii, and xxxii. "Seront les juges etablis en tous les dits lieux," etc. *Edits et Ord.*, vol. i, pp. 46, 57.

[5] "... à l'egard du siége de la prévôté et justice particulière de Québec, que nous avons éteint, et supprimé, éteignons et supprimons; voulons et ordonnons que la justice y soit rendue par le Conseil en première instance, ainsi qu'elle l'etoit auparavant l'etablissement de la Compagnie." *Ibid.*, p. 78.

would expedite justice and might decree concerning seizures of property and other matters, of which the sovereign court could not take cognizance in first instance. In 1677 he therefore re-established the provost court of Quebec.[1] At the same time, the King created the Provost of the Maréchaussée as a police officer, to be assisted by six "archers" in his task of maintaining order on the highroads and among the soldiers.[2] When any causes which interested him were to be tried in the Council, he was allowed to participate in the deliberations.

Two events happened in 1693 and 1707 which marked the spread of royal, at the expense of feudal, justice. In 1693 the Seminary of St. Sulpice in Paris surrendered to the King jurisdiction over Montreal. A royal court to administer justice in that district was straightway created. The Isle de Ville-Marie and the manor of St. Gabriel were still exempt from the King's justice. In 1707 the high justice of the seigniory of Sillery and of a fief in Three Rivers belonging to the Jesuit fathers was suppressed by the Intendant under the King's orders.[3] Thenceforth the inhabitants of the former pleaded their causes in first instance in the provost court of Quebec and those of the latter in the royal court of Three Rivers, thence by appeal to the Superior Council. Thus one of the three steps in Canadian litigation was abolished, and justice was administered more expeditiously. To carry a suit from the feudal court to one of the local royal courts and the appeal to the Supreme Court required some time, and made judicial work very heavy. Where it was impossible to cut out the feudal court, Canadian jurists sought to skip the second stage by carrying causes directly from feudal courts to the Supreme Court.[4]

[1] *Archives des Col.*, vol. xiii, pt. vii, p. 169, *et seq.*

[2] *Edits et Ord.*, vol. i, p. 97.

[3] *Ibid.*, vol. iii, p. 328.

[4] Minister to Raudot. *Supplement Canadian Archives Report* for 1899,

Meanwhile another court had been making encroachments, chiefly on the jurisdiction of the lower courts. In 1659 Bishop Laval had been given letters patent authorizing him to create an ecclesiastical court. In 1675 such a court claimed the right to try Father Morel, who was already on trial before the Sovereign Council. The ecclesiastical court or officialty consisted of a judge or "official" and a prosecuting attorney called a "promoteur". The latter now produced such proofs of the legal basis of the officialty that Father Morel was turned over to its jurisdiction.[1] Subsequently the Council formally recognized the existence of the Officialty of Quebec, condescended to receive appellants from its jurisdiction, and governed its procedure.[2]

In 1717, regular admiralty courts were established in New France. Hitherto, admiralty causes had been tried in the provost court of Quebec, in which sessions the officials of that court (a judge, a prosecuting attorney, and a clerk) were called "les officiers de la Prévôté et admirauté". The Council records from 1710 to 1715 indicate the increasing number of such cases. After the creation of special courts to treat them, the Superior Council remained constitutionally in the same relative position of an appellate court, although it was given more *immediate* control over admiralty business. For example, the courts of admiralty had to obtain the confirmation of the Council in extraordinary session assembled, before provisional judgments could be executed. Furthermore, the admiralty courts, and, on appeal,

[1] For the titles of this ecclesiastical court, see *Jugements et Délib.*, vol. i, p. 960.

[2] For example, in 1714, the Council judged that both "official" and "promoter" had contravened the criminal ordinance and ordered that the Bishop appoint others in their places. *Edits et Ord.*, vol. ii, p. 163. For another illustration, see *Jugements et Délib.*, vol. vi, p. 665.

the Council, might adjudge prizes made from freebooters in time of peace without sending a report of the procedure to the admiral.[1] Still the Council had had control of such cases before;[2] the King really made no further delegation of power to it. The only practical result was to lighten the work of the provost court of Quebec.

Council records make mention of eight or nine royal courts, several feudal courts, the admiralty, and the officialty of Quebec. From these diverse jurisdictions, appeals were carried to the Superior Council. When one considers that all cases involving life or severe corporal punishment had to be so appealed, the extent of the Council's work becomes evident. Having indicated the powers and the scope of that court's jurisdiction, let us now consider the checks upon the exercise of these powers.

In 1683, an unsuccessful effort was made to deprive the Council of jurisdiction over causes involving concessions of lands, accorded by Governor and Intendant, by the proposal that these officials should judge them jointly, but the King replied that cognizance of them must be reserved to the Sovereign Council. Royal support of the Council's jurisdiction failed,[3] however, in the eighteenth century, and the King by acts of 1743 and 1747 gave such cases to the Governor and Intendant. The home government seems to have tried by one measure after another to restrict the original jurisdiction, authorized by the Edict of Establishment.

[1] See Regulations governing Admiralty Courts. *Edits et Ord.*, vol. i, pp. 359-360.

[2] Previous to 1684 the Governor had assumed some control of the provost court of Quebec in the trial of admiralty causes. In this year, the King ruled that the Governor had no authority over such causes and no control over the officers who rendered justice in that regard. *Corres. Gen.*, series C xi, vol. vi, pt. ii, p. 322, *et seq.*

[3] Cugnet, *Abstract of Royal Decrees and Declarations*, p. 13.

In the first place, the judicial powers granted to the Intendant, had they been fully exercised, would have seriously undermined the position of the Council as a Supreme Court. There were two parts to his commission. The first part authorized him to supervise generally the prosecution of offenders and the second, to act as judge of civil cases in last resort. His judgments should be as valid as those emanating from the King's sovereign courts.[1] Fortunately the Intendant prized his position as president of the Council of Quebec and did not stress this second part of his commission. The minister also warned him to exercise this power but sparingly, leaving appeals to the established judges.[2] In fact, upon important matters, he actually consulted the Councillors and rendered his judgments only after hearing the conclusions of the Attorney-General.[3] Nevertheless there was, as a consequence of such delegation of power, two concurrent systems of civil justice in Canada. The Intendant established his deputies (*subdélégués*)

[1] His judicial powers are thus expressed: (1) "procéder contre les coupables de tous crimes de quelque qualité et condition qu'ils soient leur faire et parfaire leur procés jusques au jugement définitif et exécution dué-lui inclusivement, appeler le nombre de juges et gradués porté par nos ordonnances, et généralement connoître de tous crimes et délits, abus et malversations qui pourroient être commis en notre dit pays par quelque personne que ce puisse être; (2) Juger souverainement seul en matieres civiles, et de tout ordonner ainsi que vous verrez être juste et à propos, validant dès à présent comme pour lors les jugemens qui seront aussi par vous rendus tout ainsi que s'ils stoient émanés de nos Cours souveraines nonobstant toutes récusations prise-à-partie, édits, ordonnances, et autres choses à ce contraires." *Edits et Ord.*, vol. iii, pp. 34, 38, 42, 50, 56, 60, etc.

[2] Instructions of Colbert to Talon: "Enfin, bien que l'intendant ait le pouvoir de juger seul souverainement et en dernier ressort les causes civiles, *il est bon qu'il ne se serve de ce pouvoir* que rarement, laissant leur liberté aux juges établis." Clément, *Lettres, Instructions et Memoires de Colbert*, vol. ii.

[3] Lareau, *Histoire du Droit Canadien*, vol. i. p. 229.

throughout the country to act as courts of first instance in civil causes involving from 20 sous to 100 francs.[1] From them appeal was carried to the Intendant and no appeal was permitted from him to the Council. On April 21, 1670, François Bellanger was condemned to a fine of three francs for having proposed to appeal from a decision of the Intendant.[2]

For one reason or another, the King chose to transfer cognizance of certain kinds of causes from the Superior Council to the Intendant. He decreed that the former could not take cognizance of causes arising from infractions of the provisions of the Intendant's ordinances.[3] In 1738 the Council accordingly sent such a case before the Intendant. In 1715 the King gave the judgment of all suits involving frauds connected with the beaver trade, to the Intendant, although in 1709 he had given them to the Council. That transfer of jurisdiction was due to the alleged increase of fraudulent practices and the leniency with which Councillors treated the offenders, who were probably sharing profits with their judges.[4]

In still another way did the King indicate his desire to modify the judicial power of the Council. In early commissions, the Intendant was ordered to see that all the lower judges were undisturbed in the exercise of their functions and that the Soverign Council render judgments according to the royal edicts. Later commissions provided that the Intendant should see to it that the judges of the lower courts were undisturbed by the Superior Council,

[1] There were two in Quebec, one at Three Rivers, two at Montreal, one at Detroit and one at Michilimackanack. Mazeres, quoted in Lareau, *op. cit.*, *passim*.

[2] *Jugements et Délib.*, vol. i, p. 609.

[3] *Edits et Ord.*, vol. i, pp. 357-58.

[4] *Coll. Moreau St. Méry*, series F iii, vol. ix, pt. ii, p. 418.

thus making the Intendant the champion of the lower courts against the aggressions of the Council. This change in commission was probably due to the condemnation of certain lower judges, along with the reversal of their judgments. The whole series of constitutional changes which has been detailed shows how the Intendant's judicial power limited that of the Superior Council.

The Council did much to limit its own jurisdiction by refusing to judge causes. Some were accordingly judged by the Intendant in his independent capacity as sovereign judge; others were sent to France for the King's decision.[1] Appeals to French courts in order to evade Canadian justice became increasingly frequent. As early as 1681, the Council had, upon instructions from the King, ruled that there should be no appeal to other tribunals than those of Canada, "seeing the too great distance which separated old and New France".[2] The Madame de la Forest case, tried in the provost court of Quebec, the Superior Council and the Châtelet of Paris, and finally decided by the King in Council in 1708, was possibly only one of the causes which brought forth Raudot's paper against appeals to France. Easy appeal to France not only made the judgments of the Superior Council count for less, but denied the possibility of justice to the poor. Suitors who possessed sufficient means for an ocean passage and a visit to Paris or who had friends there to manage their legal affairs and funds to oil the wheels of justice, invariably appealed to the King. The poor man could not institute a suit against a rich and oppressive neighbor for fear of an appeal to the King in case

[1] The ordinary formula appearing in the records was: "Le Roy estant eu Son Conseil à évoqué à Soy les poursuites et procedures faites au Conseil Souverain de Quebec." *Coll. Moreau St. Méry*, series F iii, vol. vii, pt. ii, p. 765.

[2] *Edits et Ord.*, vol. ii, p. 93.

he obtained a judgment of the Superior Council against him.[1] Nevertheless shortsighted Councillors continued to grant appeals to French courts.

From the preceding outline of its history it will be seen that the broad powers of the Council over the administration of affairs, although never abrogated, gradually ceased to be exercised. From within a few years of its creation to the third decade of the eighteenth century there was a continual decline. By the end of this period, although holding constitutionally the same position as was granted it by the Edict of Establishment, it no longer participated to any extent in legislative and executive functions, while even in the judicial field it was limited by grants of power to the Intendant, by recognition of the ecclesiastical court, and by appeals to France.

[1] *Corres. Gen.* series C xi, vol. xxvi, p. 21, *et seq.*

CHAPTER VII

Administrative and Judicial Achievements of the Council

A study of the ordinances and judgments of the Council enables one to determine how far it participated in the actual government of Canada, what it aimed at doing, and how far its measures were effective. It is only thus that we are able to estimate the value of its services to the country. While its achievements as a court extended throughout its career, the great ordinances regulating agriculture, commerce, sanitation, and prevention of fire and crime, were passed chiefly during the first half century of its history. Later, these ordinances were supplemented by orders of the Intendant and even by royal orders. To be sure, in many cases the King indicated lines of administrative policy which the Council merely carried out, but there were many instances which illustrate independent attempts upon the part of the Council to remedy abuses, nor was the Council's judicial policy, whether of leniency towards the delinquent or of severity, dictated by the King, to whom appeals were seldom taken in ordinary criminal cases.

Agriculture

It was early recognized that agriculture was the pursuit upon which the permanence of the colony depended. Councillors were farmers and were inclined to pass measures protecting farmers. It was only gradually that the fur trade came to interest all classes of Canadians directly or indirectly, and that agriculture fell into second place. From the very beginning the home government insisted upon the duty of the seigniors to clear the land and install tenants for its cultivation.[1] In 1684 grantees were allowed six years for that purpose.[2] In 1711 the Council of State gave them one year in which to obey or lose the title to their land. The Sovereign Council, and the Intendant also, passed a series of stringent measures of like tenor, but nevertheless little additional land was put under cultivation. Between the years 1679 and 1721 the average annual increase was only 1,008 acres, great estates remaining for the most part uncleared. For example, the Seigneur de Longueil, some ten years after he had started to clear an estate nearly half a mile wide by six miles long, had put but 25 acres under cultivation. The case of the Seigneur of Rivière-Ouelle is still more striking. Nine years after he had taken possession of his large tract, he had cleared but 12½ acres and was grazing but twelve cattle.[3] Condi-

[1] "One of the causes which have retarded the peopling of Canada has been that the inhabitants who have gone thither, have settled down wherever they pleased, and without using the precaution of uniting together and making their clearances contiguous, in order to afford each other help when necessary. They have taken grants for an amount of land they have never been able to cultivate in consequence of its vast extent; and being thus scattered, they became exposed to the ambuscades of the Iroquois, who by their fleetness have always committed their massacres before those whom they surprised have been able to obtain assistance from their neighbors. For this reason the King had an order of Council issued two years ago, whereby His Majesty ordained as a remedy for these, that no clearings should be made thereafter except contiguous the one to the other, and that the settlements should be reduced as much as possible to the form of our parishes and towns (*bourgs*)." *Documents Relative to the Colonial History of New York*, vol. ix, p. 27.

[2] *Jugements et Délibérations*, vol. ii, p. 968.

[3] In 1679 after forty years of feudal régime and fifteen years of direct royal intervention only 22,000 arpents or 18,480 acres were tilled. Forty-two years later only 43,680 acres were cultivated. Gerin, "Le Gentilhomme Français," *Proceedings of the Royal Society*, series ii, vol. ii, pp. 79-80.

tions were so bad that in 1732 the decree of 1711 was repeated, giving the seigniors this time two years during which to clear their lands. A bad harvest in 1743 caused the greatest want and it was evident that new land must be tilled to supply the towns with grain. In April, 1745, with the intention of making tenants take up new lands, the Council of State passed a decree prohibiting the erection of stone or wooden houses upon a strip of land smaller than 297 feet wide by 360 to 480 rods long. Houses upon such small tracts were demolished and, according to a contemporary, the act was generally enforced.[1] But the need of concentrating to defend Quebec, Montreal, and other strategic points during the succeeding years of the critical struggle with the English, made such measures of no avail. Weeds and second growth gradually covered the cleared land, so that when the country passed into British hands, the whole region showed neglect.[2]

During the early years of its career the Council encouraged agriculture in many other ways. Realizing that the *habitants* were the ones who would clear the lands, it protected them against creditors and exempted their little crops from the tithe during the first five years of cultivation. It prevented the seizure of their grain and flour *en route* to and from Quebec or in Quebec mills during the time that the seignorial mills were under repair.[3] In 1667, it low-

[1] François-Joseph Cugnet, son of First Councillor Cugnet, who died in 1751, and elder brother of Thomas-Marie Cugnet, who had entered the Council as assistant Councillor in 1754, was a valuable aid to the English at the time of the Conquest. He was made French secretary to the Governor and judge of the court of Quebec and the conquered country. In 1763 he was made Road Commissioner (Grand Voyer), and about 1770, made with other Canadian gentlemen an abstract of French law as it obtained in Canada.

[2] Munro, *Seigniorial System in Canada*, pp. 50-51.

[3] Ordinance of November 14, 1663, see *Jugements et Délib.*, vol. i, p. 63.

ered the tithe from one-twentieth to one-twentieth-sixth of the farmer's grain. It aided the farmer to get the maximum return from the soil by punishing with a fine of 20 sous per arpent (.84 acre) delinquents who permitted their weeds to arrive at maturity uncut.[1] Growing crops were to be protected from the inroads of horses, cattle and hogs.[2] Likewise, persons who passed or hunted over sowed fields or forced the fences, were subject to a 10-livre fine. At the same time solicitude for increasing the number of cattle was shown. The salt meadows east of the St. Charles were declared open for the cattle of any colonist. Horses were limited in number that there might be enough fodder in the winter to support more cattle. That settlers might stock their holdings with livestock the King decreed in 1686 that during the next six years creditors could not seize the farmer's cattle in payment for debts.[3] Thus every encouragement was given to raise crops and cattle.

It was made easy for the *habitant* to get land. After 1680 a twentieth part of the lands remaining uncleared was to be distributed to the inhabitants of the country.[4] After 1711 the seigniors could not refuse to lease for a nominal quit-rent lands which they could not cultivate. This resulted in tenants often tilling more cleared lands than their lords.

But many *habitants* were improvident, sold their grain as soon as it was ripe and were forced later to buy seed for the spring sowing at monopoly prices. The Council sought to force the merchants, who had "cornered" the wheat market, to sell at reasonable rates. Several times the fear that this monopoly would prevent

[1] Ordinance of June 20, 1667, see *ibid.*, p. 406.

[2] See for examples, *ibid.*, vol. i, p. 613; vol. v, p. 238.

[3] Several classes of creditors were excepted. *Ibid.*, vol. iii, p. 96.

[4] *Ibid.*, vol. ii, p. 236.

the *habitants* from sowing led the Council to intervene with drastic measures.[1] For example, in the spring of 1701, the Council, faced by such a crisis, sent a committee to visit all the granaries of Quebec. Upon learning that some Quebec merchants had more than enough wheat to last them until harvest, the Council ordered the surplus to be seized and sold to the poor at a reasonable price. Still there was not enough grain thrown upon the market to plant a large crop, and the Council ordered that the farmers borrow wheat from their more fortunate neighbors, and that if proprietors found it inconvenient to sow all their arable lands, persons promising them one-third the harvest should be given the chance.[2] In this case, the Council seems to have succeeded in effecting the necessary distribution of wheat for the spring planting.[3]

Occasionally the Council had to grapple with the opposite problem of too much wheat. In 1664, owing to the abundant harvest of the year before, the *habitants* could not find sale for it, since the merchants would not take it even at a very low rate. The Council, fearing that this might lead the people to neglect the cultivation of the soil and clearing of the forests, decided to prevent the depreciation of wheat values. It ordered that 1,000 minots be purchased for the use of the royal soldiers who were expected soon to arrive, and that the farmers be paid at the rate of 5 francs a minot—monopoly prices were only 6 francs 10 sous—in merchandise, clothes, etc., sent by His Majesty and French merchants.[4] The purchase of so large

[1] In 1668 when wheat was held at 7 livres, the Jesuits sold their stock at 5 livres and broke the monopoly.

[2] *Ibid.*, vol. iv, pp. 542-544, 580.

[3] Like measures were passed by the Council and the Governor and Intendant throughout the eighteenth century.

[4] *Ibid.*, vol. i, p. 232.

a quantity of wheat at once, raised the price of the remainder. For the same reason the merchants were ordered to take wheat in payment at the rate of 4 francs a minot.[1]

When, however, desirable measures conflicted with the interests of Councillors, they were not so ready to act. That the *habitant* might avoid the long journeys to Quebec and Montreal, each seignior was ordered to build a grist mill. The royal decree of June 4, 1686, ordered the promulgation of this measure by the Sovereign Council. Auteuil the younger, who was then Attorney-General, with the connivance of the Councillors, many of whom were seigniors and wished to avoid the expense of building mills upon their estates, never published the decree. It remained a dead letter until a case arose involving the duty of a seignior to provide a grist mill for his tenants. Then it was that the deputy Attorney-General, in the absence of Auteuil, discovered the shelved decree and insisted upon its being registered, read, published and posted in the customary places.[2] Furthermore, although the Council was supposed to enforce the Coutume de Paris, burdensome feudal dues contrary to it were allowed to be exacted by seigniors without interference by the Council.[3] It remained for the King to abolish them in 1717.

[1] *Jugements et Délib.*, vol. i, p. 549.

[2] *Ibid.*, vol. v, p. 478, *et seq.*

[3] "Some seigniors had established provisions and servitudes of a most onerous kind, among others: statute labor; a ground rent for the use of the common used as pasture land; the privilege of recovering possession of lands granted by them, whenever sold, on refunding to the purchaser the amount of the purchase money; the reservation of the right to take from the lands granted all the wood they might want; the preference in buying what produce the farmer might have for sale; the reservation of all pine and oak trees; the eleventh part of the fish caught by the farmers in front of their lands gratis; the obligation to use the grist mill of the Seignior, etc." Abstract from *Supplement Can. Archives Report*, 1899, p. 122.

As long as Councillors were primarily interested in the cultivation of the soil, numerous measures of protection and relief were passed. The lot of the Canadian farmer was made attractive, yet we have seen how slowly lands were cleared. Councillors themselves lost interest as they came to supplement their salaries, and incomes from agriculture, by huckstering and petty trade, and later by frank participation in the fur trade. At the same time the actual supervision of the farmer passed into the hands of the Intendant, and it is doubtful whether some of the later Intendants did not prefer to discourage self-sustaining farms, with a view to the sale of the King's stores. A memoir of 1750 concerning Cape Breton Island might equally well apply to Canada. After speaking of the meadows which were capable of supporting 30,000 black cattle instead of the sixty which grazed there, the writer thus proceeds: "But it would not have been for the interest of the Intendants that the Island should produce the necessary subsistence for its inhabitants, since the means of their heaping up riches proceeds from the immense number of ships sent yearly from France loaded with flower and salt provisions, which they embezzle (from France) for their profit, and often sell to favorites, who resell to the people at exorbitant rates. This employment, happily unknown in the British constitution, is the utter ruin of the French colonies and the hindrance to a flourishing population, as exists in the British establishments, by their tyranny and robberies."[1] This description might apply to the Bigot régime, but hardly to that of Beauharnois and Hocquart, during which the Council's policy of securing cheap wheat for planting was followed.

The Council's encouragement of agriculture belongs then in the early part of its career. Its efforts were wisely di-

[1] The translation appears in *Documents rélatifs à l'Histoire de Nouvelle France*, vol. iii, p. 469.

rected, but it had to fight the spirit of adventure in the colonists and the easy road to wealth that was offered by the Indian trade. Its policy failed; the fur trade advanced more rapidly than forest clearings. It was obvious to all that the English colonies were based upon the firmer foundation of compact agricultural settlements,[1] but the immediate interests of the French colonists forbade like success in Canada.

Commerce

It was comparatively easy for the Sovereign Council to achieve tangible results in its commercial policies. Canadian commerce consisted of the fur trade, the trade with France, and community trade. In each case, the Council stood for free trade, that is, equal privileges for all Canadians. It desired to give all a chance to participate in the profits of the fur trade. While the beaver was still plentiful about the settled country and the distant Indians had not been drawn into the fur trade, the Council ordered the neighboring Indians to bring their furs to Quebec, Montreal, and Three Rivers, allowing them to sell there in the open market to the highest bidder. This plan gave the Indian a much better bargain, and kept the *habitant* at the cultivation of the soil. Formerly the latter had sought out his red brother in the Indian village, had baited him with brandy and obtained his peltries for a "song." The Indian had at the same time been relieved of coming to the white settlements where his creditors were ready to seize his furs.[2]

[1] See the interesting letter of the minister to Dupuy, May 24, 1728. *Ibid.*, p. 142.

[2] *Jugements et Délib.*, vol. i, p. 558; vol. ii, pp. 124, 337. The rules for the annual fairs passed in 1683 are further illustrative of the Council's policy. Rule 6 forbade interference with, or intercepting of, the Indians on their way down the rivers. Rule 7 forbade debauching the savages in order to get their trade at the fairs. Rule 8 forbade going to the wigwams of the Indians for trade and confined traffic to

In 1676, 1700, and again in 1707, this policy of having the Indians bring their beaver skins to Quebec, Montreal and Three Rivers was reaffirmed. The ordinance of 1707 referred to the non-French Indians and the Iroquois at the Sault and the Mountain, whom Frenchmen had been plying with brandy by opening cabarets just outside their villages.[1]

As beaver became scarce and the neighboring Indians had to make long journeys after skins, or more distant tribes had to be sought out, interchange of peltries for merchandise in the towns was obviously impossible. The King therefore bestowed upon the Governor, as early as 1675, the right to grant permits to traders to go into the Indian villages for furs. These permits were legally worth 250 livres apiece, but in reality the Governors received as much as 1,000 livres, the amount depending upon the point of destination.[2] Officers of the distant outposts shared with these privileged traders the profits of the trade. They were rarely prosecuted.[3]

The Council's policy of prohibiting trading except in the towns and the system of excluding all but a few from commerce with distant tribes, caused the rise of a class of men who insisted upon the fruits of the fur trade and yet had not the money necessary to purchase the legal right. This class of "bushrangers" or coureurs de bois vexed King and Sovereign Council not a little. In 1669, the latter forbade dealing in brandy and skins at the tepees of the Indians, and hunting permits were required. Ten years later, the King forbade hunting beyond a limit of three leagues

[1] *Collection Moreau St. Méry*, series F iii, vol. ix, pt. i, pp. 69, *et seq.* and series F iii, vol. viii, pt. ii.

[2] Kalm, *Travels Into North America*, vol. iii, p. 309.

[3] The prosecutions in 1700 were so farcical in their nature that they called forth a rebuke from the King. *Jugements et Délib.*, vol. iv, pp. 499-503.

from the French settlements, except between January 15 and April 15. These measures were followed by a vigorous prosecution of the coureurs de bois by the Council. In 1681 a general amnesty was declared and freedom of trade was established until 1698 when the system of licenses was resumed. In spite of recurrence to this restrictive method of trade, the number of coureurs de bois was never again so large, although the problem of their defiance of law and unlicensed behavior occasionally disturbed the Council.[1]

It was part of the Council's plan of free trade in the cities to permit the qualified use of brandy as a commodity of exchange. It could be sold to the Indians in places where they could be restrained from violence, but carrying liquor to the Indian villages, where excesses might be expected, was forbidden. In 1668, after considerable hesitation, the Sovereign Council permitted the French inhabitants of New France "to sell or trade all kinds of liquors to Indians, who might wish to buy or trade". Indians, however, were warned not to get drunk on pain of a fine of two fat beavers.[2] The Bishop made the traffic a *cas réservé,* thus removing it from the sphere of all civil and ecclesiastical action. The representations of the Bishop to the King concerning the disastrous effects of brandy upon the Indians resulted in the submittal of the question to twenty of the most prominent citizens of Quebec. These men declared unanimously in favor of free trade in spirituous liquors. In the face of such unanimity, the Bishop consented to give up his *cas réservé,* and the King issued a qualified prohibi-

[1] The Sieur Catalogne, the engineer, says that in 1712 only a score of coureurs de bois set out from Montreal with merchandise for the Indian villages, although he admits that a hundred more might have gone except for the high cost of living. *Correspondance Générale,* series C xi, vol. xxxiii, pt. i, p. 297.

[2] *Jugements et Délib.*, vol. i, p. 534.

tion of the traffic in liquors. Still an occasional edict against the use of liquor, the employment of licenses or the monopoly of the trade by some company, and the confining of the fur sales to the French market, prevented the beaver trade from reaching the proportions that it should have attained.[1]

The Sovereign Council exercised considerable control over French merchants during the first two decades, but it gradually lost control until, in the eighteenth century, it was practically superseded in this supervision by Governor and Intendant. Its early records are filled with regulations which show that it aimed at keeping down the price of French merchandise. To effect this end, it determined to what profits French merchants were entitled. This process was the easier, as the Council had the means of knowing just what the merchandise, offered for sale, was worth in France, for the Sovereign Council had inherited from the Avaugour régime the administration of a 10 per cent impost upon merchandise. In order to know what sums to collect, it was necessary to inspect the invoices and to see that goods and invoice corresponded. Having thus ascertained the value of the goods, it was easy to determine what profits the merchants should enjoy as recompense for their trouble and the cost of transportation. Even after the impost was transferred to liquors, in June, 1664, the Council continued to receive the invoices, and determine the profits of French merchants upon dry merchandise. Although no

[1] For example, the Company of the Indies and the King's Domain joined hands through their agents in 1724 and 1729 to prevent interloping. Guards were posted at Quebec and Montreal and it was proposed to acquire a guardhouse in Montreal to be the centre from which flying squadrons were to be dispatched. They sent as many as fifteen or sixteen men in one detachment, and exciting skirmishes occurred between them and Canadian traders. For example, the guards were sadly maltreated while on a certain inspection at the Long Falls. For interesting particulars, see *Corres. Gen.*, series C xi, vol. ii, pt. i, pp. 275, 277, 287.

longer authorized to exercise this control as part of the duty of collecting the tax, it kept up this practice with the intention of protecting the Canadian consumer until such time as His Majesty should yield to their entreaties to open the trade with France to all Frenchmen and Canadians.

The story of benevolent despotism involves the verification of the merchants' invoices, the collection of the imposts based upon them, the determination of profits to be allowed, and the verification of the actual sale of the merchandise at the prices set.

Upon the arrival of a vessel, the captain could land nothing until he had taken his invoices to the Council. In January, 1664, suspecting that certain invoices represented higher cost prices than had actually been paid in France, the Council appointed three of its members to examine these records and the books of the merchants. These Councillors were continued in office for some time. When the amount of the impost had been determined, it was paid to Tilly, Councillor, and Repentigny, collector, who as such received salaries of 200 livres each per annum. These officials were no respecters of persons, for Canadians as well as Frenchmen had to pay the duty on goods imported by them.[1]

The Council then fixed the amount of profit for the merchants. This right was no usurpation, for it had been exercised by Avaugour and by the Council's predecessor. In 1663, the latter, under the authority of La Tesserie, had made a tariff to cover certain imposts, while allowing a profit of 65 per cent on the others. Owing to a complaint that these regulations had been disregarded to the great prejudice of the people, the Sovereign Council in 1664 made a new tariff of 55 per cent profit upon dry merchandise, 100 upon liquids and 120 upon products not valued at

[1] *Jugements et Délib.*, vol. i, pp. 93, 145, 182, 193.

over 100 livres per barrel. Similar rates were given in succeeding years,[1] although fixing of specified selling prices became increasingly the rule. For example, on July 26, 1664, the price of brandy per barrel was fixed at 190 livres, and lard at 80 livres in wheat or 75 in silver, while a 55 per cent profit was allowed upon other commodities.

In its efforts to facilitate the cheap passage of persons and freight to and from Canada, the Council passed several measures. In 1664, the cost of passage was about 33 livres, but later, passengers for France were charged 40 livres, even though messing with the sailors. The freight rates on beaver skins were not to exceed 10 livres per hundred-weight and 12 sous per elk skin. Freight rates might not exceed 60 livres per barrel payable in beaver skins.[2]

The fixing of retail prices was done in several different ways. The Council sent commissioners to the stores and shops in order to see, examine and appraise, the cloths, stuffs, linens, etc., and to have each tagged with a price slip bearing the King's arms. The merchants were to keep detailed books of sales and of stock still on hand, recording the date of each sale, the name of the purchaser and the price obtained. These books were to be submitted to the Council at its discretion. Furthermore, in order to give the people the advantage of direct purchase and to cut out the profits of the middle man, the merchants were ordered to expose their wares for sale in Quebec for one month, and not over one-tenth could be sold at wholesale. After this first month the merchants might dispose of one-fourth their wares in Three Rivers and Montreal, observing the rate, and informing the Sovereign Council of the sales they had made, etc.[3]

[1] *Jugements et Délib.*, vol. i, pp. 222, 537.

[2] *Ibid.*, vol. i, pp. 194, 268, 694.

[3] *Ibid.*, pp. 226, 228.

How the Council enforced these regulations develops an interesting story. On October 22, 1664, the syndic of Quebec represented that the June and July tariffs had not been followed, various merchants having sold at much higher rates. On November 12, the Council, acting upon more definite evidence, convicted La Mothe of having sold goods at an exorbitant rate and without the price tag, and fined him 100 livres. During the following months, it became apparent that the merchants, not caring to bring similar fines upon themselves, had adopted a policy of withholding their goods until scarcity should force the Council to fix higher prices. On December 17, Damours was appointed to investigate what merchants had thus sequestered goods, and the syndic was authorized to address a warning to the offenders. Having made out a list of those who were withholding merchandise, the syndic went to the Bishop to have it promulgated, but the latter refused. The Council accordingly published it. Still merchandise continued to cost twice as much as in France, and the Council continued to try by examination of invoices, affixing of price tags and threats of punishment, to fix prices to the advantage of the colonists.[1]

At the same time, the Council did not wish to make the Canadian market so unprofitable that French merchants would stop sending goods. It therefore showed some leniency in its judgment of offenders. In 1664, fines of 500 livres against three merchants for failure to submit account books were cancelled because the Council accepted their excuse of ignorance of an ordinance posted in Quebec while they were absent. Some years later it fined La Mothe only 23 livres, after he had been convicted of selling wine at 100 livres per cask and tobacco at 3 livres per pound, although

[1] *Jugements et Délib.*, vol. i, pp. 285, 309, 433.

the conciliar rate of 1666 was but 80 livres and 2 livres respectively.[1] Still the merchants continued to grumble at the hard conditions imposed upon them and it was not until free trade with France was obtained that regulation of an onerous character ceased.

To attain free trade the Council sought the abolition of the Company of the West Indies, which controlled the Atlantic trade. It favored the formation of a company of Canadians to conduct this trade, and asked the Intendant to write to the Crown for approval.[2] The next year the Council attacked the Company administration in a letter to Colbert. It complained that certain people were kept from Canada because of inability to get their goods transported; the Company's ship had not brought what the people needed, and the captain had charged exorbitant prices. He had brought too much liquor which had debauched many and ruined their families. The colonists desired free trade, a company consisting of Canadians, or at least better service, and a more judicious selection of imports, if the old Company was to continue its functions.[3] This letter had no immediate result but was undoubtedly influential in causing the King to resume the colony in 1674 and thereby establish free trade with France.

Besides coveting the foreign trade for Canadians, the Council jealously excluded French merchants from the retail trade and the fur trade with the Indians. This was likewise a policy inherited from the Council of 1648. One regulation of the Council of 1648 forbids all foreign merchants to sell liquor at retail, or less than a pound of tobacco, or to trade either directly or indirectly with the Indians.[4]

[1] *Jugements et Délib.*, vol. i, pp. 306, 369; also Chapais, *Jean Talon, Intendant*, p. 223.

[2] *Jugements et Délib.*, vol. i, p. 457.

[3] *Ibid.*, p. 525.

[4] *Ibid.*, vol. ii, p. 56. Ordinances of 1653, 1654 and 1655.

The Sovereign Council took the same stand. In 1683, upon appeal of the native merchants, the following code of restrictions was enacted, summarizing previous similar measures of the Council.[1] (1) Foreign merchants might sell goods at retail for only two months, from August 1 to September 30, after which they could sell commodities only by wholesale or in bulk, except powder and lead which they might sell by the pound; (2) foreign merchants were prohibited from selling shirts, hats, greatcoats, suits, etc., upon which the small profits of manufacture might turn to the advantage of the inhabitants; (3) to keep French merchants from participating in the Indian fur trade, they were forbidden to trade at Three Rivers, Montreal and other posts, or upon the upper waters of the rivers from June 1 to October 31; (4) it was prohibited to inhabitants to lend their names to foreign tradesmen.

Such restrictions meant two things, either evasion or a high price for French imports. The Council left a loophole by omitting to mention ship captains in the prohibitions. Vaudreuil and Bégon thought that selling at retail by ship captains tended to lower prices; the more merchants the greater competition and the more chance to get rid of home products. The Superior Council therefore in 1720 refused to act upon the complaints of Quebec merchants to make more stringent rules. Governor and Intendant soon began to show a divergence of opinion. On November 2, 1724, the former complained that the retailing of merchandise had been carried on without regard to the ordinance of 1683 of the Supreme Council, that foreign merchants should be prevented from scouring the "coasts" and setting up shops; that such actions meant that *habitants* had had to pay exorbitant prices fixed by the majority of the merchants.

[1] *Jugements et Délib.*, vol. i, pp. 72, 861-862.

On the same day, Bégon wrote that he was against cutting off ship captains and French merchants from the retail trade, because ship captains would have to accept whatever prices retailers offered them or take their cargoes back to France; that such retailers could get a cargo at their own price and retail it at monopoly prices.[1] Competition in the retail trade was the only remedy for high prices.

The one thing certain in the controversy is the great expense of French merchandise. For example, a riot broke out near Quebec on August 23, 1714, during which the mob threatened to march upon the city unless the price of merchandise was reduced.[2] The Council prosecuted the ringleaders in a half-hearted way, but was soon involved in more important results of its protective policy. So high were the merchants' prices that the people sold their finest flour directly to the vessels in order to secure merchandise at first hand. Consequently wheat flour remaining in the country was sold at prohibitive prices, and in bad years, cargoes of flour had to be sent from France, because there was no surplus in Canada.

If the Council was indirectly responsible for the high prices of French merchandise, it tried on the other hand to facilitate the exchange of the products of the country. Since a large part of French merchandise consisted of ribbons, gaily-colored fabrics, laces, trinkets, brandy, wines, and tobacco, the Council was really discouraging idle luxury in making them too dear to buy, while the necessities of life, most of which were produced in Canada, were made available at competitive prices by the establishment of markets. The first mention of such a market occurs in 1666, when it was ordered that one should be established

[1] *Corres. Gen.*, series C xi, pt. i, vol. xlvi, p. 118, *et seq.*

[2] *Jugements et Délib.*, vol. vi, p. 997.

in Quebec, to be held Tuesday and Saturday of each week, at which meat and produce were to be sold. Later, a hall was built in the Lower Town, where produce was sold daily.[1] No butcher could sell meat elsewhere than at the stalls in the market, the rent of which went into the city treasury.[2] The Council tried to discourage huckstering, in order to bring the products of the farm directly to the consumer. Wholesale business was of course prohibited. Thrifty housewives and other small purchasers were given a couple of hours start of the innkeepers and other large purchasers. Usually the latter were forbidden to come to market before the eight o'clock bell.[3] An exception was made in 1711 of three innkeepers who had to feed soldiers and people of quality to whom picked-over vegetables and meats could not be served. On October 11, 1676, the Sovereign Council ordered the establishment of public markets in Quebec, Three Rivers and Ville Marie, and forbade trade in other places.

As a specimen of the market regulations, the following of the year 1707 may be quoted: "In conformity with the regulations of May 11, 1676, all restaurant-keepers, innkeepers, retail-dealers, and hucksterers of this city and its suburbs are forbidden to go into the environs to buy poultry, game, eggs, butter, and other small provisions, or to go out along the shore to meet those who are bringing in provisions in canoes and boats, or to buy anything except what is exposed in the market, after nine o'clock (in the morning) in the summer and ten in the winter, in order to give time to the citizens of the town and country to provide themselves with what they need."[4]

[1] *Jugements et Délib.*, vol. i, p. 871.

[2] *Ibid.*, vol. ii, pp. 126, 139.

[3] *Ibid.*, vol. vi, pp. 257, 270.

[4] *Ibid.*, vol. v, p. 239.

Further to facilitate commerce, the Council regulated weights and measures and scales, to secure uniformity.[1] During its early history it also fixed the currency. In 1644 it ordained that liards should pass at no more than 3 deniers and a few months later it reduced them to 2 deniers each.[2] A few years earlier the colony owed it a debt of gratitude for lowering the inflated "marked" sous or Parisian sous to their market value. A Parisian sou was worth 15 deniers in France, but 20 deniers in New France. In 1662 the Council of Avaugour by ordinance raised the value to 24 deniers. Forthwith some enterprising persons inundated the country with these sous, so that there was no longer any other kind of money. The Council ordered that after February 1, 1667, these marked sous should pass at the rate of 20 deniers. Meanwhile, those who would suffer were ordered to turn their coins into the hands of the Sieur Aubert de la Chesnaye and his assistants in Montreal and Three Rivers. These commissioners paid 24 deniers for each sou and gave it back at the rate of 20 deniers, thus losing 4 deniers on each sou. To cover the losses donations were received from high officials, the Company of the West Indies and a number of merchants, the sum amounting in all to 2,875 livres.[3] This fund of 1,150,000 deniers enabled the receivers to restore 287,500 sous to the market value of 20 deniers. There is a mention of one of these commissioners returning promissory notes for sous turned in. It is probable that to avoid paying the extra 4 deniers per sou more than once on the same coin, the commissioners retained all the money in their possession up to a certain date, at which time they redeemed their promissory notes.[4] In

[1] *Jugements et Délib.*, vol. iii, pp. 110, 328.

[2] *Ibid.*, vol. i, p. 171.

[3] *Ibid.*, vol. i, pp. 370, 377.

[4] Chapais attributes this clever bit of finance to Talon, *Jean Talon, Intendant*, p. 221.

subsequent ordinances the Council regulated the rate of exchange of different foreign coins, French money continuing to pass at a premium of 33⅓ per cent over Canadian. When after 1685 colonial paper currency supplemented metal, the Council ceased to figure as regulators of coinage.

The Council also controlled trade carried on outside of markets and fairs. During the seventeenth century, it fixed the price of bread, meat and liquors, seeking to secure uniformity in amount, quality and price. This was no arbitrary process. As early as 1676 the Council provided for an assembly consisting of the chief inhabitants, to meet semi-annually, on June 15 and November 15, and decide upon the price of bread and upon means of increasing and enriching the colony. Two Councillors or the lieutenant general of Quebec were to preside at these meetings. In accordance with the report of this assembly the Council was to fix prices. Accordingly, when the high price of wheat made the baking of the standard loaf for the specified price unprofitable, upon request of the bakers, the lieutenant general of Quebec would usually appear before the Council and ask that one or two of its members be deputed to preside over the assembly. Thereupon the Council usually waived its right to send a president and instructed the lieutenant general to convoke the assembly, preside over its deliberations and report its conclusions. Although it was complained that the assembly was not held regularly twice a year, yet so satisfactory was the method that in 1705 the assembly was given the control of meat prices also.[1] The assembly of citizens and the Council determined just how much white, brown and black bread could be made and for what price. They figured, for example, that when wheat stood at 55 sous a minot, a twelve-pound loaf of white

[1] *Jugements et Délib.*, vol. v. p. 195.

household bread could be made at 18 sous and the baker yet obtain a fair profit.[1] It was the duty of the lieutenant general of Quebec to make frequent visits to the bakeshops and see that the loaves weighed what they were marked. Liberty was left to the bakers to buy wheat wherever they could get it.

This system was not always strictly enforced. For example, in 1710, there were four bakers in Quebec, who were obeying the ordinances but indifferently, and the Council therefore decided to permit Pierre Joly to establish a bakeshop, where bread should be made for the public according to the regulations of the Council.[2] Where there was a disposition to be law-abiding, and the Council was persuaded of the error of its calculations, the grievances of bakers, butchers, and cabaret-keepers were readily redressed.[3]

The Pierre Joly incident suggests the fact that there was no exclusive right to exercise a craft.[4] There were no gilds, and organization of craftsmen was only suggested in the ordinance of 1676, when it was proposed that masters of each craft be elected by the artisans to supervise their respective productions.[5] This provision was never carried into effect and the Council realized that the needs of society would determine the number of craftsmen in each line of work. It was for this reason that it referred François Fleury to the assembly when he sought to be admitted to

[1] *Jugements et Délib.*, vol. iii, p. 205.

[2] *Ibid.*, vol. vi, p. 113.

[3] *Ibid.*, vol. ii, p. 241; vol. v, p. 282.

[4] These were the words of the Council when it decreed that since there was in that city neither exclusive right to work at any craft or profession, notably those of roofers and joiners, each one should be permitted to follow his choice. *Col. Moreau St. Méry*, series F iii, vol. xi, p. 363.

[5] *Jugements et Délib.*, vol. ii, p. 67.

the number of bakers in Quebec. The assembly decided that there were enough bakers at that time (1683).[1] In the case of the request of Quebec surgeons that the Council exclude ship surgeons and Frenchmen from the exercise of their profession in the town, that body refused to accede to such a monopoly measure,[2] but where a monopoly would obviously keep down the prices of the necessities of life, the Council pursued an opposite policy. For example, in 1716, it granted the exclusive right of killing and selling meat in the market to those butchers who would guarantee to sell meat at 8 sous a pound throughout the year.[3]

Commercial activity depends largely upon easy means of communication. The rivers of Canada afforded such facilities for travel by boat, snowshoes, or sledge, that roads were but slowly introduced. The beginnings were primitive. Land travel followed the banks of the St. Lawrence, and to permit this, farmers were ordered to start their enclosures at least two perches (eleven yards) back from the high-water mark. In August, 1664, *habitants* with lands abutting upon the *Grande Allée* of Quebec were ordered to make it a free road and passable to wagons, within a fortnight, or else the work would be done at the delinquent's expense. This ordinance had been ignored and on September 3, the Council fined the delinquents 20 sols for each arpent in front of their possessions. They were enjoined to place the road in condition by the coming of the snows, under pain of a very heavy fine.

Having enforced its will in this case the Council by 1690 had become insistent upon the paving of the adjoining streets. Proprietors in the Lower Town were threatened

[1] *Jugements et Dé'ib.*, vol. iii, p. 5.

[2] *Ibid.*, vol. vi, pp. 429-430.

[3] *Ibid.*, vol.. vi, p. 119.

with seizure and sale of property upon failure to comply with the ordinance. They were allowed to reimburse themselves from their renters. The level of the streets was determined by experts in the presence of the *grand voyer*, or road commissioner, and the lieutenant general of Quebec.[1] The winding Street of the Mountain between the Upper and Lower Town was repaired in 1694 by the Governor's soldiers and the teamsters, through the contributions of citizens.[2] In 1749, Peter Kalm describes the streets as being paved with black lime slates, which were quarried from the side of the Mountain. These cobblestones made a rugged surface, which was very troublesome to foot-passengers and carriages. The streets in the Lower Town were comparatively narrow and almost always damp, owing to the height of the houses, which were usually of three or four stories.[3]

The first highway between outlying hamlets and Quebec was made in 1667. Some inhabitants of Sainte Geneviève and Saint Michel recommended to the Council a route from those places to Quebec. The Council after hearing a report from its commissioner, specified in minute detail where the road should run. Since it was possible to take advantage of old lanes, the task of cutting down hills and filling gullies was not very great. Only a few leagues had bad spots to keep in repair.[4] In 1796, the Council delegated wide powers to the *grand voyer*.[5] The course of new roads and the repair of old ones from one seigniory to another were to be determined by him in conjunction with the pro-

[1] *Jugements et Délib.*, vol. iii, p. 330; *Coll. Moreau St. Méry*, series F iii, vol. vi, p. 500.

[2] *Jugements et Délib.*, vol. iii, p. 871.

[3] Kalm, *Travels into North America*, vol. iii, p. 98, *et seq.*

[4] *Jugements et Délib.*, vol. i, p. 409.

[5] *Ibid.*, vol. v, p. 238.

prietors. In the latters' absence the local judge and six of the most prominent inhabitants, or the captain of the militia, were to advise the *grand voyer*. The Council demanded passable roads of twenty-four feet in width, and the erection of bridges over streams. No one was to infringe upon the road with enclosures. The captain of the militia in each district was to make an annual report to the Council upon the state of the roads.

Nevertheless, in spite of these measures, the condition of town and country roads continued to be the subject for official complaint well on into the eighteenth century. In 1712, the Sieur Catalogne, engineer, proposed that fines and certain forfeitures should be employed to repair the streets of Quebec the majority of which he claimed were almost impassable because of rocks and mudholes.[1] In 1735, the road commissioner reported that the streets were at once a source of discomfort and of danger to the health of the passersby. He said: "The streets have their natural slope towards the river and by compelling each owner to pave before his lot, it would mean little cost to the individual and great public advantage. The citizens themselves demand that the streets be paved. Two have already commenced to pave before their houses, but others do not fall in with the plan. I have done my best to persuade them. The limestone for paving may be cheaply brought by barges from the seigniory of the Guardian Angel, three leagues from Quebec, and this work, which as a whole appears to be a considerable project, would be but a small undertaking for each individual."[2]

Although the Council had striven to widen the narrow

[1] *Corres. Gen.*, series Cxi, vol. xxxiii, pt. i.

[2] Lanouillier de Boiscler to the minister October 31, 1735. *Ibid.*, vol. lxiv, pt. i, p. 111.

streets, it was not until 1735 that Three Rivers obeyed the Council's ordinances. Here the road commissioner succeeded in adding twelve feet to their width. "It was no hard matter," he reported, "to get the streets lined up anew as the wooden houses were old and in a ruinous condition."[1]

The same tardy execution of the Council's orders occurred in regard to highroads. It was not until 1730 that there was a good road even between Quebec and Montreal,[2] and the much-needed road to Acadia was entirely too great a venture for Canadian enterprise.

In conclusion, the main commercial achievements of the Council may be summarized as (1) the opening to Canadian merchants of the trade with France, while (2) the fur trade was carefully kept out of the hands of French traders; (3) partial success in keeping down the price of French merchandise by removing the import duty from necessities to liquors and by permitting only reasonable profits; and (4) the encouragement of local trade by wise adjustment of the coinage, by the creation of markets, by the improvement of roads and by the standardizing of weights and measures. While it did not undertake large enterprises such as the construction of a road to Acadia or the subsidizing of shipbuilding for the codfisheries, its more modest deeds may be heartily commended.

Efforts at Sanitation

The Sovereign Council was persistent in its attack upon unsanitary conditions. It took many years to wean the people from old practices. Under the impression that bad smells infected with sickness, the Council consistently waged

[1] *Corres. Gen.*, series C xi, vol. lxiv, pt. i, p. 111.

[2] So good was the road that the journey by chaise from Quebec to Montreal occupied but four and a half hours. *Ibid.*

war upon the causes of such smells. The problem of keeping the streets free from fire-inviting, disease-breeding matter, involved ordinances upon several subjects. Every effort was made to have the streets paved that they might be more easily swept, for the unpaved streets became veritable quagmires in the spring and served as dumping grounds for filth and straw. At first the Council simply waged a spring-cleaning campaign. Each proprietor in the Lower Town was to clean the street in front of his house under pain of a 10-livre fine.[1] At a later period he was required to keep it free from snow and ice to prevent a winter's accumulation of filth. These provisions were executed. The streets before the houses of delinquents were cleared of snow by soldiers, and payment was exacted by seizure of property.[2] After 1694, a regular, paid scavenger with horse and cart worked in spring, summer and autumn.[3] Yet these measures of the Council were so far ineffectual that the *grand voyer* in 1735 reported unpaved streets in the Lower Town to be almost impassable during rainy weather or during the melting of the snows. He feared infection from the stench, from the filth and human excrement (*boues et vuidanges*) deposited in these streets.[4]

This was the condition of the streets after the Council had endeavored for seventy years to force the people to build privies, and thus simplify the problem of street-cleaning. Partial success was attained, although Quebec never obtained a regular sewage system until 1843.[5] The Council

[1] *Jugements et Délib.*, vol. i, p. 187.

[2] For an interesting case, see the Sieur André de Leigne's letter to the minister October 6, 1723. *Corres. Gen.*, series xi, vol. xiv, pt. i, p. 282, *et seq.*

[3] *Jugements et Délib.*, vol. iii, p. 871.

[4] Lanouillier de Boiscler to the minister October 31, 1735. *Corres. Gen.*, series C xi, vol. lxiv, pt. i, p. 111.

[5] Douglas, *Quebec in the Seventeenth Century.*

was not to blame for such slow progress. It began in 1676 with a stringent measure giving householders or occupiers until spring to build privies upon their lots. Occupiers of houses or lots too small for such sheds were held to clean the streets before their dwellings each morning. If proprietors were delinquent, costs of construction were to be taken out of their rents, and they were to pay besides a fine of 20 livres. If a mason, carpenter, etc., worked on a new house not having a privy, a fine of 20 livres was to be levied on him.[1] The enforcement of this order was left to officers of the provost court of Quebec. They reported considerable opposition. Some persons claimed that it was impossible to build on their lots. Finally in 1710 the city officers were ordered to take an architect and decide whether the complaints were justifiable. After some delay they asked to be excused, and the Council appointed one of its own members to carry out the inspection and order the prives to be built where he thought it practicable.[2] This arrangement met with but partial success, and the people submitted to these orders only gradually.

Smells of the pigsty, wharves and slaughter-house led to the enactment of ordinances, the frequent repetition of which indicated persistent evasion. In the crowded Lower Town dirty stables and pigsties were clearly unsanitary. In 1676, the owners were ordered to clean their places every week and carry the manure to the river. Then, the number of pigs for each family was reduced to one, and finally, in 1706, none was to be kept in the populous parts of the Lower Town during the summer.[3] The water front was to be kept free from smells. For instance, in 1689, the Cul de

[1] *Jugements et Délib.*, vol. ii, p. 60, *et seq.*

[2] *Ibid.*, vol. v, pp. 336, 344, 353.

[3] *Ibid.*, vol. v, p. 233, *et seq.*

Sac and the quay before the Sieur Le Bart's house were to be cleaned at the expense of the skippers using them.[1] The slaughtering of animals in the Lower Town by any individual was first regulated, then forbidden. In 1676 the waste parts were ordered to be carried immediately to the river to prevent the infection which they might cause. In 1687, the slaughtering business was put into the hands of regular butchers and the shambles were banished to the edge of the town. Later ordinances provided against uncleanliness and smells.[2]

In 1706, it became necessary to put certain restrictions upon the *habitants* who brought slaughtered meat into the city. Henceforth they were to bring certificates from the local judge or parish priest that the cattle had not been attacked by any disease nor come to their end through accident, poison or drowning. Furthermore, the royal attorney of Quebec was to inspect all meat before it was put on sale in the market. Uninspected or rejected meat was subject to confiscation. No calves under a month old were to be slain.[3] If the meat passed inspection, the owners were given, free of charge, a permit to sell. Heavy fines were placed upon the *habitant* who offended in any one of these particulars.

In these measures for pure food, the Council seemed to be thoroughly alive to the dangers of diseased meat. It did not, however, insist upon a pure water supply. The people of Quebec drank river water. In 1687, the Council ordered the digging of wells both in the Lower and the Upper Town, not so much for the sake of purer water as to create a more accessible supply for indi-

[1] *Jugements et Délib.*, vol. iii, pp. 111, 331.

[2] *Ibid.*, p. 110; vol. v, p. 233, *et seq.*

[3] *Ibid.*, vol. iii, p. 235.

vidual use and public use in case of fire.[1] In 1689, it abandoned the idea of a well in the Upper Town, but ordered an assembly of citizens to decide where one should be made in the Lower Town. I have met with no document of later date describing such a well. In fact, throughout the French period, the people continued to use river water. The boys of most families trained their dogs to draw barrels mounted upon wheels into the river, thence home to the family barrel in the cellar.[2] Under English rule horses replaced the dogs, but the same method was pursued. Writing in the first decade of the twentieth century, James Douglas says: " Many of us can remember the watercart backing into the dirty water of Cul de Sac, bucketing the turbid fluid into barrels, and distributing it at 12½ cents per barrel ".[3] Not until 1843 did Quebec acquire a sanitary water system.

Perhaps the reason that the Council did not force through its plan of supplying the town with well water was that no epidemics arose during its administration from the drinking of the river water. Auteuil wrote that the only epidemics occurring before 1714 were brought from New England or from the French vessels.[4] Epidemics from these sources suggest the need of proper quarantine measures and the segregation of contagious diseases; yet I have met with but one hint at such an endeavor. In 1664, permission was given to a surgeon to put a certain person attacked with a dangerous disease into one of the casements of the fort to

[1] " Ordonne aussy qu'il sera fait des puys à la haute et basse ville aux lieux qui seront Estimez les meilleurs et plus commodes, afin que l'on puisse facilement avoir Leau En hiver Et En Este tant pour l'usage d'un chacun En particulier, que pour le bien public En cas d'Incendie." *Ibid.*, vol. iii, p. 111.

[2] Kalm, *Travels into North America.*

[3] Douglas, *Quebec in the Seventeenth Century*, not quoted verbatim.

[4] *Corres. Gen.*, series C xi, vol. xxxiv, pt. i, p. 169, *et seq.*

be treated with medicine.[1] Hospitals there were, but the Council was not connected with their administration. It established no smallpox houses, and does not appear to have done any thing to check the spread of the foreign-born epidemics, which found such fertile ground among the robust Canadians.[2]

Fire Prevention and Fighting

Destructive fires occurred repeatedly during the French régime. After some great fire the Council would issue detailed ordinances aimed at preventing a repetition of the disaster, or providing for better fire-fighting facilities. But after the second burning of the Palais de Justice, in 1725, the Intendant assumed the responsibility for the preservation of property. Dupuy issued two long sets of ordinances and Hocquart carried through most elaborate plans to make the Palace fireproof. Brick and stone floors and stairs were introduced. The apartments of the second floor were connected by a corridor, so that the three outside stairways were made accessible, while an inside staircase was removed as a road for fire.[3]

Still, during the period of conciliar activity, the people were forced to take many precautions, which undoubtedly lessened the number of fires. Careless persons persisted in carrying firebrands and live coals or smoking tobacco along the narrow streets of the Lower Town, littered with fodder from stables and shavings from carpenter shops, with woodpiles between the tall cramped houses. Or, thrifty *habitants,* camping along the St. Lawrence on the eve of market days, rather than patronize the taverns of

[1] *Jugements et Délib.*, vol. i, p. 182.

[2] *Corres. Gen.*, series C xi, vol. xxxiv, pt. 2, p. 169, *et seq.*

[3] *Ibid.*, vol. li, pt. i, pp. 199-205.

Quebec, lit great camp fires near the shingle-roofed houses. Dirty chimneys sent out showers of sparks to fall in the midst of this combustible material; or wood placed on top of them (*mettent du bois au haut d'Icelles*) to prevent smoking, caught fire and fell upon the shingles below. The Council prohibited these abuses, punished delinquents with fines, and sought to lessen the chances of fire by removing combustible materials. All persons were forbidden to keep fodder in their houses or in other places susceptible to fire, or to winter cattle in the Lower Town "because of accidents from fire which happen there too often". Inhabitants were not to throw straw or other combustible material into the streets, and carpenters and coopers were to carry their shavings to that receptacle for all refuse, the St. Lawrence. People had to remove their piles of wood to a public wood-yard maintained on land formerly acquired by Talon.[1] After 1688 no more houses were to be roofed with shingles. This measure was modified the following year to allow chestnut and walnut shingles for dormer roofs.[2]

When the people forgot such prohibitions and local officials grew lax, conciliar ordinances had to be repeated. Eternal vigilance was the price of safety. Take, for example, the Council's measures against dirty chimneys. In 1676 that body required that chimneys be swept every two months. By 1710 the frequency of fires made it insist upon a monthly sweeping. A certificate to this effect signed by two neighbors was to be presented by the householder to the lieutenant general of Quebec. The Council shrewdly made the owner of dirty chimneys legally responsible for

[1] I have followed these measures closely from 1663 to 1716. The most important are to be found among the ordinances in *Jugements et Délib.*, vol. i, p. 617; vol. ii, p. 64, *et seq.*; vol. iii, pp. 11, 206, 328, *et seq.*; vol. vi, p. 39.

[2] *Ibid.*, vol. iii, pp. 206, 329.

any damage caused by them.[1] It insisted that all chimneys should be of sufficient size to admit sweeps and itself undertook to provide those dwarfed workers. After 1688 it appointed experts to assist the lieutenant general to inspect chimneys, reporting to the Sovereign Council for prosecution persons whose chimneys were not large enough for a sweep.[2] The lieutenant general probably showed partiality, for his report was by 1707 superseded by a sworn statement of experts alone.[3] These men were instructed to fix the responsibility for certain fires.[4] Thus the Council seems to have taken all reasonable precautions against fires, which, once started, were so destructive. Prevention was stressed because fire-fighting facilities were primitive and ineffective.

In the early times, good citizens, at the first sound of the bell, ran to the fire with bucket or kettle. Carpenters and artisans were obliged to attend, hatchet in hand,[5] for Canadians depended more upon tearing down houses in the way of the conflagration,[6] than upon putting the fire out. In 1689 twelve iron hooks were ordered for this purpose. In order that they might easily get at dirty chimneys or fires upon the roofs, proprietors were bound to have ladders fastened from eaves to ridgepole and also at least one portable ladder capable of reaching from the ground to the eaves.[7]

Although not trusting to the ability of a bucket brigade

[1] *Jugements et Délib.*, vol. ii, p. 64; vol. vi, p. 39.

[2] *Ibid.*, vol. iii, p. 206.

[3] *Ibid.*, vol. v, p. 555.

[4] For example, was the burning of Rey Gaillard's house in 1707 due to his son's carelessness with artillery fuses, to two shots heard some time before the fire, or to a dirty chimney? *Ibid.*, vol. v, pp. 513, 520.

[5] *Ibid.*, vol. ii, p. 64, *et seq.*; vol. iii, p. 329.

[6] "pour couper chemin au feu." *Ibid.*, vol. iii, p. 330.

[7] *Ibid.*, vol. ii, p. 946.

to extinguish fires, the Council tried to make that method of fire-fighting as effective as possible. We have seen its attempts in 1687 and 1689 to have wells bored for a supply of water during the months when the river was frozen. Later, it furnished buckets, which the volunteer firemen appropriated for private use. Finally, in 1706, it ordered a hundred more. These were to be paid for by a 20-sou tax on chimneys and were not to be taken away from the Château, the Palace, and other specified places, except during a fire.[1] This was as far as the Council got, and the Intendant went no further along the road of progress. No attempt was made to force the river water to higher levels by means of fire engines with the use of hose. Quebec and Montreal can be compared only unfavorably with New York and Philadelphia in this regard. Philadelphia bought an engine as early as 1718 and in 1730 purchased three larger engines, two hundred leather buckets, twenty ladders and twenty-five hooks with axes. New York, in 1731, purchased two engines and later three others. In 1738 New York had a regular force of twenty-four firemen; while two years earlier the Union Fire Company had been started in Philadelphia through the efforts of Benjamin Franklin.[2]

Preservation of Good Order

The chief function of the Sovereign Council was the preservation of order. It acted in this regard in two ways: it passed wise measures to prevent crime and imposed swift justice upon the delinquent who disregarded its warnings. It aimed to keep the people busy upon their lands and helped them accordingly. In 1663 it distributed clothing

[1] *Jugements et Délib.*, vol. v, pp. 281, 529.

[2] For these and other interesting facts about these colonial cities, see *Minutes of the Common Council of Philadelphia*, pp. 157, 297, 307, 343; *Minutes of the Common Council of the City of New York*, vol. iv, pp. 54, 404, 439; Watson, *Annals of Philadelphia*.

and provisions among the poor, and in the following year sent the useless back to France.[2] It sought to stamp out begging which, in 1671, was introduced into Quebec by four or five women from places near by. These persons communicated their boldness to others, even to men who were able to work and to young persons who were needed as servants. The Commissioner appointed in 1674 to investigate conditions, reported the number of beggars at three hundred. They had been such a burden upon the citizens and had committed so many disorders that it was to be feared they might pillage the chief houses of the city—as they had threatened to do. On August 31, the Council issued orders for them to leave the town within a week, to return to the habitations whence they came, to raise crops, etc.[1] People were forbidden to give ablebodied beggars anything at their house doors on pain of a 10-livre fine. By 1683, however, the beggars had returned. They built huts about the town, which had become scandalous and disorderly places, the dens of vagabonds, and they brought up their children in ways of idleness so that they would not become servants. After a week, quoth the Council, a healthy beggar caught in Quebec would be put in the pillory; a second offence would bring a whipping.[2] Necessitous persons, however, were allowed to beg if they received licenses from their local judge or parish priest. This privilege was abused. To avoid the bad influence of pauperized parents upon the rising generation, the Council in 1688 established poor boards to determine who were really the worthy and necessitous poor. These were aided; begging was forbidden.

This system of poor relief provided for three members on

[1] *Jugements et Délib.*, vol. i, pp. 18, 163-164.

[2] *Coll. Moreau St. Méry*, series F iii, vol. iv, pt. ii, p. 806.

[3] *Jugements et Délib.*, vol. ii, p. 871.

each board. One director was to determine the merits of applicants and report to the others. His duties were to find work for those able to work and to make an agreement with the employer about the rate of wage. A second director was to be treasurer to receive contributions and money from the alms boxes placed in the churches and to account for receipts and expenditures. A third director was to record the deliberations of the bureau and the exact condition of the poor that were given alms. Contributions of money, clothing and provisions were solicited each month by two women volunteers, who were followed by a person with a basket. The Sovereign Council appointed the members of the city boards, but in the seigniories and parishes the people elected two *habitants* to serve on the parish board with the priest. A poor man must live at least three months in a place before he could receive help. The worthy poor and the aged were to be given relief but mendicancy was forbidden, on pain of corporal punishment. The poor boards were given power to imprison, to put on bread and water, and to withhold provisions, at their discretion.[1] How this system worked cannot be determined from the Council records.

The Council had to deal with a class of white servants, most of whom had come over in earlier times. The Council of 1648, in order to increase the number of colonists in Canada, had forced ship owners to send one person with every ten tons of freight. Ship owners gave those starting for America 30 livres worth of clothing and outfit, and Canadian purchasers paid the same sum plus 30 livres for passage. Each immigrant served for three years at 75 livres a year, and built a house that he might marry and cultivate the land after the expiration of his term of service.[2]

[1] *Jugements et Délib.*, vol. iii, pp. 219-223.

[2] Auteuil to the Regent, December 9, 1715, *Cor. Gen.*, series C xi, vol. xxxiv, p. 170.

For over a decade the Council was confronted with the problem of keeping these bound servants sober and at work. The unsatisfactory character of these servants was, probably, responsible for the abandonment of the old Council's plan to bring immigrants to Canada. Some indentured servants refused to work, some ran away and after a carousal of several days sought new masters. In 1663, the Council forbade any persons to hire servants without a written dismissal from their previous masters, and laid a fine of 10 livres upon the servant and 4 livres for each day's absence, the latter to go to the injured master. This penalty was changed in 1667 to a fine of 50 sous for each day's absence, plus the amount which the master considered his crops, cattle, etc., to be damaged. The Council forbade all persons to drink with servants or to sell them liquor. These ordinances were enforced, and where runaway servants could not make restitution they were punished by imprisonment until they were willing to work, or were confined for a couple of hours in the pillory, with the inscription, "Engaged servant who has left the service of his master under false pretences", pinned across the stomach, or, on a second offence, were beaten or branded. This irresponsible class gradually disappeared, as servants became tenants and freeholders, and the Council records almost ceased to mention runaway servants.[1]

The Council sought to prevent intoxication and its attendant crimes, and to maintain the sacredness of the family tie. It exercised strict supervision over the inns. Tavern-keepers had to give proof of good character before they could obtain licenses. The old French law of 1617 against swearing, gambling, etc., in taverns was enforced. Innkeepers were warned against selling liquor in any quantity

[1] *Jugements et Délib.*, vol. i, pp. 76, 77, 104, 310, 382, 589, 747, 762.

to irresponsible persons. Prostitution was not tolerated and delinquents were driven into the woods or sent back to France. In 1676, all persons were forbidden to give shelter to or befriend girls of evil life or masqueraders of either sex.[1]

But in such a society as existed in Canada, these prohibitions and warnings were inadequate, and the preservation of the peace meant the execution of swift justice. Although Canadians were fond of the chase and of travel, the length and rigor of the winters inclined them to laziness, and idleness sometimes fostered passions which, stirred beyond control by the fires of brandy, resulted in atrocious crimes. That these crimes were so few is a tribute at once to the character of the Canadians and to the severe repressive measures of the Council. The frontier life of neighbors of different social grades living on easy terms with each other, fostered a wholesome self-respect.[2] This high opinion of themselves made them scorn continuous application to the arts, agriculture, and commerce, but it also made them sensitive to ridicule and to the slightest punishments designed to humiliate them. This characteristic accounts for the emphasis upon certain ceremonies which will be described in the punishment of criminals. The worst element in Canada were the more recent arrivals from France. A letter of 1730 shows how the incoming Frenchmen complicated the problem of preserving order: "We beg Monseigneur not to continue to send men of loose life into the colony. There are already too many of them, and it is more difficult to repress them in this country than anywhere else,

[1] For example, *ibid.*, p. 973.

[2] Beauharnais and Hocquart could not commend this spirit of independence in a province of an absolute monarchy and asked the minister in 1730 for a hundred and fifty Swiss to establish a stronger government. Nothing came of the proposal. *Cor. Gen.*, series C xi, vol. lii, pt. i, pp. 58-60.

on account of the ease with which they can get away and the difficulty of convicting them of the thefts and acts of violence that they often commit, the inhabitants of this country being naturally inclined to give asylum even to the guiltiest. The crimes continue to go on and the criminals are very difficult to discover." [1]

As the frontier characteristics of the colony began to disappear and the struggle for existence and the rough joys of the senses gave way to the increasing opportunities to accumulate property and to a desire to amass it by a short process, there was a change in the nature of the crimes most frequently committed. Seventeenth-century Canada was essentially a man's country. The King probably sent few women out to the colony after Talon's administration, whereas the immigration of unmarried men or husbands without their wives continued. It is not hard therefore to understand why rape, adultery and murder were the most frequent crimes of that period. In the eighteenth century, however, these crimes are for the most part replaced by stealing, counterfeiting, forging signatures and other methods of securing money under false pretences. The more serious crimes did not occur in waves although any suspension in the execution of justice resulted in the increase of crime, if we may believe the partisan statements of our informants. For example, the encroachments of the Intendant upon the jurisdiction of the Superior Council in 1706 was responsible according to Auteuil for the commission of crimes with impunity. He says: "People have been seen in broad daylight in the very streets baptizing dogs and imitating in derision the ceremonies of the mass. Murders from ambush have become common, and so has adultery, abandonment of infants (*suppression de part*), incest, and a list of crimes too long to specify." [2]

[1] *Cor. Gen.*, series C xi, vol. iii, p. 68.

In like manner Hocquart reports the evils of the previous administration and the efficiency of his own: "The government's lack of firmness in the past accounts for the present insubordination, but during the last few years crimes have been punished and disorders suppressed by proportionate penalties. The police regulations as to public roads, cabarets, etc., have been better observed and the inhabitants have conducted themselves better than formerly." [1]

A study of the criminal records of the Council reveals three interesting features in the administration of justice: first, the swiftness with which the criminal was usually punished, while the moral effect upon the agitated public was at its strongest; second, the frequency with which the Council modified many of the sentences of the lower courts; and, third, the severity of the penalties which seemed sometimes to be necessary. After a trial generally lasting not more than a couple of days the condemned prisoner was handed over to the executioner, and punishment was inflicted on the same day that the judgment was pronounced. Prison sentences were very rare, the prisons being used chiefly to secure the accused until the pronouncement and execution of the verdict.

The following cases illustrate at once a diversity of crimes and the modifications of sentences made in the interest of mercy. (1) A soldier accused of a grave offence was condemned by the provost of Quebec to go naked except for his shirt, to kneel before the church door and ask God for pardon, and then to be hanged. The Sovereign Council upon appeal ordered that the accused be put to the torture (*question ordinaire et extraordinaire*), and upon his testimony thus extorted it annulled the sentence of the provost court, discharged him from the accusation, and sent

[1] *Cor. Gen.*, series C xi, vol. lxvii, pt. i.

him away absolved. It ordered further that the record of his trial be closed and kept secret unless opened by decree of the Council.

(2) Jean Dupuy, who committed suicide in 1735, was convicted of the crime of having made away with himself and was sentenced by the lower court to be dragged on a sledge behind a cart with his face to the ground, to be hanged by the feet for a day, and then to be cast into the water in default of a cesspool, and his goods were to be confiscated. The Council merely deprived him of Christian burial, proof having been shown that he had betrayed symptoms of insanity long before the suicide.

(3) In 1734, a negress slave had been sentenced to have her hand cut off and to be burned alive, because she had set fire to and caused the burning of a part of Montreal. By the modified sentence of Council, she was hanged first and burned afterwards.

(4) In 1742, a soldier of the garrison of Montreal by the name of Beaufort was sentenced to capital punishment for having profaned the sacred words of the New Testament and the representation of Jesus Christ crucified, by using them both in fortune-telling and in other profane and illegal practices. He was even convicted of having scorched the hands and feet of the said crucifix by holding it to the fire in order to dry the drugs with which he had covered part of it. The Council modified the sentence, condemning the delinquent to be scourged and to spend three years in the galleys.[1] Several times this cummuting of life penalties to galley sentences occurred.

(5) In 1690, François Laurens was convicted of having improvised certain contracts (*obligations*): to wit, one

[1] *Cor. Gen.*, series C xi, vol. lxiv, pt. iv, p. 15, *et seq.*; *Jugements et Délib.*, vol. iii, pp. 421-425.

transfer (*transport*) unsigned, and three notes with names of witnesses forged. The judge of Montreal sentenced him to be hanged, his property confiscated, his victims reimbursed, and the Seigniors of Montreal presented with the fine of 400 livres. Upon appeal to the Sovereign Council he was condemned to be put in the pillory (*d'Estre appliqué au carcan et y demeurer attaché par le Col pendant trois heures*), with an inscription across his stomach bearing these words, "Author of false notes", to restore what he had fraudulently received, and to pay 50 livres fine for expense of trial. He was, further, warned not to repeat the offense on pain of the halter, and to act as a servant for three years.[1]

(6) The same judge of Montreal had condemned a miller of Costeau to be hanged for stealing 84 minots of wheat and obtaining money from various customers on the promise of furnishing them flour. The Council amended this sentence to a scourging of the shoulders and branding with a fleur-de-lis upon the shoulder, a 50-livre fine, and a prohibition from the further exercise of his trade as a miller.[2]

(7) Sometimes the Council, although dealing out rigorous sentences because French law specified such penalties, connived at the omission of the more barbarous features. For example, when, in 1668, Jacques Bigeon, criminal and assassin, was sentenced to have his right hand cut off and nailed to a post and to be strangled by hanging to a gallows, the criminal did not hang there with his bleeding stump, for the hand was cut off only after his death.[3]

The turbulent character of the frontier town of Montreal perhaps accounts for the extreme severity of the sentences inflicted by the local judge of that city, for most of the sen-

[1] *Jugements et Délib.*, vol. iii, p. 421.

[2] *Ibid.*, p. 424.

[3] *Ibid.*, vol. i, p. 486.

tences which the Council modified in the interests of mercy were laid by that official. Still there were very severe sentences pronounced by the supreme court when it seemed necessary to make an example of evil doers. Only the severest punishments could repress criminals who through isolation or natural depravity were capable of dastardly and heinous crimes like incest and the rape of daughters. Four cases occurred between 1668 and 1686 in which little girls of seven years and up were raped. The Council condemned the criminals to be hanged; or beaten, branded with a fleur-de-lis on the cheek, and banished for ever; or banished with shaved head and lacerated back, to serve nine years in the King's galleys.

One adulterous woman was merely compelled to beg on bended knee the pardon of her husband, while another was to be shaved and beaten with rods at the chief crossroads of the city, and to be kept in a strong place at her husband's expense provided he did not wish to take her back. The men involved were condemned in one case to prison in chains and on bread and water, and in the other to banishment from all the French possessions in the new world and to confiscation of property. In 1684, the irate husband who killed the adulterer *in flagrante delicto* was released from prison after five months of confinement, was given the freedom of the city and of three leagues around, and later permitted to go to Montreal to carry on his business.

The Sovereign Council several times ordered promulgation of the ordinance of Henry II of 1556 respecting women guilty of infanticide or abandoning their children. In 1671, one woman was convicted of having concealed her pregnancy, of having cared for herself three times and taking medicine to lose her fruit, and finally of having given birth, the day after her second marriage, to a child which she immediately killed and buried. She was put to the torture to see whether or not she had arranged the death trap in which her first husband was murdered, and was then hanged.[1]

The murderer usually received a death penalty, although he was sometimes banished. The ceremonies attending the execution of a prisoner were designed to impress the populace with the heinousness of his crime. These ceremonies may be illustrated by the case of Jacques Bigeon, who in 1668 was convicted of having deliberately murdered Nicolas Bernard, and of numerous other crimes. He was led before the door of the church, naked except for his shirt, with a rope around his neck and a torch in his hand. There, upon his knees, he asked pardon of God, of the King, and of justice, for his crimes, and was strangled by hanging to a gallows placed in the Upper Town. After death his head and right hand were cut off and nailed to a post set up in a conspicuous place for a warning. From his property 25 livres were spent in masses for the soul of the murdered Bernard and 500 livres went to the Seigniors of Montreal. The humiliating march, the petition for mercy before the door of the church or of the victim's house, the fines for the souls of the victims or for the hospital, were usual features of capital punishments.[2]

Theft was sometimes punished by death, but usually the thief was scourged and branded.[3] Prison sentences were rare, the prisons being used chiefly to secure the accused until the pronouncement and execution of the verdict. From 1706 on there were proposals to repair the prisons and dungeons, as well for the security of the prisoners who were confined there as for preventing their communication

[1] For these and other cases, see *ibid.*, i, pp. 485, 517, 530, 649, 660, 973; ii, pp. 328, 969; iii, pp. 44, 424, etc.

[2] *Ibid.*, vol. i, p. 485; vol. iii, p. 425.

[3] *Ibid.*, vol. i, p. 975; vol. ii, p. 82.

with each other. In 1730, by the aid of outsiders several prisoners escaped before their condemnation. The dungeons being so deadly that no man could live in them continuously, it was proposed to build a wall about the prison to enable the prisoners to take the air.[1] The Attorney-General had the prisons cleaned and the straw changed once a month. He furnished the prisoners with the necessities of life, persons of consideration paying for their maintenance.

The greater part of the Council's judicial business consisted of civil suits. The people were litigious, and usually carried their suits to the higher court when the judgment of the lower court was adverse. So frequent were these appeals even when the justice of the judgment was obvious to all, that a fine of 3 livres was laid for frivolous and inadmissible appeals. The Council indeed tried to prevent persons becoming involved in lawsuits by recognizing settlements made out of court.[2] These cases, however, were comparatively few.

Contemporaries claim that justice was cheap and the

[1] Beauharnais and Hocquart to the minister October 15, 1730. "Vous devez estre informé, Monseigneur, que les prisons Royales estoient si peu sures que ces criminels avant leur condamnation avoient trouvé le secret de couper leurs fers et rompre les grilles par la communication qu'ils avoient avec les personnes de dehors par le moyen d'une fenestre a rez de chaussée qui donnoit dans une cour fermée simplement de pieux de façon que M. Le Marquis de Beauharnais a la requisition de M. Hocquart a esté dans la necessité d'y establir un corps de garde pour empescher leur évasion par la suitte et celle des autres prisonniers. D'ailleurs les cachots sont si malsains par l'humidité qui y regne qu'il n'est pas possible a des hommes d'y pouvoir séjourner continuellement, et c'est ce qui nous a déterminé de faire faire une enceinte de muraille à la cour des dites prisons autant pour la seureté des prisonniers que pour leur faire prendre l'air quelque fois comme dans un préau." The charge of the King for this wall and a small dungeon for a girl thief amounted to 2087 livres 7 sous and 10 deniers. *Corres. Gen.*, series C xi, vol. lii, pt. i, p. 69.

[2] *Jugements et Délib.*, vol. i, pp. 898, 1014.

abandon with which men went to law over trivial sums seems to support this claim. The defendant was given a week or a fortnight in which to produce the papers for his defence, and at the meeting at the end of this period the case was definitely settled. The ordinary suit occupying so short a time could hardly have cost heavily.

Yet justice was sometimes rather expensive. For example, a record of April 24, 1669, shows the expenses of an appeal, which was not entertained, to have been as follows:

To the bailiff for summoning witnesses	8 livres 10 sous
To the guard	40 sous
To the clerk for recording the testimony of, and reading previous evidence to, the witnesses	8 livres 10 sous
Interrogatory process	30 sous
Sentence	30 sous
To witnesses for expenses	26 livres 10 sous
Execution of the decree refusing the appeal	30 sous

The appellant was therefore charged 50 livres to get a hearing before the Council.[1] It must be noted, however, that over 43 of the 50 livres were expended on account of witnesses, the judical fees being slight in comparison. In cases requiring few witnesses the costs may well have amounted to little, and we may believe the boast of the Canadian as to the cheapness of justice under the French régime.

[1] *Jugements et Délib.*, vol. i, p. 555.

APPENDIX A

THE PERROT TRIAL

On January 30, the matter was brought before the Council. Tilly and Dupont were appointed to investigate acts of violence practiced by Perrot.[1] On January 31 and February 2, these commissioners tried to interrogate Perrot but he refused to reply and challenged the whole Council. He was repeatedly questioned but continued to object to the Council as his judge. On February 16, Frontenac wrote that the object of Councillors was to take depositions, conduct the trial, and report the evidence to the King for his decision. Perrot probably saw that if he could successfully challenge all commissioners, the Council could not collect evidence sufficient to condemn him in the eyes of the King. He adopted these tactics on June 11, when he addressed a very offensive petition to the Sovereign Council.[2] He held that the Governor wished to destroy him utterly in order to put another in his place, that the person temporarily replacing him was a relative of Tilly, who wished to ruin him in order to keep the said relative in office; that the Councillors, whose tenure was during the Governor's pleasure would act as the Governor desired. For these reasons he refused to recognize the Governor and his Council as his judges. The Council declared his objections inadmissible, detained Tilly as commissioner, and ordered that the examination of witnesses should proceed. The process was expensive: eleven witnesses came down from Montreal, one of whom was paid 100 livres and all of whom received considerable sums.[3] On August 17,

[1] *Jugements et Délib.*, vol. i, pp. 790-792.

[2] *Ibid.*, pp. 805-807.

[3] *Ibid.*, pp. 808, 810, 812.

Perrot addressed another petition to the Council, taking exception not to the whole body but to Frontenac, Tilly, Peiras and Vitré. On the 28th the Council ordered the exclusion of all those challenged, since they could not vote upon the competency of each other, and ordered the appointment of five officials to judge the ground of Perrot's challenges.[1] The prisoner at once challenged one of these emergency judges and this challenge was referred to the Council, which declared it inadmissible.[2]

On September 3, the unchallenged Councillors began their sessions by ordering the commissioners, who had commenced the trial, to complete the investigation, that all documents relating to the suits might be sent to the King for judgment.[3] But they timidly avoided passing upon the grounds of Perrot's charges and consequently upon the competence of Frontenac, Tilly, Peiras and Vitré to sit as his judges. Again on September 6 they declared their incapacity to do this, whereupon the Governor said the Council had found them capable and judge it they must or pay a fine.[4] But the Council relieved them from this dilemma by ordering that the reasons and pleas for Perrot's challenges be sent to France there to be judged, and that for purposes of facilitating that judgment, the old commissioners should proceed with the interrogation of the prisoner.

On September 17 and 23, October 15, 22, and 28 and November 5, the Council considered petitions written by Perrot, asking his release, that he might arrange his affairs in time to go to France that autumn. He had not succeeded in preventing the gathering of evidence; he sought freedom to go to Versailles, confident in the influence of Talon at Court or in

[1] *Jugements et Délib.*, p. 829.

[2] *Ibid.*, p. 830.

[3] "Dict a esté que le proces sera parachevé d'instruire par les Commissaires qui l'ont encommencé, pour estre le tout avec la prise à partie Et recusations envoyé en Cour afin d'estre jugé." *Ibid.*, p. 831.

[4] "Et qu'ils jugeroient ou payeroient l'amende." *Ibid.*, vol. i, p. 838.

the justice of his cause. The refusal of the officials called in to judge whether or not his accusations were true enough to incapacitate Frontenac and others from sitting in judgment in his case suggests that perhaps there was some truth in his claims. His petitions show increasingly the anger of a man exasperated beyond the bounds of self-control by his long confinement.[1] Thorough investigation of the charges had been made, when in the middle of November, he was permitted to sail for France, where owing to the evidence thus collected, he was imprisoned for three weeks in the Bastille.[2] This trial undoubtedly strengthened the Sovereign Council as a criminal court. When working in harmony with its president, no one could with impunity defy it.

[1] His last petition of November 5 was exceedingly bitter. He asserted that Frontenac planned to keep him another year in prison. He declared that he would exonerate himself at the expense of the Council, which he would accuse of negligence and would cast blame upon the shoulders of the Attorney-General who ought to complete the legal examination and not leave it to a " Governor and President," who was his accuser. He asked the Council, since after its decree of September 3 and 6 the Governor was no longer its master, to declare that it was not the Council but the Governor, who was keeping him in prison, when it was necessary for him to go with the papers of the trial to the Court to answer by word of mouth. *Ibid.*, p. 878.

[2] Clément, *Lett. Instr. et Mem. de Colb.*, vol. iii, pt. ii, p. 590.

APPENDIX B

The Damours Affair

On August 16, 1681, Madame Damours presented a letter to the Council explaining the circumstances of her husband's arrest and demanding that he be made acquainted with the accusations brought against him and that his trial proceed in the ordinary way.[1] Damours claimed that he was in the Lower Town superintending the unloading of his boat when a guard asked him to come to the Château St. Louis. Here the Governor took him into his inner office and asked why he had had his boat cleared for Matane without a permit from him. Damours replied that he had come to the Governor in April to obtain a permit for a canoe which he intended to despatch before the ice melted sufficiently for the passage of his boat. The Governor had agreed provided that Boisseau, collector of the King's customs, had no objection. The latter made no difficulty about allowing a canoe to make the journey to Matane until conditions should permit the boat to make the trip. When Damours made these statements, the Governor replied that the permit was for the canoe and not for the boat; whereupon Damours said: "Monsieur, I ask pardon. I did not think it was necessary to take out another license, since it was only a question of going to a house on land that the King has given me. I thought that the license you gave us ought to suffice. I believe that it is the intention of the King to permit free access to the lands that he has granted."[2] The Governor flew

[1] "Il vous plaise ordonner qu'il sera informé des accusations qui peuvent estre faites contre luy a la requeste de Monsieur le procureur general pour ensuite luy estre son proces fait par les voyes ordinaires Et vous ferez justice, signé Damours." *Jugements et Délib.*, vol. ii, p. 640.

[2] "...que l'on aille fort librement sur les terres qu'il nous a donnees; Sur quoi Monsieur le Gouverneur s'emportant tout d'un coup de collere dit au supant, allez vous les aprendrez les intentions du Roy Et vous demeurerez en prison jusques a ce que vous les sachiez." This is from the narration of Damours, found in *ibid.*, p. 639.

into a rage at this speech and told Damours that he could go learn the intentions of the King in prison and remain there till he knew them. The guards were summoned and Damours was lodged in prison with a coureur de bois by the name of Duluth.

Frontenac stated in the Council that if Damours had made the slightest apology for his insolent words or for his fault in clearing a boat at night without clearance papers or reporting his act to the officer in charge at Quebec during the Governor's absence, he would have accepted it and have made his punishment merely nominal; [1] but Damours had now added to these offences a greater one by tempting the Council to undertake something beyond its jurisdiction. It was not Damours's place to inform against the Governor, since the latter could not be made an ordinary defendant.[2] The Governor thought Damours's scorn of his authority and the appeal to the Council were inspired by others.

The speech of Duchesneau threw some light upon this phase of the matter. Upon learning of Damour's arrest, the Intendant and the Attorney-General had sought the Governor to inquire if it would be agreeable to him if the Council were assembled to hear the complaints which he might make against the said Damours, in order to try him. The Governor answered that it was a matter that did not concern the Council. It was possible that Madame Damours carried suggestions from the Intendant and Attorney-General which prompted the appeal of the prisoner to the jurisdiction of the Council. It is impossible to think that the three had *previously* planned the series of events for the sake of humiliating Frontenac by scorning his authority and making him amenable to the Council. The nature of the offense was too rash and blundering to have been the result of such plans. Damours's act was ill-considered and may have been due to the ignorance of clearing

[1] "Il les auroit volontiers receus Et se seroit contanté de l'avoir retenu quelques jours aux arrests pour l'example." *Ibid.*, p. 642.

[2] "...qu'il n'en ayt une common parere du Roy." *Ibid.*

formalities that he professed. The wording of the pass for the canoe might have excused his failure to obtain another for his boat,[1] but the secrecy and irregularity of the departure for the boat are features of the episode that excite suspicion. Still they prove no more than that this Councillor, who was undoubtedly a victim of inflated ideas about his position and the privileges of his office, disregarded some of the regulations. I do not believe that the action was due to conspiracy. Damour's record of eighteen years in the Council would forbid such a belief. Governors during that time had had grounds to rebuke several of the Councillors but none of them had complained of Damours. Even Mésy had spoken well of him and had reappointed him. His assumption to interpret the intentions of the King was undoubtedly insolent: Frontenac claimed that function as the sole representative of the King's person in France. He had often made use of the words now used by Damours. To a man without a sense of humor it was an irritating situation. To Frontenac, Damours's next step was the culminating display of insolence. To Damours it seemed but right that he should be tried by the Council. Arbitrary imprisonment was not in accordance with his ideas of the privileges of Councillors. Trial by one's peers was an old feudal privilege. He was simply asking that privilege; but in view of the recent movements to make the Governor amenable to the court, his demand inevitably raised that issue. Would the Council be able to effect the release of Damours, or failing that, would it be recognized as the court to try an action which involved the Governor and one of its members?

On the day Madame Damours presented the letter to the Council the issue was joined. The session had been called to register the King's Edict of Amnesty for the coureurs de bois,[2]

[1] "Nous permettons au Sr Damours etc. d'aller dans un Canot a la R^e^ Matane . . . Et en attendant leur barque puisse les aller joindre au dit lieu a la fonte des glaces." *Ibid.*, p. 642.

[2] See *Edits et Ord.*, vol. i, pp. 248-250.

and a further edict which prohibited going into the depths of the forest to trade. The Governor pointed out that Damours should have drawn up a petition and had it presented by one of the Councillors and that this irregularly presented letter should be considered only after the important business of the session had been despatched. The Intendant argued that they ought not to refuse the request of Damours, who was an old Councillor and one whose conduct had always been most prudent; that all the Councillors should be present for the important work of the meeting, a necessity which had influenced the Council at the instance of the Governor himself to terminate the Tilly-Peyras affair in order that they might give their opinions. Frontenac said that a full attendance was desirable but not necessary. The Attorney-General concluded that the Council should attend to the business of the King only after the affair of Damours was settled; and that the letter be read at once. And so it was voted.

In the speeches that followed the reading, Duchesneau requested the Governor to set Damours at liberty, in order that he might give his opinion concerning the registration of the edicts of the King. The Governor refused. The morning had been consumed by these discussions and as the noon hour sounded, the Intendant bade the clerk come with him. The Governor said that he would prevent his departure until the minutes had been signed. The Intendant requested that he be allowed to go to his house with the clerk, in order to look over the minutes at his leisure, for as he was responsible for their correctness, he always verified before signing them. The Governor implied that the Intendant changed the minutes to suit himself, and insisted that they should be signed then and there so that nothing could be changed. The Intendant refused and attempted to leave the Council chamber, when Frontenac placed himself before the door, again asking the Intendant to sign the minutes, and said that he would do service as usher himself. But Duchesneau replied that he would rather make his exit through the window or stay there all day than comply with the request of the Governor,[1] and he protested against these violent measures which kept the whole Council in the chamber, and asked to be assigned a place where he could examine the minutes in freedom and quiet. The Governor relented and permitted him to go into his own office to examine and sign the registers.

On August 18 the Governor again refused to set Damours at liberty and said that this was not an affair that concerned the Council. The Attorney-General demanded that the Governor be asked to agree that all the documents pertaining to the case be sent to the King for his decision. The Council so voted. On the 20th, the same officer submitted further reports on the Damours case, which the Council ordered to be attached to the other documents which were to be sent to the King. These hostile votes were obtained by giving the Intendant a vote and excluding the Governor as an interested party.[2] The Governor remarked that these added documents would further enlighten the King as to the purity of motive displayed by the Attorney-General and some of the Councillors. He stated that the King would be informed that Tilly, Dupont, and Peyras had not participated in the deliberations concerning the Damours affair as they considered it not within the jurisdiction of the Council and as infringing upon the authority of the Governor. The majority of the Council, however, had succeeded in taking the first steps in the trial of Damours and intended to submit the results of their investigations to the King. The steady resistance of the Governor prevented any greater success for their plans. Damours remained in prison until the autumn recess.

[1] "Il [M. le Gouverneur] se seroit mis devant la porte et auroit dit qu'il serviroit plutost d'huissier pour empescher qu'il ne l'ouvrist Et l'ouroit encore prié de vouloir faire une chose qui est si fort dans les formes, dont il auroit encor fait reffus Et dit qu'il sortiroit plutost par la fenestre, ou qu'il demeureroit tout le jour icy." *Jugements et Délib.*, vol. ii, p. 643.

[2] "L'affaire mise en deliberation, Monsieur l'Intendant dit qu'il ne prenoit point l'avis de Monsieur le Gouverneur puisque c'estoit une affaire qui le regardoit." *Ibid.*, p. 661.

APPENDIX C

The Callières and Desjordy Cases

Meanwhile St. Vallier had further played his rôle as "scourge of Canada," as Laval called him. At a religious ceremony which was to take place at the house of the Recollets of Ville Marie, and at which the Bishop and Callières, the Governor of Montreal, were to be present, the Bishop, remarking that the stall of honor had been reserved for Callières, had it removed. Callières arriving shortly afterward had it put back into its former place. The Bishop issued a mandate ordering the Recollet fathers to close their church, to refrain from celebrating any ceremonies, and from administering any sacraments therein, for not having obeyed his orders as to the *prie-dieu*. He then issued three monitories, in which after explaining at length the reasons for his interdict, he referred to the scandalous conduct of Callières with the sister of the Superior of the Recollets. Callières being a high-spirited man brought the matter before the Sovereign Council. On October 31, he presented a petition begging to be allowed to have cited before the court the Bishop and the ecclesiastics who had published the mandate and monitories. He demanded that these defamatory acts should be declared null and that the Bishop and ecclesiastics should be held to make reparation to him. The petition was referred to the Bishop for his answer, to be given at the next meeting of the Council. The Bishop attempted no defence but limited himself to a review of the violent measures taken by Callières. He was astonished, he said, that M. de Callières' friends the Recollets should have given him the originals of the mandate and third monitory; that M. de Callières should have answered with a libel, full of outrages, promulgated to roll of drums at the church portal during divine service and at various public places in the city; that he had constituted himself judge of the ecclesiastical quarrel and had decided in favor of the Recollets. On December 13, the Council voted to suspend action until the King should express himself upon the matter. This tribunal had lost jurisdiction over Mareuil because it would not allow the Bishop's conduct to be questioned, it now gave up jurisdiction of this cause for the same reason.[1]

Upon the same day the same course was pursued in a similar cause. The act of aggression complained of in this case was not performed by the Bishop in person but by his agents. The parish priests of Batiscan and Champlain, in accordance with a mandate of Bishop St. Vallier, interdicted the Sieur Desjordy, half-pay captain, and the wife of one M. Desbrieux from entering the churches in those places, on the ground of adultery and scandalous conduct. In March 1694 Desjordy petitioned the Council to make Bishop and priests show just cause for their accusations. The Attorney-General did not act vigorously. The parish priests, secure in the protection of the Bishop, did not appear. On December 13, the Council voted to suspend judgment until the arrival of the vessels the next year.[2] Bishop St. Vallier was advised by his Archbishop to come to Paris at once to influence in his favor the settlement of all these disputes in which he was involved. Thus the Council awaited the settlement by other institutions of all the embarrassing disputes, in which the ecclesiastical power had become involved.

[1] *Jugements et Délib.*, vol. iii, pp. 960-962.

[2] *Ibid.*, pp. 957-960.

BIBLIOGRAPHY

I. Unpublished Material

(1) In the small archives room of the Legislative Building at Quebec, there are seventy volumes of *Jugements et Délibérations du Conseil Supérieur*, which contain the records of civil and criminal cases. Each volume contains from 140 to 185 pages and is prefaced by the announcement that the register was initialed by the Intendant of justice, police and finance in New France, and was used to register decrees which might be rendered by the Superior Council of the country sitting in that city, done at Quebec on such a day of such a year. To each the Intendant's signature was affixed.

(2) A second series A to K, volumes i to xi, entitled *Registre des Insinuations du Conseil Supérier depuis 1663-1683*, etc., contains all the documents registered by the Council. These volumes are indexed chronologically.

(3) Much more available because copied in a fair hand are the following series of documents, copied for the most part in France and installed in the manuscript room of the archives building in Ottawa. *Les Archives des Colonies*, series B, as described by Mr. Parker, consists "of registers or letter-books in which were copied despatches, memoranda and other papers sent by the King and the minister to officials, ecclesiastics, and private persons in the colonies, and to others interested in the possessions of France beyond the seas. While orders of the King (*ordres du roi*) and despatches of his minister form the core of the series, the amount of miscellaneous correspondence and papers is very large. The series is calendared as follows: volumes i-xlii in Richard's *Supplement to the Report on Canadian Archives* for 1899, pp. 245-548; 42-74 in the Report for 1904, Appendix K; 75-189 in the Report for 1905, vol. i, part vi." Mr. Richard did not calendar some documents that the series contains. The abstracts he does give however may be trusted for accuracy.

(4) The *Correspondance Générale*, or C xi series, in the Canadian Archives is very valuable. Most of the volumes are indexed, so that any document is quickly available. The following calendars are not sufficiently detailed to give much aid to the student: vols. i-xxx in an appendix to the *Report on Canadian Archives* for 1885, pp. xxix-lxxix; vols. xxxi-lxxv in an appendix to the Report for 1886, pp. xxxix-cl; vols. lxxvi-cxxii in an appendix to the Report for 1887, pp. cxl-ccxxxvi.

Helpful abstracts of the Raudot-Pontchartrain correspondence however may be found in Richard's *Supplement to the Report on Canadian Archives* for 1899, pp. 201-230.

(5) A still more valuable mass of documents is a collection made by Moreau de St.Méry (1750-1819), the statesman, administrator, and historian. Although many of the originals may be found in series C xi and series B, this collection is the only source of information for phases of certain important trials and constitutional struggles. Trustworthy abstracts of vols. ii-xvi may be found in Richard's *Supplement to the Report on Canadian Archives* for 1899, pp. 30-91. For less interesting abstracts of later volumes, see the *Report on Canadian Archives* for 1905, vol. i, pt. vi, pp. 447-505. Only a few of the later volumes have been copied however.

(6) Manuscript copies of works written during the eighteenth century by "M. Petit, député des conseils supérieurs des colonies françaises" may be classed as source material. The most important is a copy of *Le Droit Public ou Gouvernement des colonies françaises d'après les lois faites pour ces pays*, 2 vols., published by Délalain in Paris in 1771. Of the greatest use is his *Memoires sur l'administration des colonies françaises en Amerique et projets de legislation pour lesdites colonies*, in the Bibliothèque Nationale, Fond François, 12081, fair copy in the Dominion Archives.

II. Alphabetical Bibliography of Published Sources and Secondary Works

Brymner, D. *Reports on Canadian Archives*. 78 vols., Ottawa, 1872-1903.

Casgrain, H. R. *Une Paroisse Canadienne au XVIIe Siècle*, Québec, 1880.

Chapais, T. *Jean Talon, Intendant de la Nouvelle-France*, Québec, 1904. Treats the administration of the colony at some length.

Charlevoix, F. X. *Histoire et Description de la Nouvelle-France*, ed. by J. G. Shea, 6 vols., New York, 1866-72.

Clément, P. *Lettres, Instructions, et Mémoires de Colbert*, 7 vols., Paris, 1861-70.

Collection de Manuscrits contenant Lettres, Mémoires et autres Documents Historiques ré atifs à l'Histoire de la Nouvelle-France, recueillis aux archives de la Province de Québec, ou copiés à l'étranger, 4 vols., Quebec, 1883-85.

Chéruel, *Dictionnaire historique des Institutions, Moeurs et Coutumes de la France*, 2 vols., 6th ed., Paris, 1884.

Cugnet, F. J. *Digeste des Edits, Declarations*, etc. and, in the same volume, "Traité de la Police," Quebec, 1775.

Desmaze, Charles Adrien. *Le Parlement de Paris; son organization,*

. . *avec une notice sur les autres parlements de France* (1334-1860), Paris, 1860.

Doughty, A. G. *Reports on Canadian Archives*, Ottawa, 1904-1914.

Douglas, J. *Quebec in the Seventeenth Century*, Cleveland, 1905.

Doutre, J. and Lareau, E. *Histoire Générale du Droit Civil Canadien*, Montreal, 1872.

Edits, Ordonnances Royaux, Déclarations, et Arrêts de Conseil d'Etat du Roi concernant le Canada, 2 vols., Quebec, 1803-1806. New edition enlarged and improved, 3 vols., Quebec, 1854-56. A very good collection although the old French spelling is not retained.

Faillon, M. E. *Histoire de la Colonie Française en Canada*, 3 vols., Ville-Marie, 1865-66.

Ferland, J. B. A. *Cours d'Histoire du Canada*, 2 vols., Quebec, 1861-65.

Garneau, F. X. *Histoire du Canada*, 4 vols., Montreal, 1882-83.

Gaspé, P. R. de. *Les Anciens Canadiens*, Quebec, 1863.

Gerin. "Le Gentilhomme Français," in *Proceedings of the Royal Society of Canada*, series ii, vol. ii, pp. 79-80.

Gosselin, A. "Un Episode de l'Histoire du Théâtre au Canada," in the same series, vol. iv.

Gosselin, A. *Vie de Mgr. de Laval, premier Evêque de Québec et Apôtre du Canada*, 2 vols., Quebec, 1890.

Harrisse, H. *Notes pour servir à l'Histoire . . . de la Nouvelle-France*, Paris, 1872.

Isambert, F. A. *Recueil Général des Anciennes Lois Françaises depuis l'an 420 jusqu'à la Révolution de 1789*, 30 vols., Paris, 1822-33.

Journal des Jésuites, 2 vols. supplemented by "Extraits des Journaux des Jésuites" from 1710-1759 in *Canadian Missions, Parkman Collection*, Harvard Library.

Juchereau, Soeur. *Histoire de l'Hôtel-Dieu.*

Jugements et Délibérations du Conseil Souverain de la Nouvelle-France, 6 vols., Quebec, 1885-91. In vol. v the title is changed to *Jugements et Délibérations du Conseil Supérieur de Québec.*

Kalm, P. *Travels into North America*, translations, 2 vols., London, 1772. By a Swede who visited America in 1749-50.

Kingsford, W. *History of Canada*, 10 vols., Toronto, 1887-98.

La Hontan, Baron de. *Nouveaux Voyages*, 2 vols., The Hague, 1705, and many subsequent editions. See also Thwaites, R. G., for well-Englished version.

Lareau, E. *Histoire du Droit Canadien depuis les Origines de la Colonie jusqu'à nos jours*, 2 vols., Montreal, 1888-89.

La Tour, Abbé de. *Mémoire de la Vie de M. de Laval.*

Lorin, H. *Le Comte de Frontenac*, Paris, 1895. A good and scholarly work.

Luchaire, A. *Manuel des Institutions Françaises*, Paris, 1892.

Mandements, Lettres Pastorales, et Circulaires des Evêques de Québec, ed. by H. Tétu and C. O. Gaynon, 6 vols., Quebec, 1887-90.

Margry, P. *Rélations et Mémoires inédits, pour servir à l'Histoire de la France dans les Pays d'Outre Mer, tirés des archives du Ministère le la Marine et des Colonies*, Paris, 1865. Of little use to the constitutional historian.

Marie de l'Incarnation, Mère. *Lettres Historiques*, Paris, 1857.

Moroni. *Dizionario di erudizione storico-ecclesiastica*, 103 vols., Venice, 1840-61.

Munro, W. B. *The Seigniorial System in Canada*, New York, 1907.

Munro, W. B. "The Office of Intendant in New France," *American Historical Review*, October, 1906, pp. 15-38.

New York. *Documents relating to the Colonial History of New York*, ed. by O'Callaghan and Fernow, 15 vols., New York, 1853-83. Vol. IX contains documents collected in France.

Parkman, F. *Count Frontenac and New France under Louis XIV*, Boston, 1877.

Parkman, F. *The Old Régime in Canada*, 2 vols., Boston, 1874.

Parkman, F. *A Half-Century of Conflict*, 2 vols., Boston, 1892.

Parkman, F. *Montcalm and Wolfe*, 2 vols., Boston, 1884.

Roy, J. E. "Les Intendants de la Nouvelle-France," in *Proceedings of the Royal Society of Canada*, 1903.

Royal Society of Canada. *Proceedings*, First Series, 11 vols., Ottawa, 1882-94. Second Series, 19 vols., Ottawa, 1895-1914.

Shortt, A. and Doughty, A. G. *Canada and its Provinces*, 14 vols., Ottawa, 1913.

Sulte, B. "L'Ancienne Noblesse du Canada," in *Revue Canadienne*, May-September 1885, pp. 298-556 *passim*.

Tanguay, C. *Dictionnaire Généalogique des Familles Canadiennes, depuis la fondation de la Colonie jusqu'à nos jours*, 7 vols., Montreal, 1871-90.

Thwaites, R. G. ed. *Lahontan's New Voyages to North America*, 2 vols., Chicago, 1905.

Weir, R. S. *The Administration of the Old Régime in Canada*, Montreal, 1897.

Bei Fragen zur Produktsicherheit wenden Sie sich bitte an:
If you have any questions regarding product safety,
please contact:

Walter de Gruyter GmbH
Genthiner Straße 13
10785 Berlin
productsafety@degruyterbrill.com